Tourism Destination Evolution

Outlining the need for fresh perspectives on change in tourism, this book offers a theoretical overview and empirical examples of the potential synergies of applying evolutionary economic geography (EEG) concepts in tourism research. EEG has proven to be a powerful explanatory paradigm in other sectors, and tourism studies has a track record of embracing, adapting and enhancing frameworks from cognate fields. EEG approaches to tourism studies complement and further develop studies of established themes such as path dependence and the Tourism Area Life Cycle. The individual chapters draw from a broad geographical framework and address distinct conceptual elements of EEG, using a diverse set of tourism case studies from Europe, North America and Australia. Developing the theoretical cohesion of tourism and EEG, this volume also gives non-specialist tourism scholars a window into the possibilities of using these concepts in their own research. Given the timing of this publication, it has great potential value to the wider tourism community in advancing theory and leading to more effective empirical research.

Patrick Brouder is a Banting Postdoctoral Fellow at the Department of Geography, Brock University, Canada. He is also a Senior Research Fellow at the School of Tourism and Hospitality, University of Johannesburg, South Africa, and a Research Associate at the Department of Tourism Studies and Geography, Mid Sweden University, Sweden.

Salvador Anton Clavé is Full Professor of Regional Geographical Analysis at Rovira i Virgili University, where he serves as Director of the Doctoral Program in Tourism and Leisure. His research concentrates on the analysis of the evolution of tourism destinations, tourism and city design and planning, the globalization of theme parks and attractions, the impact of ICT on tourism, and tourism policies and local development.

Alison Gill is a Professor at Simon Fraser University in Vancouver, with a joint appointment in the Department of Geography and the School of Resource and Environmental Management. Her research interests are in the evolution of destinations with respect to issues of growth management, sustainability and governance.

Dimitri Ioannides is Professor of Human Geography at Mid Sweden University, Sweden. He has varied research interests in tourism, including the economic geography of the tourism sector as well as tourism within the context of sustainable development.

New Directions in Tourism Analysis

Series Editor: Dimitri Ioannides, E-TOUR,
Mid Sweden University, Sweden

Although tourism is becoming increasingly popular both as a taught subject and an area for empirical investigation, the theoretical underpinnings of many approaches have tended to be eclectic and somewhat underdeveloped. However, recent developments indicate that the field of tourism studies is beginning to develop in a more theoretically informed manner, but this has not yet been matched by current publications.

The aim of this series is to fill this gap with high quality monographs or edited collections that seek to develop tourism analysis at both theoretical and substantive levels using approaches which are broadly derived from allied social science disciplines such as Sociology, Social Anthropology, Human and Social Geography, and Cultural Studies. As tourism studies covers a wide range of activities and sub fields, certain areas such as Hospitality Management and Business, which are already well provided for, would be excluded. The series will therefore fill a gap in the current overall pattern of publication.

Suggested themes to be covered by the series, either singly or in combination, include - consumption; cultural change; development; gender; globalisation; political economy; social theory; sustainability.

Tourism Destination Evolution

Edited by Patrick Brouder,
Salvador Anton Clavé, Alison Gill
and Dimitri Ioannides

LONDON AND NEW YORK

First published 2017 by Routledge

2 Park Square, Milton Park, Abingdon, Oxfordshire OX14 4RN
52 Vanderbilt Avenue, New York, NY 10017

Routledge is an imprint of the Taylor & Francis Group, an informa business

First issued in paperback 2020

British Library Cataloguing in Publication Data
A catalogue record for this book is available from the British Library

Library of Congress Cataloging in Publication Data
A catalog record has been requested for this book

ISBN: 978-1-4724-5399-0 (hbk)
ISBN: 978-0-367-66825-9 (pbk)

Typeset in Times New Roman
by Sunrise Setting Ltd, Brixham, UK

Contents

Illustrations

Contributors

Salvador Anton Clavé is Full Professor of Regional Geographical Analysis at Rovira i Virgili University where he serves as Director of the Doctoral Program in Tourism and Leisure. His research concentrates on the analysis of the evolution of tourism destinations, tourism and city design and planning, the globalization of theme parks and attractions, the impact of ICT on tourism, and issues concerning tourism policies and local development.

Patrick Brouder is a Banting Postdoctoral Fellow at the Department of Geography, Brock University, Canada. He is also a Senior Research Fellow at the School of Tourism and Hospitality, University of Johannesburg, South Africa, and a Research Associate at the Department of Tourism Studies and Geography, Mid Sweden University, Sweden.

Doris Anna Carson is a researcher and lecturer at the Department of Geography and Economic History, Umeå University, Sweden. Her research focuses on the nexus between mobilities, innovation processes and economic development opportunities in rural and remote communities. She has published a number of peer-reviewed articles on tourism development in resource peripheries, local systems-of-innovation dynamics and short-term population mobilities (including tourist, labour and Indigenous mobilities), with a particular focus on remote South Australia and the Northern Territory, Australia.

Dean Bradley Carson is a Professor of Human Geography interested in the population dynamics of rural and sparsely populated areas. Dean's particular interest is in how the mobility of people into, out of and around rural areas impacts prospects for economic and social development. Dean has a background working with large demographic and social datasets in Australia, Canada, Scotland and Sweden. Dean's PhD examined the use of Internet technologies in peripheral tourism destinations.

Christopher Fullerton is Associate Professor and Chair at the Department of Geography, Brock University, Canada. He is also a member of Brock's Environmental Sustainability Research Centre. His research interests include rural community economic development and land use planning, as well as urban public transit planning and policy.

Alison Gill is a Professor at Simon Fraser University in Vancouver, with a joint appointment in the Department of Geography and the School of Resource and Environmental Management. Her research interests are in the evolution of destinations with respect to issues of growth management, sustainability and governance.

Henrik Halkier is Professor of Regional and Tourism Studies at Aalborg University, Denmark. His main research interests are destination development, food tourism and destination governance.

Robert Hassink is Professor of Economic Geography at Kiel University, Germany, and Visiting Professor in the School of Geography, Politics & Sociology at Newcastle University, UK. His main research areas are theories of economic geography, regional innovation policies, industrial restructuring and regional economic development in Western Europe and East Asia, particularly South Korea.

Dimitri Ioannides is Professor of Human Geography at Mid Sweden University, Sweden. He has varied research interests in tourism, including the economic geography of the tourism sector as well as tourism within the context of sustainable development.

Laura James is an Associate Professor in the Department of Culture and Global Studies at Aalborg University, Denmark. Her main research interests are regional development, food tourism and cross-sectoral knowledge dynamics.

Mulan Ma is a researcher and lecturer in tourism management at Shanghai University of International Business and Economics. She received her PhD in Geography at Kiel University, Germany. Her research interests include evolutionary economic geography, tourism economics, tourism management and planning.

Jasper F. Meekes is a PhD researcher in the Department of Spatial Planning and Environment at the Faculty of Spatial Sciences, University of Groningen and the European Tourism Futures Institute (ETFI) at Stenden University of Applied Sciences, the Netherlands. His dissertation deals with the role of leisure in regional development in the Dutch province of Fryslân. In this project the topic of leisure serves as a test case for exploring how a perspective based on complexity thinking can be applied in spatial planning. The project is part of the research programme of University Campus Fryslân (UCF), financed by the Province of Fryslân.

Piotr Niewiadomski is an economic geographer interested in the worldwide development of the tourism production system, the global production networks of tourist firms and the impact of tourism on economic development in host destinations. His research mainly focuses on Central and Eastern Europe (CEE) and the context of post-communist restructuring in CEE after 1989. He is now Lecturer in Human Geography in the School of Geosciences, University of Aberdeen, UK.

Constanza Parra is a social scientist, with interdisciplinary interests in the ways societies relate to the natural environment and deal with contemporary sustainability challenges. She was trained as a sociologist in Chile and obtained her PhD in France working on multi-level governance of protected areas. She is an Assistant Professor at the Division of Geography & Tourism, Department of Earth & Environmental Sciences, University of Leuven, Belgium. Previously, she was Rosalind Franklin Fellow at the University of Groningen, the Netherlands, and an AFR/Marie-Curie postdoctoral fellow at the University of Luxembourg. She researches and writes on social sustainability, nature–culture interactions, governance of socio-ecological systems and sustainable (eco)tourism.

Gert De Roo is Professor of Spatial Planning at the Department of Spatial Planning and Environment, University of Groningen, the Netherlands, and Visiting Professor at Newcastle University, UK. His research focuses on non-linear development of urban space and place, relating complexity thinking and planning theory, decision-making models concerning interventions within the urban environment, and managing transitions of space. De Roo has been President of the Association of European Schools of Planning (AESOP) and co-chair of the International Urban Planning and Environment Association (UPE). He is editor-in-chief of AESOP's digital platform InPlanning and editor of the Ashgate Publishing Series on Planning Theory.

Cinta Sanz-Ibáñez is a PhD candidate in Tourism and Leisure at the Department of Geography at Rovira i Virgili University, Catalonia. Her research has been funded by a PhD research grant from the Spanish Ministry of Education. Her work mainly focuses on tourism destination evolution, with a particular interest in contributing to integrate this field of research into the whole discussion around evolution of places and regions within the economic geography mainstream.

Peter W. Williams is a Professor Emeritus, geographer and planner in the School of Resource and Environmental Management at Simon Fraser University in Vancouver, Canada. His research focuses on identifying policy, planning and development approaches that lead to more sustainable tourism destinations.

Julie Wilson is a researcher and lecturer in the Faculty of Tourism and Geography of Rovira i Virgili University and a lecturer at the Open University of Catalonia (UOC). She has been a Marie Curie Intra-European Fellow (2004–7) and a Fulbright Schuman Advanced Research Scholar (2008–9). She is a Member of the International Geographical Union (IGU) Commission for the Geography of Tourism, Leisure and Global Change, and has edited a number of research monographs, with several articles published in international refereed journals.

Foreword

It is estimated that over 1 billion tourists travel abroad every year and that the tourism industry generates an economic impact of well over 2 trillion US dollars, representing about 3 percent of global GDP (statistics vary according to sources). More importantly, indirect contributions of this sector, as well as domestic tourism, generate benefits that are of an even considerably higher magnitude. As such, tourism frequently constitutes a vital component of the economic system across all spatial scales. From the transformation of difficult-to-reach mountain villages into international ski resorts to the promotion of whole regions built around landscape characteristics and culinary offerings, tourism seems to permeate the entire globe, from metropolitan cities to rural hinterlands.

Considering the widespread economic impact of this particular sector, as well as its spatial extent, tourism should be given special attention in economic geography. While there has been substantial research effort over the past decades, much work remains to be done. This is particularly true when it comes to the incorporation of evolutionary approaches to the study of service sectors and the economic trajectories of places, something that has recently gained popularity within the field of geography. The present edited volume constitutes an important step in this direction, and thus it is a key contemporary contribution that will significantly advance future research efforts aiming to untangle the complexity of 'tourism destination evolution'.

One could argue that tourism is an ideal playground for Evolutionary Economic Geography (EEG). Above all, this sector is more place-bound and reliant on local institutional conditions, production systems and socio-historical constructs of reality and imagination than many other segments of the economy. On the one hand, it is embedded in the complex social and political relationships which uniquely characterize places, while, on the other hand, it also experiences heightened exposure to constantly evolving extra-local trends, consumer preferences, and cultural and lifestyle fashions. The potentially low entry barriers combined with the power to transform the economic fortunes of places across the entire spectrum of localities indeed raise the question of why tourism is not an evolutionary science. The constant balancing act of having to re-invent itself by means of adaptation and branching processes, while battling institutional lock-in and managing co-evolution with other sectors in the economy, suggests that EEG provides an ideal framework to study tourism.

The present volume is a testimony to the usefulness of EEG approaches in the study of tourism, but it also points to many open avenues for future research efforts, encouraging others to contribute to this exciting and highly relevant line of inquiry.

Dieter F. Kogler
Dublin, 22 December 2015

1 Why is tourism not an evolutionary science?

Understanding the past, present and future of destination evolution

Patrick Brouder, Salvador Anton Clavé, Alison Gill and Dimitri Ioannides

Introduction

More than a century ago, Thorstein Veblen (1898) famously asked 'Why is economics not an evolutionary science?'. At its core, Veblen's paper of the same name questioned the dominant thinking of the day that economic systems tended towards equilibrium, arguing instead that economies evolve over time. Thus, it is not enough to merely describe the economy, but rather conceptualize it in terms of long-term change processes and development (Boulton 2010). While the study of economic systems has slowly opened up to account for Veblen's ground-breaking thinking, there is no denying that the epistemological parameters of classical economics still dominate scholarship on economic systems well over 100 years later.

Evolutionary economics has emerged as an important part of economic studies in recent decades (Dosi and Nelson 1994), and its natural progression to economic geography was heralded as recently as 1999 in Boschma and Lambooy's crossover paper 'Evolutionary economics and economic geography' (Boschma and Lambooy 1999). In the decade which followed, many geographers presented the case for a distinct sub-discipline of 'Evolutionary Economic Geography' (EEG), where 'we start from the definition of economic geography as dealing with the uneven distribution of economic activity across space. An evolutionary approach specifically focusses on the historical processes that produce these patterns' (Boschma and Frenken 2011: 286).

EEG has had a marked influence on economic geographers, prompting certain observers to ask whether this amounts to 'yet another turn' in the subject's progression, following so-called turns such as the critical turn and relational turn (Grabher 2009). Empirical research has delivered results in studies of industrial clusters and regions with historical legacies in manufacturing (e.g. Klepper 2007), clearly focusing on the regional level (e.g. Neffke *et al.* 2011). The *Handbook of Evolutionary Economic Geography* was published in 2010 (Boschma and Martin 2010a) and the sub-field continues to be adopted by geographers working in various regional environments. Tourism appears to lend itself particularly well to an EEG empirical approach, especially within localities that depend heavily on this sector for their economic revival and diversification (Brouder 2014a).

Has tourism research been limited by a lack of an evolutionary perspective? Many tourism researchers have long been interested in the development of destinations over time, though they have resisted the temptation for simplistic modelling of destination development with early calls for multilineal models of tourism development (Cohen 1979). The most influential model for the evolution of tourism destinations was put forward by Butler (1980) in the Tourist Area Life Cycle (TALC) Model. The primary concern of the TALC model was understanding resource management under conditions of increasing visitor numbers, but the stages of the model from exploration (in the early stage) to consolidation (during the peak stage) and beyond certainly implied ongoing evolutionary processes at work. EEG is one approach for helping academics understand change processes at the destination level and, as such, tourism geographers have become increasingly eager to utilize an EEG lens in their empirical studies.

This volume brings together a group of scholars who have been conducting research on tourism destinations using evolutionary approaches and, in particular, EEG perspectives. This introductory chapter offers an overview of EEG and tourism research to date and presents the empirical chapters that follow.

Evolutionary economic geography

Boschma and Martin (2010b) argue that EEG is a distinct sub-discipline in economic geography and not a subset of either neoclassical or institutional approaches. EEG research pays attention to the long-term processes of change in the spatial economy, with an empirical focus on individuals and firms at the regional level. EEG theorists have been inspired by Schumpeter (1934) and emphasize novelty and innovation through human creativity as the main drivers of economic evolution. Thus, there is a focus on knowledge creation and dissemination throughout firms and within regions. While knowledge creation is inherently a dynamic process, EEG theory also deals with long-term change and the barriers to dynamic knowledge creation are just as important as the aids.

EEG has three antecedent theoretical pillars on which it has developed: path dependence, complexity theory, and Generalized Darwinism (Boschma and Martin 2010b). Path dependence is an established area of research within economic geography (Arthur 1994; David 1997). It implies that history matters and that feedback loops in, for example, a region's economy become self-reinforcing over time. This can lead to increased product and market development for a particular sector and can result in increasing sectoral productivity and regional prosperity over time. However, path-dependent regional economic evolution also tends towards regional 'lock-in', whereby the processes of knowledge creation and sharing, regional institutions and political support for the dominant path tend to reinforce that path over time. Lock-in can prove successful for decades, but behind the overt success is a hidden change in the exposure of the regional economy – by placing all of the regional 'eggs in one basket'. This classic pattern of success followed by collapse is most notable in the former industrial regions of Europe and the 'rustbelt' of North America. Much of the research on EEG has been inspired by the 'industrial ruination' (Mah 2012), which has affected formerly prosperous regions, with scholars hoping to understand ways to break away from regional path-dependence before ruination occurs. As tourism has reached maturity in many destinations, the same worries relating to the negative outcomes of path dependence have become concerns of researchers but also locals. In many mass tourism destinations, tourism's status as a single-sector economy thus raises the spectre of future regional ruination.

Martin and Sunley (2015:10) argue that 'local and regional economies are complex, multilayered systems, both connected to and in part also constitutive of their (competitive) environments, and that to understand fully their evolutionary development over time requires analysis of their multi-scalar and interdependent character'.

Entrepreneurs and labour operate in complex, multiple environments (e.g. social, cultural, technological, institutional, industrial), and these environments are interdependent and marked by reciprocal causality (Martin and Sunley 2015). Neither is any one sector self-contained and there is interaction between sectors as well as within sectors. While this point is obvious, it is important to remember since most empirical studies, and this is certainly the case in tourism studies, tend to be reduced to single-sector examinations. An evolutionary perspective opens up for broader conceptualizations, which may be incorporated into empirical studies. For example, the concept of co-evolution is utilized in EEG studies and shows that new paths may emerge endogenously and grow independently of the dominant path (or paths) while still interacting with those paths due to the complex environment at the regional level. Co-evolution within the region or between sectors thus negotiates the tension between the interdependent environments and the individual agencies.

The terminology of generalized Darwinism is the most obvious marker of EEG studies. Generalized Darwinism includes the concepts of novelty and continuity, variety, selection and retention. It is promulgated as a universal, multi-level approach to studies in social and economic evolution (Hodgson and Knudsen 2010). In EEG it is the widely used terminology for understanding how knowledge is constantly produced and reproduced in a given region. Some scholars argue that institutions are an important part of a generalized Darwinian framework of economic evolution (Essletzbichler 2009; Hodgson and Knudsen 2010), while others argue that the evolutionary project in economic geography cannot supplant institutional geography (MacKinnon *et al.* 2009). An important distinction in EEG (in comparison with other regional development frameworks, e.g. innovation systems and agglomeration economies) is that regions are not seen as units of selection, but rather as selection environments upon which evolutionary processes operate (Boschma and Martin 2010b). An important focus in generalized Darwinism is the desire for variety, in contrast to diversification per se, as a driver of regional innovation and growth. The distinction between variety and diversification centres on the idea that it is related variety, which is similar enough to other things going on in the region that it is complementary without being in direct competition. This would lead to a situation which is optimal for regional development. This idea is readily applicable at the destination level since tourism is a sector made up of a number of related industries.

Destination evolution

Since the emergence of interest in studying tourism as an activity that creates and develops productive spaces, a range of significant studies on destination evolution has appeared (Saarinen 2004; see also Table 1.1). Pioneer approaches such as those of Gilbert (1939) were followed by further endeavours through the 1950s, which combined empirical and theoretical considerations within the frame of different regional academic traditions of tourism geography (especially the French, German and Anglo-American approaches). These analyses mainly focused on the role of tourism demand as the main driver of economic and spatial change (Wolfe 1952; Christaller 1964). Several models (e.g. Plog 1973; Doxey 1975; Miossec 1977; Stansfield 1978; Cohen 1979) revealed that the impacts of tourism are linked to specific stages of destination development. These frameworks also provided the ability to build in acceptance that destinations can experience processes of rejuvenation if they are able to adapt themselves to the changing habits and preferences of the visitors (see Pearce 1989). Parallel to this is a long tradition of empirical research, mainly focused on the analysis of the specific history of each destination. Usually these studies portray destination evolution as a process mainly caused by the growth in the number of tourists and by changes in the provision of services, facilities and infrastructure for tourists (see Brey *et al.* 2007 for a complete review).

Inspired by the aforementioned literature and, especially, the concept of the Product Life Cycle (Vernon 1966; Cox 1967), Butler's TALC model (Butler 1980) appeared as a fundamental framework for analysing the evolution of destinations. The TALC model has been used to study a myriad of destination cases and has also been a source of inspiration for further conceptual work on destination development. For instance, Haywood (2006) has called for an adjustment of approach to how tourism scholars utilize the TALC, by arguing for the necessity to move away from the notion of changed stages or states and instead to focus on the actual processes of change. Others have sought to validate it (see Butler 2006a, 2006b) and to modify and extend it (Hovinen 1981; Haywood 1986; Cooper 1992; Getz 1992; Ioannides 1992; Benedetto and Bojanic 1992; Meyer-Arendt 1993; Agarwal 1997; Baum 1998; Priestley and Mundet 1998; Faulkner 2002; Russell and Faulkner 2004). The TALC has generated the most relevant destination evolution research stream. It is even more relevant than historical studies related to specific destinations (see, for instance, Walton 2000; Cirer 2009; and Battilani and Faure 2011).

Nevertheless, parallel to the adoption of the TALC model as a convenient theoretical framework, other longitudinal models have also been proposed since the 1980s. For example, the French analyst Chadefaud (1987) built a useful

Table 1.1 Selected papers on destination evolution with approaches other than Evolutionary Economic Geography.

Authors	Main contribution	Year
Gilbert	Changes and growth of the built-up area in seaside health resorts acting as residential population attractors with a spatial development perspective.	1939
Wolfe	Interest on the processes of change of tourism destinations and its potential effects with special interest in second-home areas.	1952
Christaller	Tourist flows and patterns explaining the spatial distribution of tourist places from a demand perspective.	1964
Plog	Changes in the tourist market are related to subsequent changes in the destinations visited. Destinations decline is predictable and inevitable.	1973
Doxey	Model suggesting that communities pass through a sequence of reactions as the impacts of tourism in a destination become more pronounced.	1975
Miossec	Destination evolution is driven by the continuous adaptation of demand and supply with 5 phases from a pioneering stage to a congestion stage.	1977
Stansfield	Seminal case-study about rejuvenation of tourism destinations. Rejuvenation is possible if destination emphasises its (unique) locational advantages.	1978
Cohen	Discussion of the need to conceive multilineal models of tourism development illustrated by an elaboration of MacCannell's fundamental concepts.	1979
Butler	Seminal model – Tourism Area Life Cycle (TALC) – starting a long trend of research on the evolution of tourist-area demand. Defines pattern and stages in the tourist area's evolution.	1980
Gormsen	Spatio-temporal model explaining common factors in the development of destinations over increasingly peripheral zones of the world.	1981, 1997
Chadefaud	The 'collective myth' – the mental representations of demand – as the driver of the tourism product's evolution.	1987
Smith	Focus on development from a spatial perspective. Tourism development linked to urbanization process. Comparative spatial evolutionary model for contemporary beach resorts.	1991, 1992
Gill	Uses growth theories to highlight importance of social and political processes in the evolution of resort destinations.	2000
Agarwal	Exploration of the theoretical relationship between Butler's TALC and the restructuring thesis.	2002
Equipe MIT	Distinction between types of spaces created by tourism and types of spaces transformed by tourism and exploration of links between them.	2002, 2005, 2011

(*Continued*)

Table 1.1 (Continued)

Authors	Main contribution	Year
Papatheodorou	Theoretical model of tourism evolutionary patterns from an economic geography perspective, illustrating the interaction of market and spatial forces in destination evolution and development	2004
Prideaux	Multidimensional model – Resort Development Spectrum – based on the long-term evolution of demand in a destination.	2004
Andriotis	Identification of the principal characteristics determining morphological change of coastal resorts in a predictable sequence of stages.	2006
Agarwal	Relevance of relational spatiality for spatial planning in coastal resort restructuring.	2012
Anton Clavé	Categorization of different types of mature Mediterranean mass coastal destinations according to the (re) development strategies implemented by decision-makers.	2012
Weaver	Paper positioning sustainable mass tourism as the desired outcome for most destinations. It defines three distinctive paths: the market-driven organic, the regulation-driven incremental, and the hybrid induced.	2012
Pavlovich	Critique of the linear models of destination evolution based upon the concept of networks as rhizomic. Change as anti-hierarchical, self-organised and locally inspired.	2013
Clivaz *et al.*	Development of the concept of 'touristic capital' of resorts in order to analyse their specific trajectories over time.	2014

diachronic model to analyse the evolution of destinations/products based on the relationship between the dominant and dominated classes' mental representations (see Suchet 2015). The spatio-temporal model of Gormsen (1981, 1997) defined stages in temporal development of tourism in seaside resorts according to the following aspects, taking an evolutionary, global scope: availability of specific tourist services; source of capital for development; origin of supplies (local, regional or further afield); effects of tourist traffic; and the environmental stress imposed upon the coastal area. Additionally, Smith (1992) identified coastal-area tourism development as a process of urbanization that could be clearly defined in terms of physical expansion, functional diversification and environmental impacts.

Following in this vein, the new millennium has seen the appearance of several new contributions. For example, Agarwal (2002) framed the analysis of the destination evolution processes within the concept of restructuring, and Gill (2000) examined social and political dynamics in the evolution of a new mountain-resort destination. Building a comprehensive general theory of tourism development, the Equipe MIT (2002, 2005, 2011) in France strongly argued how tourism has the capacity to allow places to emerge with new systems of actors and new social and urban practices (see also Stock 2003). Parallel to this, Prideaux's (2004) Resort Development Spectrum (RDS) related the evolution of destination resorts to long-term changes in demand, while Papatheodorou (2004) theoretically explored the evolutionary patterns of destinations linking markets and spatial evolution. Additionally, Andriotis (2006) returned to the domain of morphological studies such as those of Meyer-Arendt (1993) and Smith (1992) and defined the morphological transformation of Mediterranean coastal destinations through a number of development stages. Beyond the specific value of each of these separate constructs, their most important contribution was their ability to introduce new perspectives to the issue of the evolution of destinations and to continue the debate about the utility, the limitations and the findings obtained from the well-established TALC model.

More recently, other approaches have appeared, reflecting that the evolution of destinations is highly dependent on enacting human agency. Anton Clavé (2012a) categorized different types of mature Mediterranean mass coastal destinations according to the redevelopment strategies implemented by decision-makers. Clivaz *et al.* (2014) used the concept of *tourist capital of resorts* to discuss how collective agency could generate a metamorphic dynamic able to facilitate the conversion of resorts into urban places. Pavlovich (2014) adopted the Deleuzian concept of networks as *rhizomic*, in the sense that they are anti-hierarchical and change can occur in an unexpected manner in any direction, and thus, through collaboration, network connections are fundamental in destination change. In notable contrast with other previous approaches, these contributions focus the analysis on the evolution of destinations as places instead of analysing changes of tourism in places. Also during this period, Weaver (2012) differentiated between organic, incremental and induced paths in mass tourism, and Agarwal (2012) went back to the restructuring approach. In her 2012 paper she utilizes Healey's (2004) conceptualizations of space and place and explores the role of relational spatiality in destination restructuring.

All of the cited papers were produced with a general evolutionary (but non-dependency) interest and they illustrate how the study of destination development dynamics has been a relevant issue in tourism studies. Nevertheless, much has to be done to synthesize the diversity of concepts used by these authors in order to develop a coherent approach. However, taken together, they indicate the existence of certain key issues other than the evolution of demand, facilities and services that should be discussed when analysing destination evolution. Obviously, these approaches could also be linked to other tourism analysis perspectives, such as resilience (Tyrell and Johnston 2008; Calgaroa *et al.* 2014; Lew 2014), the well-established research on sustainability development (Bramwell and Lane 2012) and tourism geography relational approaches (Pastras and Bramwell 2013), including, in this last case, the aforementioned research on destination regeneration as viewed from a relational perspective (Agarwal 2012).

In contrast with early frameworks focused on the role of demand in destination evolution, the most recent understanding of destination change includes the role of the social, economic and political context in enabling and constraining change processes. Both Haywood (2006) and Butler (2004) state that analysis needs to be context specific to fully identify causes and effects of tourism destination evolution. Moreover, Agarwal (2005) points out that resort changes have to be examined in a global context, linking resort development with global change, local governance and collective action. Nevertheless, most models focus overwhelmingly on the evolution of tourism activities and in so doing they offer inadequate explanation of change dynamics at the destination level (Agarwal 1994). Thus, tourism destinations, like other places, evolve by means of dynamic processes, including the necessary mobility of people (not only tourists), of capital, of goods and of information (Jackson and Murphy 2002). Currently, most analyses acknowledge that it is not possible to study the evolution of destinations without also including social, cultural, economic, and environmental changes and challenges (Amin 2002). So, analyses of destination evolution need further conceptual development of the local and global contextual forces inducing change (Butler 2004; Agarwal 2005; Dodds 2007), and research must encompass the idea that destinations are complex places with residential, productive and social functions extending beyond tourism with co-evolving trajectories (Equipe MIT 2002).

Also, when analysing the evolution of destinations, researchers increasingly consider tourism development as a socially constructed process. According to Verbole (2003: 152), tourism development might be 'seen as a dynamic, on-going socially constructed and negotiated process that involves many social actors (individuals, groups and institutions) who continuously reshape and transform it to fit it to their perceptions, needs, values and agendas'. In this sense, as widely evidenced, research on destination evolution must focus on analysing the impact of stakeholders' decisions and interventions in response to either external or internal influences (Haywood 1986, 2006; Cooper and Jackson 1989; Ioannides 1992; Anton Clavé 2012b; Pavlovich 2014; Clivaz et al. 2014).

Furthermore, current approaches to tourism destination evolution tend to avoid the implicit determinism outlined by many initial demand-oriented evolution models. This determinism has been linked to the existence of a carrying-capacity threshold for a destination that, when reached, forces it to regenerate in order to survive. There are well-known cases of mature destinations that have been able to overcome declining paths and increase their ability to attract markets (Russell and Faulkner 2004; Aguiló et al. 2005; Ivars et al. 2013). A central lesson from these destinations is that renewed success and survival are the result of a shared strategic vision and the deep involvement of key stakeholders in the construction of an atmosphere of political, entrepreneurial and social consensus for new development. Forgetting this lesson could lead to incorrect forecasts about irreversible tendencies towards decline as has been the case in some of the best-known second-generation Mediterranean destinations (Knowles and Curtis 1999). From a critical analysis approach, Stock (2003) further questions the existence of deterministic demand growth thresholds since the determining (and deterministic) impacts leading to decline are more of an ideological a priori than actual scientific observation. Stock claims that such a priori positioning comes from the frontal rejection of mass tourism, which many authors adopt (Stock 2003).

All in all, current developments point out the strong need to explore and discuss how these different perspectives are contributing to a deeper understanding of destination evolution and how research can move from the 'what' to the 'how' and 'why' (Brouder 2014b). Within tourism geography, Brouder and Eriksson (2013a) and Ma and Hassink (2013) have started to deal with the synergies between the TALC and EEG, while other authors have begun adopting certain EEG concepts as a way to better understand the specific mechanisms behind the evolution of destinations as places (e.g. Gill and Williams 2011, 2014).

EEG, which has been used to analyse the evolution of other specialized places and regions (Boschma and Frenken 2006; Boschma and Martin 2010a), is now emerging as a promising framework of tourism research in order to enhance understanding of 'how' and 'why' tourism destinations evolve over time (Ioannides *et al.* 2015). As is discussed in the following chapters of this volume, EEG has released within tourism studies the potential of powerful economic geography notions such as branching (Brouder and Eriksson 2013b), co-evolution (Brouder and Fullerton 2015; García-Cabrera and Durán-Herrera 2014; Ma and Hassink 2013; Larsson and Lindström 2014; Randelli *et al.* 2014), path creation (Gill and Williams 2011, 2014), path dependence (Bramwell and Cox 2009; Chen and Bao 2014; Ma and Hassink 2013; Williams 2013), path plasticity (Halkier and Therkelsen 2013) and survival (Brouder and Eriksson 2013b). Additionally, bridges between conventional EEG research development and other economic geography approaches are also in the works, for example, with relational economic geography (Sanz-Ibáñez and Anton Clavé 2014) and, in attempts to determine the role of coupling between global and local stakeholders in destination evolution, with Global Production Network analysis (Niewiadomski 2014; Sanz-Ibáñez and Anton Clavé 2016). Moreover, specific research approaches to single types of tourism destinations have also been proposed, for example the dynamic and contested state of urban tourism (Brouder and Ioannides 2014).

To sum up, EEG concepts are creating a new framework to aid not only in understanding how destinations evolve over time, but also in interpreting the role of tourism as a way of accumulating capital in destinations and its implications in terms of the dynamics of economic variety, environmental (in)equity and social justice. EEG also highlights how transformations of destinations as places help them survive as communities. All in all, it can be argued that by incorporating an EEG lens in tourism research we can begin to respond to Britton's (1991: 466) critical perspective about the geography of tourism when he stated that 'by treating tourism almost solely as a discrete economic subsystem, many revealing links have been missed between tourism and other politically and theoretically important geographic issues which demonstrate the wider role and position of tourism in capitalist accumulation'. The eighteen papers already published on tourism and EEG (see Table 1.2) and the eight empirical chapters included in this volume are an initial attempt by tourism scholars to engage with EEG and, as shall be seen, a lot of important work has been done and has opened the door to further avenues of enquiry.

Table 1.2 Tourism papers incorporating Evolutionary Economic Geography theory.

Authors	Description	Publication	Published[a]
Gill & Williams	Case study of path dependence in Whistler Resort, Canada	*Journal of Sustainable Tourism*	2011
Brouder & Eriksson	Regional Branching towards tourism in north Sweden's resource-based regions	*Tourism Geographies*	2012
Ma & Hassink	Case study of path dependence and co-evolution in Gold Coast, Australia	*Annals of Tourism Research*	2012
Halkier & Therkelsen	Path dependence and 'path plasticity' in Denmark's coastal tourism regions	*Zeitschrift für Wirtschaftsgeographie*	2013
Larsson & Lindström	Co-evolution of new tourism with traditional boat-building in Sweden	*European Planning Studies*	2013
Brouder & Eriksson	Conceptual overview of the nexus of EEG and tourism studies	*Annals of Tourism Research*	2013
Williams	Understanding of tourism mobilities as path-depending or path-creating	*Journal of Sustainable Tourism*	2013
Randelli *et al.*	Path creation and regional lock-in within rural tourism in Italy	*Land Use Policy*	2014
Brouder	Review of 'EEG and Tourism' sessions at AAG Meeting 2013	*Tourism Geographies*	2014
García-Cabrera & Durán-Herrera	Co-evolution of tourism firms and institutional change in a crisis context	*Annals of Tourism Research*	2014
Chen & Bao	Path dependence in the evolution of resort governance models in China	*Tourism Geographies*	2014
Brouder	Review of EEG and tourism papers to date and list of future research paths	*Tourism Geographies*	2014

(Continued)

Table 1.2 (Continued)

Authors	Description	Publication	Published[a]
Gill & Williams	Path Creation through 'Mindful Deviation' of stakeholders in Whistler	*Tourism Geographies*	2014
Ma & Hassink	Path dependence and regional lock-in within tourism in Guilin, China	*Tourism Geographies*	2014
Sanz-Ibáñez & Anton-Clavé	Conceptual paper linking tourism destination evolution to agglomerations and relational economic geography	*Tourism Geographies*	2014
Brouder & Ioannides	Urban tourism through an EEG lens	*Urban Forum*	2014
Niewiadomski	Framework for analysing hotel industry using EEG and Global Production Network theory	*Tourism Geographies*	2015
Brouder & Fullerton	Co-evolution of multiple tourism paths across the Niagara Region, Canada	*Scandinavian Journal of Hospitality and Tourism*	2015
Sanz-Ibáñez & Anton-Clavé	Analysis of how local–global coupling among stakeholders hints at destination upgrading	*Annals of Tourism Research*	2015

Note:[a] Published date is when the paper was first available online, volume and issue date is available in the references.

Summary of this volume

The theoretical pillars on which EEG is built – path dependence, complexity and generalized Darwinism (Boschma and Martin 2010b) – also inform each of the studies in the present volume to a greater or lesser extent. Several chapters focus on path dependency in various contexts. From the Danish coast (Chapter 2) to the Whistler resort municipality in Canada (Chapter 3) to a selection of remote communities in Australia (Chapter 6), the chapters highlight institutional lock-in in particular. Tracing attempts to break from existing paths to creating new paths, these three chapters, taken together, point to the need for long-term perspectives in understanding destination evolution. For example, Gill and Williams' work (Chapter 3) is based on decades of research in Whistler and reinforces the academic necessity of long-term engagement with communities, in particular for qualitative studies of destination evolution. Gill and Williams (Chapter 3) cite Hall's (2011) work on why a lack of policy learning restricts the development of sustainable tourism governance over the long term. This central evolutionary question of learning in regions is also in focus in Carson and Carson's study (Chapter 6), where institutional lock-in has limited the development of sustainable tourism. Carson and Carson acknowledge the inter-sectoral pressures of institutions in resource-dependent communities, but they also go deeper to show how intra-sectoral failures in tourism seem to be repeated over time as a lack of learning from the past limits the future. Thus, these three chapters show that learning is key for sustainable governance in tourism destinations and that only localized strategic learning leads to contextualized strategic action.

Complexity theory is also a major element of several of the chapters in this volume. Halkier and James (Chapter 2) and Meekes, Parra and de Roo (Chapter 9) choose to utilize a complex adaptive systems (CAS) approach in their studies. In Chapter 9 the authors attempt to merge notions of CAS with EEG concepts and to capture the CAS for tourism and recreation in one region of the Netherlands. While the study is more of a snapshot in time rather than a longitudinal study, the authors highlight the usefulness of evolutionary concepts such as self-organization and emergence in understanding complex change. At the same time, Halkier and James (Chapter 2) tie the extant studies on CAS in tourism (e.g. Farrell and Twining-Ward 2004) to the emerging use of resilience approaches in tourism geography (Lew 2014). Halkier and James's use of Boschma's (2014) notions of adaptation and adaptability in regional resilience is of particular interest in understanding how complex change includes both short-term adjustment to circumstance and long-term strategic planning.

In Chapter 5, Sanz-Ibáñez, Wilson and Anton Clavé focus on key 'moments' in destination evolution, arguing that at certain points in time there is a clear and marked shift in a destination's path trajectory and that analysing such shifts alongside and in addition to the general development trajectory over time will lead to a more nuanced understanding of human agency in destination evolution. Niewiadomski's study (Chapter 7) examines the regional development implications of one key moment in Central and Eastern Europe – the post-communist opening of markets and the resultant influx of international hotel chains. By focusing on knowledge transfer, Niewiadomski shows how EEG concepts are useful in understanding how external knowledge helps to create new paths during hotel operations and, ultimately, how post-communist regions 'de-lock' themselves from their unproductive past.

Related to the concept of complexity discussed above, co-evolution features as an important theme of several chapters in this volume. In Chapter 4, Hassink and Ma present a research framework for co-evolution in tourism areas. They see co-evolution as a cognate concept to the TALC (Butler 1980), arguing that an understanding of co-evolution is not just necessary but, in fact, well suited to tourism-area analyses since such areas are marked by a myriad of products, sectors and institutions operating at various levels in a destination. Moreover, Hassink and Ma argue that co-evolution strengthens work on tourism regional innovation systems and so adds to the depth of understanding in tourism geography. Brouder and Fullerton (Chapter 8) use the concept of co-evolution to interrogate the assumed unilineal development of tourism in the Niagara region of Canada. They argue that even within tourism in one small region there are multiple, co-evolving paths and that these distinct, albeit inter-related, paths have their own nuanced institutional environment. This intra-regional disjuncture means that sustainable tourism development is not optimized. While these studies do not engage deeply with generalized Darwinism, the presence of co-evolution in the empirical cases means there is scope for deeper engagement going forward.

In summary, we believe that the contributions to this volume are timely as concerns about the sustainability of maturing tourism destinations increase and as tourism development continues to expand to ever more communities and regions across the globalizing world. In the following chapters, the reader will find a set of research papers which explore long-term change in a diverse set of tourism destinations, with all studies drawing inspiration from EEG. The concluding chapter by Ioannides and Brouder reflects on the evolution of tourism research over time and the central place EEG will have in the direction of future research.

References

Agarwal, S. (1994). 'The resort cycle revisited: Implications for resorts'. In C.P. Cooper and A. Lockwood (eds) *Progress in Tourism, Recreation and Hospitality Management*. Chichester: Wiley (pp. 194–208).

Agarwal, S. (1997). 'The resort cycle and seaside tourism: An assessment of its applicability and validity'. *Tourism Management* 18, 65–73.

Agarwal, S. (2002). 'Restructuring seaside tourism: The resort lifecyle'. *Annals of Tourism Research* 29(1), 25–55.

Agarwal, S. (2005). 'Global–local interactions in English coastal resorts: Theoretical perspectives'. *Tourism Geographies* 7(4), 351–72.

Agarwal, S. (2012). 'Relational spatiality and resort restructuring'. *Annals of Tourism Research* 39(1), 134–54.

Aguiló, E., Alegre, J. and Sard, M. (2005). 'The persistence of the sun and sand tourism model'. *Tourism Management* 26(2), 219–31.

Amin, A. (2002). 'Spatialities of globalisation'. *Environment and Planning* 34(3), 385–99.

Andriotis, K. (2006). 'Hosts, guests and politics: Coastal resorts morphological change'. *Annals of Tourism Research* 33(4), 1079–98.

Anton Clavé, S. (2012a). 'Rethinking mass tourism, space and place'. In J. Wilson (ed.) *Routledge Handbook of Tourism Geographies: New Perspectives on Space, Place and Tourism*. London: Routledge (pp. 217–24).

Anton Clavé, S. (ed.) (2012b). *10 Lessons on Tourism: The Challenge of Reinventing Destinations*. Barcelona: Planeta.

Arthur, W.B. (1994). *Increasing Returns and Path Dependence in the Economy*. Ann Arbor: University of Michigan Press.

Battilani, P. and Faure, F. (2011). 'The rise of a service-based economy and its transformation: Seaside tourism and the case of Rimini'. *Journal of Tourism History* 1(1), 27–40.

Baum, T. (1998). 'Taking the exit route: Extending the tourism area life cycle model'. *Current Issues in Tourism* 1(2), 167–75.

Benedetto, C.A. di and Bojanic, D.C. (1992). 'Tourism area life cycle extensions'. *Annals of Tourism Research* 20, 557–70.

Boschma, R. (2014). 'Towards an evolutionary perspective on regional resilience'. *Papers in Evolutionary Economic Geography*, no. 14/09. Utrecht University, Utrecht.

Boschma, R. and Frenken, K. (2006). 'Why is economic geography not an evolutionary science? Towards an evolutionary economic geography. *Journal of Economic Geography* 6, 273–302.

Boschma, R. and Frenken, K. (2011). 'The emerging empirics of evolutionary economic geography'. *Journal of Economic Geography* 11(2), 295–307.

Boschma, R. and Lambooy, J. (1999). 'Evolutionary economics and economic geography'. *Journal of Evolutionary Economics* 9, 411–29.

Boschma, R. and Martin, R. (eds) (2010a). *The Handbook of Evolutionary Economic Geography*. Cheltenham, UK: Edward Elgar Publishing.

Boschma, R. and Martin, R. (2010b). 'The aims and scope of evolutionary economic geography'. In R. Boschma and R. Martin (eds) *The Handbook of Evolutionary Economic Geography*. Cheltenham, UK: Edward Elgar Publishing (pp. 3–39).

Boulton, J. (2010). Introduction to a reprint of: 'Why is economics not an evolutionary science?'. *Emergence: Complexity and Organisation* 12(2), 41–69.

Bramwell, B. and Cox, V. (2009). 'Stage and path dependence approaches to the evolution of a national park tourism partnership'. *Journal of Sustainable Tourism* 17(2), 191–206.

Bramwell, B. and Lane, B. (2012). 'Towards innovation in sustainable tourism research?'. *Journal of Sustainable Tourism* 20(1), 1–7.

Brey, E.T., Morrison, A.M. and Mills, J.M. (2007). 'An examination of destination resort research'. *Current Issues in Tourism* 10(5), 415–42.

Britton, S. (1991). 'Tourism, capital and place: Towards a critical geography of tourism'. *Environment and Planning D: Society and Space* 9, 451–78.

Brouder, P. (2014a). 'Evolutionary economic geography: A new path for tourism studies?' *Tourism Geographies* 16(1), 2–7.

Brouder, P. (2014b). 'Evolutionary economic geography and tourism studies: Extant studies and future research directions'. *Tourism Geographies* 16(4), 540–5.

Brouder, P. and Eriksson, R.H. (2013a). 'Tourism evolution: On the synergies of tourism studies and evolutionary economic geography'. *Annals of Tourism Research* 43, 370–89.

Brouder, P. and Eriksson, R.H. (2013b). 'Staying power: What influences micro-firm survival in tourism?'. *Tourism Geographies* 15(1), 124–43.

Brouder, P. and Fullerton, C. (2015). 'Exploring heterogeneous tourism development paths: Cascade effect or co-evolution in Niagara?'. *Scandinavian Journal of Hospitality and Tourism* 15(1–2), 152–66.

Brouder, P. and Ioannides, D. (2014). 'Urban tourism and evolutionary economic geography: Complexity and co-evolution in contested spaces'. *Urban Forum* 25(4), 419–30.

Butler, R.W. (1980). 'The concept of a tourist area life cycle of evolution: Implications for management of resources'. *The Canadian Geographer* 24(1), 5–12.

Butler, R.W. (2004). 'The tourism area life cycle in the twenty-first century'. In A.A. Lew, C.M. Hall and A.M. Williams (eds) *A Companion to Tourism*. Oxford: Blackwell (pp. 159–69).

Butler, R. (ed.) (2006a). *The Tourism Area Life Cycle: Applications and Modifications*. Clevedon, UK: Channel View.

Butler, R. (ed.) (2006b). *The Tourism Area Life Cycle: Conceptual and Theoretical Issues*. Clevedon, UK: Channel View.

Calgaroa, E., Lloyd, K. and Dominey-Howes, D. (2014). 'From vulnerability to transformation: A framework for assessing the vulnerability and resilience of tourism destinations'. *Journal of Sustainable Tourism* 22(3), 341–60.

Chadefaud, M. (1987). *Aux origins du tourisme dans les Pays de l'Adour. Du mythe à l'espace: un essai de géographie historique.* Pau: Département de géographie et d'aménagement de l'Université de Pau et des Pays de l'Adour, et Centre de Recherche sur l'Impact Socio-spatial de l'Aménagement.

Chen, G. and Bao, J. (2014). 'Path dependence in the evolution of resort governance models in China'. *Tourism Geographies* 16(5), 812–25.

Christaller, W. (1964). 'Some considerations of tourism location in Europe: The peripheral regions – underdeveloped countries – recreation areas'. *Papers in Regional Science* 12(1), 95–105.

Cirer, J.C. (2009). *La Invenció del Turisme de Masses a Mallorca.* Palma: Institut Balear d'Economia.

Clivaz, C., Crevoisier, O., Kebir, L., Nahrath, S. and Stock, M. (2014). *Resort Development and Touristic Capital of Place.* Neuchâtel: Maison d'Analyse des Processus Sociaux. Universite de Neuchâtel.

Cohen, E. (1979). 'Rethinking the sociology of tourism'. *Annals of Tourism Research* 6(1), 18–35.

Cooper, C. (1992). 'The life cycle concept and strategic planning for coastal resorts'. *Built Environment* 18(1), 57–66.

Cooper, C. and Jackson, S. (1989). 'Destination life cycle: The Isle of Man case study'. *Annals of Tourism Research* 16(3), 377–98.

Cox, W.E. (1967). 'Product life cycles as marketing models'. *Journal of Business* 40(10), 375–84.

David, P.A. (1997). *Path Dependence and the Quest for Historical Economics: One More Chorus of the Ballad of QWERTY.* Oxford: University of Oxford.

Dodds, R. (2007). 'Sustainable tourism and policy implementation: Lessons from the case of Calvià, Spain'. *Current Issues in Tourism* 10(4), 296–322.

Dosi, G. and Nelson, R.R. (1994). 'An introduction to evolutionary theories in economics'. *Journal of Evolutionary Economics* 4(3), 153–72.

Doxey, G.V. (1975). 'A causation theory of visitor-resident irritants: Methodology and research inferences'. Proceedings of the Travel Research Association 6th Annual Conference. San Diego: Travel Research Association (pp. 195–8).

Equipe MIT (2002). *Tourismes 1. Lieux Communs.* Paris: Belin.

Equipe MIT (2005). *Tourismes 2. Moments de Lieux.* Paris: Belin.

Equipe MIT (2011). *Tourismes 3. La Révolution Durable.* Paris: Belin.

Essletzbichler, J. (2009). 'Evolutionary economic geography, institutions, and political economy'. *Economic Geography* 85(2), 159–65.

Farrell, B.H. and Twining-Ward, L. (2004). 'Reconceptualizing tourism'. *Annals of Tourism Research* 31(2), 274–95.

Faulkner, B. (2002). 'Rejuvenating a maturing tourist destination: The case of the Gold Coast. Gold Coast Tourism Visioning Project'. *Current Issues in Tourism* 5(6), 472–520.

García-Cabrera, A.M. and Durán-Herrera, J.J. (2014). 'Does the tourism industry co-evolve?' *Annals of Tourism Research* 47, 81–3.

Getz, D. (1992). 'Tourism planning and destination life cycle'. *Annals of Tourism Research* 19(4), 752–70.

Gilbert, E.W. (1939). 'The growth of inland and seaside health resorts in England'. *Scottish Geographical Magazine* 55, 16–35.

Gill, A.M. (2000). 'From growth machine to growth management: The dynamics of resort development in Whistler, British Columbia'. *Environment and Planning A* 32, 1083–103.

Gill, A.M. and Williams, P.W. (2011). 'Rethinking resort growth: Understanding evolving governance strategies in Whistler, British Columbia'. *Journal of Sustainable Tourism* 19(4–5), 629–48.

Gill, A.M. and Williams, P.W. (2014). 'Mindful deviation in creating a governance path towards sustainability in resort destinations'. *Tourism Geographies* 16(4), 546–62.

Gormsen, E. (1981). 'The spatio-temporal development of International tourism: attempt a centre-periphery model'. *Etudes & Mémoires. Centre des Hautes Etudes Touristiques d'Aix-en-Provence* 55,150–70.

Gormsen, E. (1997). 'The impact of tourism in coastal areas'. *Geo Journal* 42(1), 39–54.

Grabher, G. (2009). 'Yet another turn? The evolutionary project in economic geography'. *Economic Geography* 85(2), 119–27.

Halkier, H. and Therkelsen, A. (2013). 'Exploring tourism destination path plasticity: The case of coastal tourism in North Jutland, Denmark'. *Zeitschrift für Wirtschaftsgeographie* 57(1–2), 39–51.

Hall, C.M. (2011). 'Policy learning and policy failure in sustainable tourism governance: from first- and second-order to third-order change?' *Journal of Sustainable Tourism* 19(4–5), 649–71.

Haywood, K.M. (1986). 'Can the tourist area life-cycle be made operational?' *Tourism Management* 7(3), 154–67.

Haywood, K.M. (2006). 'Legitimising the TALC as a theory of development and change'. In R.W. Butler (ed.) *The Tourism Area Life Cycle: Conceptual and Theoretical Issues*. Clevedon, UK: Channel View (pp. 29–47).

Healey, P. (2004). 'The treatment of space and place in the new strategic spatial planning in Europe'. *International Journal of Urban and Regional Research* 28(1), 45–67.

Hodgson, GM. and Knudsen, T. (2010). *Darwin's Conjecture. The Search for General Principles of Social and Economic Evolution*. Chicago, IL.: University of Chicago Press.

Hovinen, G.R. (1981). 'A tourist cycle in Lancaster County, Pennsylvania'. *The Canadian Geographer* 25(3), 283–6.

Ioannides, D. (1992). 'Tourism development agents: The Cypriot resort cycle'. *Annals of Tourism Research* 19(4), 711–31.

Ioannides, D., Halkier, H. and Lew, A. (2015). Evolutionary economic geography and the economies of tourism destinations'. *Tourism Geographies* 16(4), 535–9.

Ivars Baidal, J.A., Rodríguez Sánchez, I. and Vera Rebollo, J.F. (2013). 'The evolution of mass tourism destinations: New approaches beyond deterministic models in Benidorm (Spain)'. *Tourism Management* 34(2), 184–95.

Jackson, J. and Murphy, P. (2002). 'Tourism destinations as clusters'. *Tourism and Hospitality* 4(1), 36–52.

Klepper, S. (2007). 'Disagreements, spinoffs, and the evolution of Detroit as the capital of the U.S. automobile industry'. *Management Science* 53(4), 616–31.

Knowles, T. and Curtis, S. (1999). 'The market viability of European mass tourist destinations: A post-stagnation life cycle analysis'. *International Journal of Tourism Research* 1, 87–96.

Larsson, A. and Lindström, K. (2014). 'Bridging the knowledge-gap between the old and the new: Regional marine experience production in Orust, Västra Götaland, Sweden'. *European Planning Studies* 22(8), 1551–68.

Lew, A.A. (2014). 'Scale, change and resilience in community tourism planning'. *Tourism Geographies* 16(1), 14–22.

Ma, M. and Hassink, R. (2013). 'An evolutionary perspective on tourism area development'. *Annals of Tourism Research* 41, 89–109.

MacKinnon, D., Cumbers, A., Pike, A., Birch, K. and McMaster, R. (2009). 'Evolution in economic geography: Institutions, political economy, and adaptation'. *Economic Geography* 85(2), 129–50.

Mah, A. (2012). *Industrial Ruination, Community, and Place: Landscapes and Legacies of Urban Decline*. Toronto, ON: University of Toronto Press.

Martin, R. and Sunley, P. (2015). 'Towards a developmental turn in evolutionary economic geography?'. *Regional Studies* 49(5), 712–32.

Meyer-Arendt, K. (1993). 'Geomorphic impacts of resort evolution along the Gulf of Mexico coast: applicability of resort cycle models'. In P.P. Wong (ed.) *Tourism vs Environment: The Case for Coastal Areas*. Dordrecht: Kluwer (pp. 125–38).

Miossec, J.M. (1977). 'Un modèle de l'espace touristique'. *L'Espace Géographique* 6(1), 41–8.

Neffke, F., Henning, M. and Boschma, R. (2011). 'How do regions diversify over time? Industry relatedness and the development of new growth paths in regions'. *Economic Geography* 87(3), 237–65.

Niewiadomski, P. (2014). 'Towards an economic-geographical approach to the globalisation of the hotel industry'. *Tourism Geographies* 16(1), 48–67.

Papatheodorou, A. (2004). 'Exploring the evolution of tourism resorts'. *Annals of Tourism Research* 31(1), 219–37.

Pastras, P. and Bramwell, B. (2013). 'A strategic-relational approach to tourism policy'. *Annals of Tourism Research* 43, 390–414.

Pavlovich, K. (2014). 'A rhizomic approach to tourism destination evolution and transformation'. *Tourism Management* 41, 1–8.

Pearce, D.G. (1989). *Tourist Development*, 2nd edition. Harlow: Longman; and New York: Wiley.

Plog, S.C. (1973). 'Why destination areas rise and fall in popularity'. *Cornell Hotel and Restaurant Administration Quarterly* 13, 6–13.

Prideaux, B. (2004). 'The resort development spectrum: The case of the Gold Coast, Australia'. *Tourism Geographies* 6(1), 26–58.

Priestley, G. and Mundet, L. (1998). 'The post-stagnation phase of the resort cycle'. *Annals of Tourism Research* 25(1), 85–111.

Randelli, F., Romei, P. and Tortora, M. (2014). 'An evolutionary approach to the study of rural tourism'. *Land Use Policy* 38, 276–81.

Russell, R. and Faulkner, B. (2004). 'Entrepreneurship, chaos and the tourism area life cycle'. *Annals of Tourism Research* 31(3), 556–79.

Saarinen, J. (2004). 'Destinations in change: The transformation process of tourist destinations'. *Tourist Studies* 4(2), 161–79.

Sanz Ibáñez, C. and Anton Clavé, S. (2014). 'The evolution of destinations: Towards an evolutionary and relational economic geography approach'. *Tourism Geographies* 16(4), 563–79.

Sanz Ibáñez, C. and Anton Clavé, S. (2016). 'Strategic coupling evolution and destination upgrading'. *Annals of Tourism Research* 56(1), 1–15.

Schumpeter, J.A. (1934). *The Theory of Economic Development: An Inquiry into Profits, Capital, Credit, Interest, and the Business Cycle*. London: Transaction Publishers.

Smith, R.A. (1992). 'Beach resort evolution. Implications for planning'. *Annals of Tourism Research* 19(2), 304–22.

Stansfield, C.A. (1978). 'Atlantic City and the resort cycle. Background to the legalization of gambling'. *Annals of Tourism Research* 5(2), 238–51.

Stock, M. (Coord.) (2003). *Le Tourisme: Acteurs, Lieux et Enjeux*. Paris: Belin.

Suchet, A. (2015). 'Pour en finir avec Butler (1980) et son modèle d'évolution des destinations touristiques: Le cycle de vie comme un concept inadapté à l'étude d'une aire géographique'. *Loisir et Société/Society and Leisure* 38(1), 7–19.

Tyrrell, T. and Johnston, R. (2008). 'Tourism sustainability, resiliency and dynamics: Towards a more comprehensive perspective'. *Tourism and Hospitality Research* 8, 14–24.

Veblen, T. (1898). 'Why is economics not an evolutionary science?'. *Quarterly Journal of Economics* 12(4), 373–97.

Verbole, A. (2003). 'Networking and partnership building for rural tourism development'. In D. Hall, L. Roberts and M. Mitchell (eds) *New Directions in Rural Tourism*. Aldershot: Ashgate (pp. 152–68).

Vernon, R. (1966). 'International investment and international trade in the product cycle'. *The Quarterly Journal of Economics* 8(2), 190–207.

Walton, J.K. (2000). *The British Seaside: Holidays and Resorts in the Twentieth Century*. Manchester: Manchester University Press.

Weaver, D.B. (2012). 'Organic, incremental and induced paths to sustainable mass tourism convergence'. *Tourism Management* 33(5), 1030–7.

Williams, A.M. (2013). 'Mobilities and sustainable tourism: path-creating or path-dependent relationships?' *Journal of Sustainable Tourism* 21(4), 511–31.

Wolfe, R.I. (1952). 'Wasaga Beach – the divorce from the geographic environment'. *The Canadian Geographer* 2, 57–66.

2 Destination dynamics, path dependency and resilience

Regaining momentum in Danish coastal tourism destinations?

Henrik Halkier and Laura James

Introduction

As Martin and Sunley (2014) note, there are many different models of change implied by evolutionary concepts. These include: gradualism, path dependence, punctuated equilibrium, branching, emergence, and life cycles. Within tourism studies, the last of these, which appears in the form of Butler's Tourism Area Life Cycle (TALC) model, has dominated conceptualization of long-term destination dynamics (Brouder and Eriksson 2013). Butler's model predicts a singular evolutionary path of involvement, exploration, development, consolidation and stagnation before a point of change where a tourism area may either be rejuvenated in some way or fall into decline. While the TALC model has inspired many studies of destination development (Lagiewski 2006; Haywood 2006), it has also been subject to critique and revision (Butler 2009), notably by combining macro- and micro-perspectives in order to avoid unilinear implications of Butler's seminal text (Ma and Hassink 2013; Sanz-Ibáñez and Anton Clavé 2014).

There has also been more work on the relationship between social institutions and social agency in destination development, including the ways in which policymakers and stakeholders attempt to broaden and rejuvenate developmental paths in a variety of destinations (e.g. Dredge 2006; Bramwell and Meyer 2007; Henriksen and Halkier 2009; Gill and Williams 2011; Anton Clavé 2012). Many tourist destinations consist of a large number of relatively small private and public actors, and such destinations are often regarded as having difficulties because of a shortage of actors with sufficient resources to engage in reinvention of the tourist experience offered (Hall and Williams 2008; Hjalager 2010; Halkier 2010). From an evolutionary perspective this suggests that such tourist destinations are likely to face difficulties creating new paths or adapting to external changes, for example in demand, because a preponderance of small or micro firms delivering labour-intensive services implies a scarcity of actors with sufficient resources to engage actively in reorientation and adaptive activities (Halkier and Therkelsen 2013). However, some destinations appear better at adapting to changing circumstances (e.g. consumer trends or new competing destinations), and hence the question of how and why this is the case comes to the fore.

In this context, resilience has emerged as an important framework for theorizing destinations' ability to adapt to new situations or recover from disruption (Farrell and Twining-Ward 2004; Allison *et al.* 2010). Originating in physics and mathematics, the most common interpretation of resilience is the 'rebound' (Hill *et al.* 2008) or 'snapping back' (Foster 2007) of a material or system to its prior state after some kind of disturbance; this is the so-called engineering resilience. In the 1970s, ecologists took up the concept, using it to define the degree of disturbance or shock a system can absorb without shifting to a new equilibrium, with attendant changes in structure and function (Holling 1973). Researchers of tourism activities have adopted both engineering resilience and ecological resilience; for example, in the study by Pizam and Smith (2000) of the impact and length of effect of terrorist acts on destinations. A third approach to resilience rejects the assumption of a single equilibrium or multiple equilibria, arguing instead for a broader approach to resilience in which socio-ecological systems should be understood as complex and adaptive. Such systems comprise firms, institutions and other actors who are continually adapting to but also interacting with their environment (see also Davoudi *et al.* 2012; Bristow and Healy 2014a, 2014b).

Folke (2006) outlines several key features of such systems. First, functions and relationships are distributed across the system at a variety of scales. Second, the boundary between the system and its environment is difficult to identify and is not fixed. Third, complex adaptive systems (CAS) are characterized by non-linear dynamics as a result of complex feedback mechanisms, demonstrating path dependency. Finally, they also exhibit emergence and self-organization; that is, macro-scale features emerge spontaneously from micro-scale processes. In some ways, this conception of resilience is quite different from the engineering and equilibrium approaches, which assume periods of stability disrupted by some shock or external force and which then snap back to the previous situation or a new status quo. However, a CAS approach is also concerned with reactions to shocks or disturbances. The difference is that these are seen as continual rather than periodic and potentially arising from unpredictable feedback mechanisms within the system as well as external forces.

There have been calls for tourism studies to adopt a CAS approach (Farrell and Twining-Ward 2004; Allison *et al.* 2010) although there have, to date, been relatively few empirical applications (Lew 2014). It should also be noted that the CAS approach these writers advocate differs from earlier calls to embrace the complexity of the tourism sector. Milne and Ateljevic, for example, highlighted the 'complexity of the global-nexus and how its economic, cultural and environmental elements interact to create local development outcomes' (2001: 374). They did not, however, advocate an approach based explicitly on complex systems theory. Their main contribution was to insist on the importance of the global–local nexus, (i.e. wider and more refined tourism geographies), rather than the temporal aspect (change over time) that is at the heart of the resilience discussion.

In this chapter we examine the development of two coastal leisure tourism destinations in North Jutland, Denmark, in the context of both 'slow burn' and more sudden economic shocks over the last 15 years. Adopting a CAS-inspired perspective on resilience, we focus particularly on the ways in which local actors have attempted to influence growth trajectories and adapt to change in the face of declining visitor numbers. In addition to the resilience literature within tourism studies, we draw on the work of researchers from economic geography and regional studies, where, in recent years, resilience – alongside other evolutionary concepts – has been applied to issues of regional and local development (Martin and Sunley 2006; Martin 2010; Christopherson *et al.* 2010; Hassink 2010; MacKinnon and Derickson 2013; Pendall *et al.* 2010; Pike *et al.* 2010; Bristow and Healy 2014a; Boschma 2014). In particular, we draw on the resilience framework developed by Martin (2012) in distinguishing between the *renewal* of previous trajectories and *reorientation* towards new activities, and Boschma's (2014) suggestion that resilience depends on the capacity of regions to overcome this trade-off between adaptation (for renewal) and adaptability (for reorientation).

The empirical data discussed here have been generated in connection with a study of coastal destinations across Denmark co-sponsored by the Danish Structural Funds programme. Methods include a series of interviews with key public and private actors, document analysis and localized statistics on destination development. The two destinations are Skagen and Klitmøller. The analysis demonstrates that the two destinations have evolved along similar paths since coastal mass tourism came to North Jutland in the 1960s on the back of massive construction of privately owned holiday homes (but to some extent rented out to visitors), especially in the 3 months of the main summer season (Halkier and Therkelsen 2013). However, both destinations have responded in different ways to a downturn in international visitation since the turn of the century.

The chapter ultimately reviews the empirical findings in the light of the resilience approach, (tentatively) arguing that a range of factors, such as governance arrangements, including intra-destination networking patterns, destination self-images and interaction with external actors, affect the ability of destinations to adapt to changing circumstances in terms of patterns of demand and competition.

Resilience and CAS

Originating in physics and mathematics, the concept of resilience is commonly understood as the 'rebound' (Hill *et al.* 2008) or 'snapping back' (Foster 2007) of a material or system to its prior state after some kind of disturbance. However, this 'engineering resilience' is only one of three main perspectives that are commonly identified (see Pendall *et al.* 2010; Lew 2014; and MacKinnon and Derickson 2013 for overviews). Engineering resilience focuses on 'stability at a presumed steady-state, and stresses resistance to a disturbance and the speed of return to the equilibrium point' (Berkes and Folke 1998: 12). This approach is often applied to disaster management, where the aim is to return to the stable state assumed to exist before an external shock. 'Ecological resilience', by contrast, is concerned with the degree of disturbance or shock a system can absorb without shifting to a new equilibrium, with attendant changes in structure and function (Holling 1973).

This is mainly used to identify thresholds between different equilibria in ecosystems although it has also been applied to economic systems (Martin 2012). A third approach is based on the concept of 'panarchy' (Gunderson and Holling 2002) and rejects the notion of stable equilibria. Instead both human and natural systems are conceived of as interdependent, nonlinear, complex adaptive systems (Farrell and Twining-Ward 2004; Martin and Sunley 2007, 2012).

CAS involves many interacting processes, with 'interdependent and integrated parts displaying unpredictable behaviour, constantly evolving, and in general not amenable to analysis by orthodox, linear, deterministic science' (Farrell and Twining-Ward 2004: 276). Such systems have the capacity to adapt their internal structure in response to an external shock or the emergence of self-organized criticality (Bak 1996, quoted in Martin and Sunley 2007). CAS is never in equilibrium and is vulnerable to 'butterfly effects', where apparently small changes in peripheral parts of the system may result in far-reaching and unpredictable consequences. In addition, 'slow burn' variables (Walker *et al.* 2012) may have gradually increasing impacts or can suddenly cause a system to 'flip' into a different state. The relevant timeframe will vary between systems. In the case of climate systems, for example, 'sudden' changes may be defined in decades; while, in social and economic systems, timeframes of days or months are more relevant.

Allison *et al.*, drawing on Folke (2006), argue that from a CAS perspective resilience refers to 'the capacity of a system to absorb disturbance and reorganize, while undergoing change, with the same or similar system retained' (2010: 505). CAS would seem to be a promising approach to the study of resilience in tourism destinations, since tourism combines social and natural resources in complex systems, which are multi-scaled, highly interconnected and unpredictable. Several commentators have called for such an approach within tourism studies (Farrell and Twining-Ward 2004; Allison *et al.* 2010), but operationalizing a CAS framework in empirical research has proven challenging, not least due to the difficulty of identifying and measuring such systems with components ranging from the local to the global scale (Tyrrell and Johnston 2008). In practice, many different approaches to resilience are represented within the tourism literature, and the precise definition of resilience varies according to the specifics of the destinations examined. Whilst this definitional imprecision could be seen as a weakness of the resilience concept, it has also allowed for cross-disciplinary communication and creativity (Espiner and Becken 2014).

Within the tourism literature, most studies have adopted an engineering or ecological approach. These include studies focusing on the recovery of destinations and tourist numbers after sudden shocks or disasters of different kinds, such as economic crises (Lew 1999), political crises (Hamzah and Hampton 2013; Biggs *et al.* 2012), natural disasters such as the Indian Ocean tsunami (Calgaro and Lloyd 2008; Biggs *et al.* 2012; Larsen *et al.* 2011) or earthquakes (Orchiston 2013) and acts of terrorism (Pizam and Smith 2000). Others, representing the ecological approach, have considered the impacts of human activity on the resilience of socio-ecological systems such as coral reefs (Coghlan and Prideaux 2009) and desert environments (Stafford-Smith and Moran 2008). Further studies have considered the 'resilience' of visitor numbers to changes in the natural environment such as the whale population (Lambert *et al.* 2010). The resilience of different types of destination to climate change has also emerged as a significant topic of research (Becken 2013); for example, in relation to alpine destinations and winter sports (Luthe *et al.* 2012), and islands and diving tourism (Hillmer-Pegram 2013).

An important point of debate is whether resilience implies destinations returning to their previous growth path or restructuring their activities more fundamentally to move to a new trajectory. Martin (2012), for example, suggests a four-part framework for assessing the resilience of a regional economy: resistance (degree of sensitivity or depth of reaction of a regional economy, e.g. employment rate, output); recovery (speed and degree of recovery from a shock); reorientation (the extent to which an economy adapts and restructures its activities in response to a shock); and, renewal (the extent to which a regional economy renews its previous growth trajectory). Some writers have criticized resilience as conservative in conceptualizing responses to disturbance primarily in terms of renewal of existing activities as opposed to reorientation (Hassink 2010: 53). MacKinnon and Derickson (2013), for example, argue that the ecological concept of resilience is conservative when applied to social relations. Resilience, they claim, is a discourse imposed on local communities who are expected to adapt to external pressures. They suggest the concept of 'resourcefulness' as an alternative which 'emphasizes forms of learning and mobilization based upon local priorities and needs as identified and developed by community activists and residents' (MacKinnon and Derickson 2013: 263–4).

Pike *et al.* also critique conservative conceptions of resilience, suggesting two types of resilience:

> adaptation can explain a form of resilience based upon the renewal of a pre-conceived and previously successful development path in the short term. . . . Resilience through adaptability emerges through decisions to leave a path that may have proven successful in the past in favour of a new, related or alternative trajectory.
>
> (2010: 62)

Seen through the lens of CAS, resilience implies an ongoing process of adjustment, adaptation and renewal, which incorporates processes and actors at a variety of scales. From this perspective 'resilience is not viewed as a return to normality, but rather as a dynamic, evolutionary capacity to adapt in response to stresses and strains' (Bristow and Healey 2014a: 94). As a result, the distinction between adaptation and adaptability is blurred, and Boschma (2014) argues that this should be regarded as a key characteristic of resilience where 'the capacity to overcome the trade-off between adaptability and adaptation' through reorientation of existing 'skills, resources and institutions in regions' (p. 5) is perceived as crucial for maintaining long-term regional growth.

These debates bring both the agency of local actors and the political struggles around resilience agendas to the fore. Two key questions here are whether local actors are able to act to renew or reorient growth paths, and what governance arrangements are required to support resilience (whether in terms of resistance, renewal or reorientation). One of the problems with adopting a systems-oriented approach to studying resilience is that it may neglect the role of human agency (Bristow and Healy 2014a, 2014b). Yet humans have an innate capacity to anticipate and take proactive action to build up resilience through collective action as well as learning and adapting to change (Berkes and Seixas 2005; Becken 2013). Human agents in CAS are 'constantly reacting to what the other agents are doing and to the environment, and are thus continually evolving through feedback and learning' (Bristow and Healey 2014a: 95). However, devising appropriate responses and anticipatory policies is clearly challenging in the context of complex systems, which are characterized by uncertainty and non-linear relationships. As Hartzog suggests, change is 'constant and to be expected, if not necessarily accurately predicted, such that the focus for policy needs to be on "responsive adaptation" rather than "predictive avoidance"' (2005: 229). At the same time CAS highlights the importance of processes and interactions that operate over many different scales, exposing the limitations of local actors' ability to affect system level dynamics (MacKinnon *et al.* 2009).

Nevertheless, a number of general prescriptions for governance arrangements and policymaking that could support resilience in tourism destinations have been put forward although, as Lebel *et al.* (2006) note, most have not been systematically assessed in the same places. First, and in particular from the CAS perspective, developing knowledge of system dynamics and how they change is crucial (Folke *et al.* 2005; Allison *et al.* 2010). This requires monitoring capacity with continuous testing and evaluation, recognizing the inherent uncertainty in CAS. Flexible institutions and multi-level governance systems are also thought to be important for a variety of reasons. Flexible institutions are more likely to be able to both anticipate and prepare for change, for example through decentralized processes of learning, as well as responding to change through collective action (Ernstson *et al.* 2010). Given the multi-level linkages and interactions within CAS, polycentricity, with inclusive governance networks including different stakeholder groups, government agencies and organizations, is also considered important (Luthe *et al.* 2012; Luthe and Wyss 2014; Berkes and Ross 2013).

In their review of the literature on governance for resilience Bristow and Healey conclude that regional and local governments seeking to build territorial resilience 'need to work collaboratively with a range of other actors and thus develop responses as part of a strategically co-ordinated, yet fluid network of governance' (2014a: 100). Polycentricity also allows for a diversity of approaches and institutions, with some overlap or redundancy reducing vulnerability to institutional failure. Finally, the importance of leadership and an appreciation of the political struggles through which resilience agendas and visions are developed and implemented has been emphasized (Larsen *et al.* 2011; Pike *et al.* 2010; Bristow and Healy 2014b).

In order to gauge destination resilience and the processes sustaining it, this text combines two CAS-inspired interpretations of regional resilience. First, Martin's four-part framework is used to assess the economic impact of external shocks, both with regard to short-term reactions (*resistance* and *recovery*) and in relation to the long-term implications for path development (*renewal* of old growth patterns or *reorientation* in new directions). Second, the process-oriented perspective advocated by, among others, Bristow and Healy helps to illuminate the role of governance and agency by highlighting the importance of *polycentricity* (diversity of institutions and stakeholder networks), *institutional flexibility* (the ability of changing strategies and governance set-ups in order to meet new challenges) and *monitoring capacity* (the ability to follow economic developments as they unfold).

The resilience of coastal tourist destinations in Denmark

National and regional contexts

Compared with other countries in north-western Europe, the arrival of international tourists has long been seen as an important contributor to Denmark's national economy (Vækstteam for Turisme og Oplevelsesøkonomi 2013). A significant part of leisure tourism in Denmark takes place along the North Sea coast, which offers visitors white beaches with more room per individual than is often the case along the Mediterranean coasts. The main group of visitors to this region is families travelling with children, from Denmark and the immediately surrounding countries, enjoying the great outdoors (Montanari 1995; Nyberg 1995; Vækstteam for Turisme og Oplevelsesøkonomi 2013). As the coastal hinterlands are generally rural and distant from the urban growth centres in eastern parts of the Jutland peninsula, this has made coastal leisure tourism an important provider of jobs in peripheral parts of the country, albeit traditionally a very seasonal one, with most of the activity concentrated in the three summer months (Hjalager and Jensen 2001; Vækstteam for Turisme og Oplevelsesøkonomi 2013). Coastal tourism as an economic activity has, therefore, become an integrated part of regional development in the westernmost parts of the country, both in economic terms and within Danish policy discourse.

However, for more than a decade coastal leisure tourism has increasingly come to be seen as being in need of remedial action by government and private stakeholders. Already at the beginning of the 2000s 'the German challenge' was a well-rehearsed metaphor referring to a declining number of visitors from the south, still by far the largest group of international visitors (Turismens Udviklings Center 2000; Vækstteam for Turisme og Oplevelsesøkonomi 2013), and the recent tourism strategy by the Danish government proceeds from the observation that

> from 2007 to 2012, Denmark has experienced a decrease in international visitation, while international tourism has generally grown in Europe. . . . This, however, reflects opposing trends: growth in city breaks and business tourism, and a significant decline in coastal and nature-based tourism.
>
> (Regeringen 2014: 7)

The decrease in international overnight stays only amounted to 4 per cent (calcu-lated on the basis of Danmarks Statistik 2014), but as this occurred in a context of tourism growth across Europe, as well as on the back of a 17 per cent reduction in international overnight stays from 1993 to 2007 (calculated on the basis of Danmarks Statistik 2014), the decline could readily be construed as a crisis in the international-visitor economy in Denmark.

In the following analysis we examine the impact of the economic crisis and longer-term changes in demand on two coastal destinations in Denmark (see Figure 2.1). Both places are located in North Jutland, the most important coastal

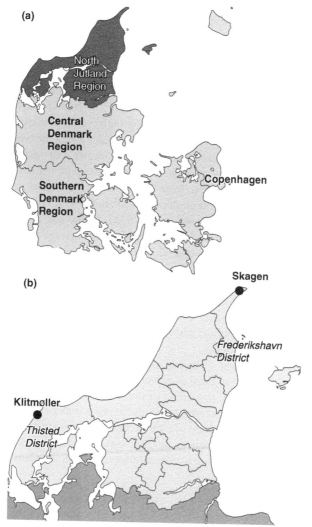

Figure 2.1 Maps of (a) Denmark and (b) the North Jutland region of Denmark.
Source: WikiCommons.

leisure tourism destination in Denmark for international visitors, and they have been chosen because they represent two different histories of coastal tourism. Skagen is a well-established, high-profile destination, combining natural and cultural resources with a strong brand in relation to the Scandinavian market; while Klitmøller is an example of a traditional, small coastal town by the North Sea, which has recently attempted to reinvent its experience offer.

The main indicator of tourism activity used by policymakers in Denmark is the number of commercial overnight stays (hotels, campsites, holiday home rentals, etc.), available in consolidated time series for more than 20 years and hence useful when assessing change over time. Moreover, the number of overnight stays is available by local government units, although unfortunately not at the level of individual destinations, and they are also available by months, serving as an indicator of structural change in visitation patterns in highly seasonal destinations. This is complemented by a second indicator, namely assessments of tourism's economic impact through so-called tourism satellite accounts (VisitDenmark 2008). These are also available at the level of local government units and aggregate economic activity generated in Denmark by international and domestic tourists through expenditure on accommodation, attractions, food, local transport, shopping and so on. From an analytical perspective their drawback is that the economic impact figures have only been available since 2006; but, more importantly, because of the considerable efforts required to produce the estimates, their publication is tardy (the most recent figures are from 2012), while data for 2 years are actually missing (2007, 2009). Thus, these indicators play a limited role in day-to-day policy debates. However, for the purpose of our research, the economic impact figures still cover the period before and after the recent financial crisis and, therefore, provide additional insights into the development of the tourism economy. Conversely, employment statistics are of less use in the context of North Jutland because the predominant form of visitor accommodation is in private holiday home rentals, normally involving little in the way of direct employment since visitors clean and do the catering themselves. Data such as these are missed by industry headings like 'Hotels & Restaurants' in Danish sectoral employment statistics.

In order to assess the policies adopted by public institutions in the face of the economic crisis and attempts to adapt to longer-term change, we have undertaken documentary analysis of tourism and economic development strategies and reports. These include documents from regional and local government as well as destination development organizations (DMOs) within North Jutland and the two case-study destinations. Moreover, so as to follow the process of change in more detail in the two case-study destinations, 20 qualitative, semi-structured interviews have been undertaken with public and private tourism stakeholders, covering local government economic development officers, local DMO executives, public and private visitor attractions, and private providers of accommodation. Interviews were conducted in connection with the VisitNordjylland project Growing Coastal Tourist Towns, the main findings of which have been published elsewhere (Jørgensen and Halkier 2013).

Responses to the visitor-number 'crisis' in North Jutland

North Jutland is the Danish coastal destination with the highest proportion of international earnings, 45 per cent as opposed to a national average of 40 per cent in 2011 (calculated on the basis of VisitDenmark 2014: 2), and the region has, therefore, been an integral part of the general story about the growing crisis of coastal tourism in Denmark. Compared with the early 1990s, nearly a quarter of international overnight stays had disappeared by 2007 (calculated on the basis of Danmarks Statistik 2014) and, after the onset of the financial crises in 2008, both domestic and international visitation first dropped and then stagnated at a lower level.

The regional DMO, VisitNordjylland, with access to ongoing monitoring data on overnight stays, as well as more detailed research of visitor preferences undertaken at the national level by VisitDenmark, has translated the perception of a visitor crisis into policy initiatives at the regional level. The regional level of tourism governance in Denmark has traditionally been associated with experience-development initiatives promoting long-term growth by adapting to new market trends; while local DMOs and private firms have been more oriented towards relying on marketing as a policy instrument that could increase visitation in the current or coming season (Kvistgaard 2006; Halkier 2008). However, a perception of acute crisis in the tourism economy and the insistence of regional government that a long-term decline in international visitors required measures oriented towards renewing the product created, surprisingly quickly, consensus around a new dual strategy for tourism development in the region.

On the one hand, and in line with the renewal perspective, attempts were made to regain lost market shares among traditional customer segments, especially German families with children. Although regional government has been somewhat reluctant to commit funding to promotion and branding 'because other industries take care of their own marketing' (Halkier 2008; Kvistgaard 2006), North Jutland has been consistent in its commitment to support destination marketing, which in recent years has accounted for more than 40 per cent of VisitNordjylland's activity expenditure (VisitNordjylland.dk 2012: 14). In addition to continued efforts to boost the number of visitors by marketing traditional North Jutland experiences to traditional groups of customers, a series of initiatives have also been launched to assist the development of new tourist experiences other than relaxing on or around temperate beaches in the summer season. This, in turn, would help to reorient the path of tourism development in the region through diversification of the experience offer that could appeal to different types of visitors, especially well-off couples travelling without children, both within and outside the main summer season. This has included support for attempts to develop and promote activities that would help diversify the experience offer and possibly extend the season. Examples include supporting new events such as food festivals and attracting the windsurfing world cup to Klitmøller, local story-telling projects that provide live interpretation of lesser-known parts of North Jutland (VisitNordjylland.dk 2008) and, more recently, initiating innovation networks for public and private actors in order to develop new visitor-relevant projects (VisitNordjylland.dk 2014).

Both the renewal-oriented marketing efforts and the reorientation efforts aimed at developing novel experiences for new target segments are coordinated by VisitNordjylland as the regional DMO, but the governance structures around the two types of activities differ. While regional marketing involves a highly routinized coordination of the efforts of local DMOs to mobilize private tourism firms to sign up to annual marketing initiatives, experience development has been undertaken through temporary project organizations. These are established by various 'coalitions of the willing', such as private tourism enterprises and local DMOs with organizational and knowledge resources previously situated outside the well-trodden path of family-oriented coastal relaxation tourism. These range from local government bodies responsible for infrastructure experiences in coastal towns to national parks, public cultural institutions and private firms providing specialized services and experiences with regard to, for instance, local food and outdoor activities.

As such, the regional-level response to the perceived visitation crisis would seem to display signs of both polycentricity (both regional and local, as well as public and private sector actors are involved) and new, intricate and overlapping patterns of cooperation developed to create scope for new initiatives to counteract the declining number of commercial overnights. This means that in practice some local tourism bodies have been engaged in complementary policy initiatives that, if successful, could result in renewal of the existing temperate-beach–family-oriented paradigm and a concurrent reorientation of parts of the accommodation capacity towards new visitors with more varied (and expensive) demands in terms of experiences and services.

The extent to which these efforts have been successful in terms of helping to stimulate the regional tourism economy will be discussed in the final part of this chapter. Here it can be noted that, measured by the one indicator which Danish destinations primarily rely on – the number of commercial overnight stays – recovery at the aggregate regional level seems to have been limited. This is because in 2013 international and total overnights had respectively declined by 18 per cent and 12 per cent compared with 2007 (calculated on the basis of Danmarks Statistik 2014). In fact these measures are both very close to the lowest levels recorded since the early 1990s.

In order to follow the development of tourist destinations in North Jutland in terms of processes of adaptation and collective initiatives such as public policies, we now turn to two cases studies, selected to represent two different experiences with regard to tourism. Both Skagen and Klitmøller originated as fishing villages, but while fishing continues to play a role in the former, both directly and in terms of repair and supply services (Stisager, Thomsen, personal interviews), it is now marginal in the latter (Odgaard, personal interview). Moreover, while Skagen has a long and illustrious history as a prominent coastal resort for well-off Copenhageners (partly based on its additional cultural capital as the home of Danish impressionism in the late nineteenth century; Hardervig 2006), Klitmøller grew as a typical holiday-home destination in the 1960s and has recently extended its experience offer by becoming a hub of windsurfing-based tourism under the *Cold Hawaii* brand (Laursen and Andersson 2014). In terms of general governance, the two destinations do, however, display similarities as they are part of a local government area with a range of different economic activities and tourist destinations, and as such they are embedded in wider governance networks, both in geographical terms and with regard to competing priorities for economic development. In the following sections, Skagen and Klitmøller are analysed in turn, starting from an outline of tourism development in each destination, then considering key aspects of the policy processes that unfolded in response to the recent financial crisis: the monitoring of tourism development; key development initiatives; and the governance structures shaping the policy response. Finally, the economic performance of tourism in North Jutland and the two local destinations during and after the financial crisis will be reviewed.

Skagen: bouncing back, branching out?

Like the rest of North Jutland, the impact of the financial crisis has also been clearly visible in the very north of Denmark: commercial overnight stays in Frederikshavn, the local government district within which Skagen is located, dropped 12 per cent from 2008 to 2010 (calculated on the basis of Danmarks Statistik 2014), but then recovered to previous levels with regard to international visitors, while domestic visitation stagnated at a lower level.

In Skagen the number of visitors is also the standard by which tourism development is measured on an ongoing basis; and therefore this relatively strong performance means that policymakers have focused primarily on building on their success by getting more international visitors and attracting additional domestic, short-stay visitors outside the summer months (Stisager, Eldh, personal interviews), something which fits not only local perceptions of current challenges, but also national priorities in extending the leisure tourism season along the Danish coasts (VisitDenmark 2007). Although some underline that Skagen is a multifaceted destination reaching from impressionist painting via folk music festivals to biker rallies with amateur stripper competitions (Ebbesen, personal interview), the general preference is clearly to maintain the destination as something slightly exclusive (Illum, Thomsen, Eldh, Gandrup, Dal, personal interviews). In practice this translates into new initiatives, primarily revolving around extending the season through a coordinated programme of events, ensuring that special-interest visitors have reasons to go to Skagen outside the main season. These range from cultural events (e.g. literature festival, history through geocaching) to gastronomy (e.g. food festival, cooking classes) to outdoor activities (e.g. winter swimming, marathon) (Stisager, Eldh, personal interviews).

The governance framework for tourism around Skagen is generally described by the tourism firms and public policymakers involved as being highly collaborative, and the local tourist association has a key role as activities' coordinator (Stisager, Eldh, Illum, personal interviews). Although certain local retailers suggest that there might still be room for improvement (Stenbroen, Dal, personal interviews), a wide range of local businesses and civil society organizations have become involved in activities to extend the season through the network Innovation Skagen 365, established in 2011 and co-sponsored by VisitNordjylland, which brought together private firms, public bodies and civil-society activists around projects to develop new visitor-relevant activities outside the main season. Moreover, relations between this dense bottom-up network of local stakeholders in Skagen and local government in Frederikshavn seem to have improved gradually, recently culminating in the formation of a joint DMO for the entire local government area, with the previous director of Skagen DMO as CEO (Stisager, Eldh, personal interviews). All in all this suggests that governance patterns have become increasingly polycentric in recent years and the stakeholders involved much more heterogeneous, in parallel with flexible policy responses to tourism-development challenges, which have become increasingly diverse. Interestingly, the focus on a deliberate programme of events spaced out through the year seems to have functioned as a way of managing potential conflicts between development agendas because different stakeholders (restaurateurs, winter swimmers, literary buffs, etc.) each became responsible for making a particular month a success, for themselves and, by implication, for the greater good of promoting all-year tourism in the destination.

Klitmøller: riding the waves?

In terms of commercial overnight stays, the impact of the economic crisis in and around Klitmøller has been significant (a reduction of 21 per cent from 2008 to 2013, calculated on the basis of Danmarks Statistik 2014) with regard to both domestic and international visitors. The impacts on each group had somewhat different timings because domestic visitation declined quickly and then stabilized, while long-international visitation held up better in terms of the number of commercial overnight stays.

As elsewhere in North Jutland, tourism is continuously monitored on the basis of the number of commercial overnight visits registered. The data outlined above have formed the basis of a shared understanding of the urgency of going beyond adjusting the existing product aimed at beach-oriented families with children and hence developing new experiences that could attract new types of visitors (Christensen, Jensen, Holler, personal interviews). In practice, based on major new initiatives in nature-based and activity-oriented tourism, this has resulted in new and very tangible developments in/around Klitmøller. These initiatives do, however, point in rather different directions. On the one hand, in 2014 a sea bath allowing swimming in the wild North Sea under safe and controlled circumstances was opened in neighbouring Nørre Vorupør (Vorupør Erhvervsforening 2014), sponsored by the Realdania Foundation (Realdania 2014). This extends the appeal of this holiday-home area as a place for family-oriented coastal holidays and can, therefore, be interpreted as a renewal-oriented strategy. On the other hand, two new developments of nature-based attractions point in different directions and could be seen as part of a reorientation strategy. Based on a national programme of promoting responsible use of protected natural habitats, a handful of national parks have been established, and thus in 2007 a substantial part of Klitmøller's coastal hinterland was designated a national park, consisting of large empty and protected swathes of coastal heath (Naturstyrelsen 2014). This caters primarily to a more grown-up market interested in nature itself rather than outdoor activities for families.

In parallel with this, Klitmøller itself has sprung to prominence as a windsurfing destination, originally pioneered by windsurfers spotting the high quality and variation in the waves along this part of the North Sea coast and later by what was quickly dubbed Cold Hawaii (Laursen and Andersson 2014). Despite initial local scepticism, Klitmøller as a windsurfing destination was quickly embraced by regional and local tourism organizations supporting the attraction of an annual event on the professional PWA world cup circuit (Friends of Cold Hawaii 2014). Since 2010 this has not only brought a very high level of activity in the destination each September, but has also boosted its profile as the place to windsurf in Denmark and, indeed, northern Europe.

In terms of governance, however, Klitmøller and the wider Thisted district are reported to have a long history of local rivalry at several levels: between incoming windsurfers and resident fishermen and women in Klitmøller itself; between Klitmøller as an up-and-coming destination and the more well-established holiday-home destination in neighbouring Nørre Vorupør; between the coast and the central-government-driven national park in the hinterland; and between the coast and the main (only) city of Thisted (Haller, personal interview). However, social and localist squabbles are also overlaid by the different types of tourism developments taking place and competing for promotional attention and development resources. Although some stakeholders claim that these three development directions support each other (Steenholm, Jensen, personal interviews), most see them as competing (Andersen, Larsen, Odder, Odgaard, Fejerskov, personal interviews). Additionally, the fact that Thisted district employs a consultant as a go-between between itself and the various stakeholders (Sodborg, Christensen, personal interviews) also suggests a lack of trust between actors within the destination. While the internal governance of Klitmøller has clearly been flexible and evolved over time (inclusion of the initially much-maligned windsurfing-based entrepreneurs), the polycentricity of its wider Thisted context would seem to verge on disjointedness, where a combination of local rivalry (Klitmøller versus Nørre Vorupør versus Thisted) and the targeting of different types of tourist experiences have been difficult to coordinate.

This is due to the fact that major stakeholders in each of the activities are external to the destination (national foundations and government agencies, an international professional sports body) and hence have agendas that do not necessarily combine easily. While the implications of this for the destination in terms of tourism activities will be discussed below, it is, however, interesting to note that Klitmøller itself is the only locality in the north-west of Jutland that has recorded a growing population, driven by incomers attracted by quality waves and a strong local buzz (Laursen and Andersson 2014).

Outcomes: overnight stays and visitor economies

Having reviewed the policy responses to the perceived crisis of tourism at the regional level and in two local destinations, it is illuminating to consider the extent to which the efforts in North Jutland, Skagen and Klitmøller have managed to make an impact on the development of the local visitor economy. According to the indicator used in ongoing monitoring by Danish policymakers, the number of commercial overnight visits, the picture is mixed. In North Jutland as a whole, international overnight stays were still in 2013 close to the all-time low recorded in 2009, and this reduction was not compensated for by a stable, but reduced, level of domestic overnight stays, as illustrated in Figure 2.2. In Skagen, recovery has largely taken place already with regard to the (less important) international overnight stays, while domestic visitation reflects the regional pattern. Finally, in Klitmøller recovery is still not in sight for either international or domestic overnight stays (calculated on the basis of Danmarks Statistik 2014). Although this type of information is generally used for ongoing monitoring of destination performance, the rather gloomy picture emerging can, however, be somewhat modified by looking at alternative indicators, because both the distribution of visitation over the year and the economic activity associated with the presence of tourists will influence the possibilities for long-term development of the destination.

The ambition to extend the season was found on the regional level, and its translation into policy initiatives was particularly pronounced in Skagen, where a schedule of events was developed to push the destination in the direction of all-year tourism. But despite much creativity in terms of policy initiatives and governance, visitation still remains concentrated in the peak season, which accounted for 66 per cent of commercial overnight stays in 2008 and 64 per cent in 2013

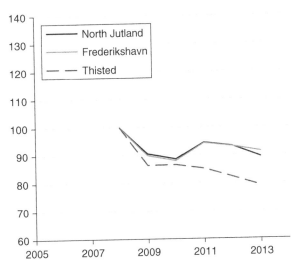

Figure 2.2 Number of commercial overnight stays (2008 = index 100).

Source: Calculated on the basis of Danmarks Statistik 2014.

(calculated on the basis of Danmarks Statistik 2014). From a wider perspective of regional development, the economic impact of tourist visitation is, however, perhaps the most important indicator to consider, because it remains the main motivation for local stakeholders to engage in the provision of tourism services and experiences. Here it is interesting to note that, both at the regional level and in Skagen, recovery would seem to be (more than) accomplished, as illustrated by Figure 2.3. The economic activity associated with tourism in North Jutland as a whole declined by 9.7 per cent from the last year before the crisis until the turning point in 2010, but already in 2011 the pre-crisis level had been surpassed (calculated on the basis of Danmarks Statistik 2014). Similarly, economic activity driven by tourism in Frederikshavn district including Skagen was severely hit, with a reduction of 18.5 per cent from 2006 to 2010, but had nearly regained lost ground by 2012. By contrast, Thisted including Klitmøller actually experienced significant growth in economic activity from 2006 to 2008 but then stagnated. Using tourism-associated economic activity as an indicator does, in other words, point towards a different interpretation of tourism development compared with the prevalent monitoring numbers of commercial overnight stays.

However, if economic indicators for activity and overnight indicators are combined, together they suggest that the long-standing ambition of the Danish tourism industry is currently being realized in North Jutland, namely to have greater earnings per overnight stay. From 2008 to 2012 this increased by 26 per cent in Frederikshavn/Skagen and 21 per cent in Thy/Klitmøller (calculated on the basis of Danmarks Statistik 2014; VisitDenmark 2008). This reflects either increasing prices for existing products or a shift in the direction of more spendthrift visitors and more value-added experience offers. Given the long-term shift towards more domestic and fewer German visitors, the latter explanation seems plausible.

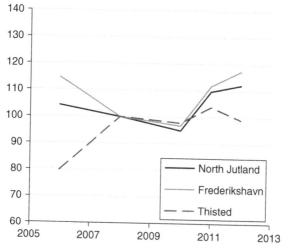

Figure 2.3 Economic impact of commercial overnight stays (2008 = index 100).

Source: Calculated on the basis of VisitDenmark 2008.

Conclusion: resistance, recovery and tourist destination resilience in North Jutland and beyond

From the perspective of destination resilience in response to the recent financial crisis, it is reasonable to conclude that the tourism sector in North Jutland displays signs of resilience. Lost ground has been recovered through a bounce-back in the economic impact of tourist activities as measured on the basis of tourism satellite accounts for the region as a whole and Skagen/Frederikshavn in particular. However, in Klitmøller the previous path of strong growth of economic activity associated with tourism has been replaced by stagnation.

Nevertheless, as policymaking to a large extent has navigated on the basis of much more alarmist figures produced by monitoring commercial overnight stays, in a bizarre sense North Jutland would seem to have experienced both the best and the worst of both worlds. Ideally, policymakers would probably prefer to have ongoing monitoring procedures available that provide reliable real-time insight into destination development generally, although in North Jutland this was not the case, as commercial overnight stays was still the dominant source of information. However, these alarmist overnight figures seem to have been an important impetus towards galvanizing efforts to reorient the experience offer and hence, presumably, helped to direct tourism development in new directions. The relatively narrow set of indicators used to measure performance in this case indicate the difficulties of monitoring, effectively and on an ongoing basis, the resistance and recovery of different aspects of tourism activity within a resilience framework.

Turning to governance structures and processes, the experience within North Jutland appears somewhat mixed. First, at the regional level the strategic reorientation towards a stronger focus on experience, and hence reorientation of the destination, would seem to have been furthered by a wide-spread consensus about acute crisis in the tourism economy and the implementation through flexible coalitions of public and private actors. Second, Skagen appears to have developed a governance structure that supports resilience: tourism development is monitored on an ongoing basis through the number of commercial overnight stays; there is a shared vision about a more desirable future for tourism in the destination (longer season, more international visitors), within an expanding and increasingly diverse local policy network that mobilizes large sections of business and civil society; and there are a wide range of activities adapted to current challenges. Being situated on a narrow peninsula with strict national-level planning constraints has pointed local stakeholders in the direction of focusing on quality tourism and high-spending visitors, something which is also in line with Skagen's long-standing reputation for being rather more upmarket than the average coastal town in North Jutland. While the methods in terms of governance and development initiatives have clearly been innovative, the development path displays a combination of renewal and reorientation.

Renewal is with regard to the overall direction of development (trying to widen Skagen's appeal as an iconic genteel coastal destination beyond the Scandinavian market) and a temporal reorientation of domestic visitation to embrace the destination beyond the summer months. And finally, tourism development in and around Klitmøller has been characterized by flexibility in the sense that many new initiatives have been introduced in recent years, but in terms of governance the picture is more uneven. While the larger picture of Thisted district comes across as disjointed rather than polycentric, Klitmøller would seem to have reinvented itself on the basis of its new profile as an international windsurfing destination. The governance of tourism development has, in other words, to a large extent been characterized by flexible and increasingly polycentric relationships, still revolving around the publically funded regional and local DMOs as hub, but drawing on a growing number of private firms and civil-society actors and associations who contribute to specific experience development projects.

Analysed within a CAS-inspired resilience framework, North Jutland has instituted destination-development strategies of a dual nature, combining attempts to renew existing forms of visitation while at the same time developing new experiences aimed at other types of prospective visitors. Although establishing causal links between development measures and realized visitation patterns is difficult, it is interesting to note that at this point in time some degree of reorientation would seem to have been realized in financial terms. This amounts to more revenue per overnight stay achieved through more domestic visitation. This economic success does not, however, only run counter to the general attempt to increase international visitation, but has also *not* been associated with a prolonging of the season.

All in all, adopting a resilience perspective has, therefore, contributed to the understanding of coastal tourism in North Jutland in several ways. First, it has underlined the importance of combining different time perspectives, not just focusing on long-term trends or short-term fluctuations, but also taking medium-term developments seriously, for instance in studying the impact of and recovery after external shocks and interpreting them on the basis of the long-term evolution of tourist destinations. Second, inspired by Martin and Boschma, the interplay between adaptation/renewal and adaptability/reorientation has been underlined, as several strategies exist and interact with the region and its local destinations. Third, by applying a resilience perspective on local destinations, the importance of local variation has been highlighted, with regard not just to the supply of services and experiences, but also to governance structures and processes. And finally, as suggested by the CAS perspective of Bristow and colleagues, the importance of taking a comprehensive approach to destination development has been underlined. Combining the headline figures, commercial overnight stays, used by policymakers on an ongoing basis to monitor destination development with indicators of the economic impact of tourism that are only available long after strategic decisions have been taken has, in other words, produced a much more nuanced picture of destination development.

The lessons learned from applying a CAS-inspired approach to resilience to the case of coastal tourism in North Jutland may, however, also be relevant for studies of other tourist destinations and regions more generally. First, inspired by the work of Martin and Boschma, the combination of adaptation/adaptability perspectives has been important in setting short-term developments in the context of long-term evolutionary trends, underlining the relevance and significance of including a medium-term analysis. Second, analysing economic development along many dimensions is clearly important. This should, of course, include indicators available on demand in real time, such as commercial overnight stays that are used by policymakers for monitoring developments on an ongoing basis. However, in order to avoid being locked into prevailing political perceptions of crisis/recovery, additional indicators such as economic impact estimates based on tourism satellite accounts, for example, could be used by independent analysts in order to bring to the fore other, equally tangible, perspectives on the long-term economic performance of destinations and regions.

Acknowledgements

Thanks are due to the editors and anonymous reviewers for constructive comments on an earlier draft of this text. The authors would also like to thank Matias Jørgensen for his contribution to data collection during research undertaken for VisitNordjylland as part of a project sponsored by the Danish European Social Funds programme. Finally, Laura James gratefully acknowledges the financial support of the Swedish *Handelsbanken* through a Browald stipend, and both authors acknowledge support provided through the KILN project, funded by the British Economic and Social Research Council (ES/J019488/1).

References

Allison, H.E., Moore, S.A., and Strickland-Munro, J.K. (2010). 'Using resilience concepts to investigate the impacts of protected area tourism on communities'. *Annals of Tourism Research* 37(2), 499–519.

Anton Clavé, S. (2012). *10 Lessons on Tourism. The Challenge of Reinventing Destinations*. Barcelona: Planeta.

Bak, P. (1996). *How Nature Works: The Science of Self-Organised Criticality*. New York: Springer Verlag.

Becken, S. (2013). 'Developing a framework for assessing resilience of tourism sub-systems to climatic factors'. *Annals of Tourism Research* 43, 506–28.

Berkes, F. and Folke, C. (1998). *Linking Social and Ecological Systems for Resilience and Stability*. Cambridge: Cambridge University Press.

Berkes, F. and Ross, H. (2013). 'Community resilience: Toward an integrated approach'. *Society & Natural Resources* 26(1), 5–20.

Berkes, F. and Seixas, C.S. (2005). 'Building resilience in lagoon social–ecological systems: A local-level perspective'. *Ecosystems* 8(8), 967–74.

Biggs, D., Hall, C.M., and Stoeckl, N. (2012). 'The resilience of formal and informal tourism enterprises to disasters: Reef tourism in Phuket, Thailand'. *Journal of Sustainable Tourism* 20(5), 645–65.

Boschma, R. (2014). 'Towards an evolutionary perspective on regional resilience'. *Papers in Evolutionary Economic Geography*, no. 14/09. Utrecht: Utrecht University.

Bramwell, B. and Meyer, D. (2007). 'Power and tourism policy relations in transition'. *Annals of Tourism Research* 34(3), 766–88.

Bristow, G. and Healy, A. (2014a). 'Der aufbau resilienter regionen: Komplexe Adaptive Systeme und die rolle der politischen intervention'. *Raumforschung und Raumordnung* 72(2), 93–102.

Bristow, G. and Healy, A. (2014b). 'Regional resilience: an agency perspective'. *Regional Studies* 48(5), 923–35.

Brouder, P. and Eriksson, R.H. (2013). 'Tourism evolution: On the synergies of tourism studies and evolutionary economic geography'. *Annals of Tourism Research* 43, 370–89.

Butler, R.W. (2009). 'Tourism in the future: Cycles, waves or wheels?' *Futures* 41(6), 346–52.

Calgaro, E. and Lloyd, K. (2008). 'Sun, sea, sand and tsunami: Examining disaster vulnerability in the tourism community of Khao Lak, Thailand'. *Singapore Journal of Tropical Geography* 29(3), 288–306.

Christopherson, S., Michie, J., and Tyler, P. (2010). 'Regional resilience: theoretical and empirical perspectives'. *Cambridge Journal of Regions, Economy and Society* 3(1), 3–10.

Coghlan, A. and Prideaux, B. (2009). 'Linking tourism and natural resource management through output indicators'. Paper presented at the conference CAUTHE 2009: 'See Change: Tourism & Hospitality in a Dynamic World'.

Danmarks Statistik. (2014). Tourism StatBank. [online] URL: www.statistikbanken.dk/ statbank5a/default.asp?w=1680 (accessed on 22 December 2014).

Davoudi, S., Shaw, K., Jamila Haider, L., Quinlan, A.E., Peterson, G.D., Wilkinson, C., Fünfgeld, H., McEvoy, D., Porter, L., and Davoudi, S. (2012). 'Resilience: A bridging concept or a dead end? "Reframing" resilience: Challenges for planning theory and practice'. *Planning Theory & Practice* 13(2), 299–333.

Dredge, D. (2006). 'Policy networks and the local organisation of tourism'. *Tourism Management* 27(2), 269–80.

Ernstson, H., Barthel, S., and Andersson, E. (2010). 'Scale-crossing brokers and network governance of urban ecosystem services: the case of Stockholm'. *Ecology and Society* 15(4), 28. [online] URL: www.ecologyandsociety.org/vol15/iss4/art28/ (accessed on 23 September 2014).

Espiner, S. and Becken, S. (2014). 'Tourist towns on the edge: Conceptualising vulnerability and resilience in a protected area tourism system'. *Journal of Sustainable Tourism* 22(4), 646–65.

Farrell, B.H. and Twining-Ward, L. (2004). 'Reconceptualizing tourism'. *Annals of Tourism Research* 31(2), 274–95.

Folke, C. (2006). 'Resilience: the emergence of a perspective for social–ecological systems analyses'. *Global Environmental Change* 16(3), 253–67.

Folke, C., Hahn, T., Olsson, P., and Norberg, J. (2005). 'Adaptive governance of social-ecological systems'. *Annual Review of Environment and Resources* 30(1), 441–73.

Foster, K.A. (2007). 'Snapping back: What makes regions resilient?' *National Civic Review* 96(3), 27–9.

Friends of Cold Hawaii (2014). Vil du være med? [online] URL: www.coldhawaii.com/ (accessed on 11 May 2015).

Gill, A.M. and Williams, P.W. (2011). 'Rethinking resort growth: understanding evolving governance strategies in Whistler, British Columbia'. *Journal of Sustainable Tourism* 19(4–5), 629–48.

Gunderson, L.H. and Holling, C.S. (2002). *Panarchy*. Washington DC: Island Press.

Halkier, H. (2008). 'Regional development policies and structural reform in Denmark. From policy segmentation towards strategic synergy?' In O. Bukve, H. Halkier, and

P.D. Souza (eds) *Towards New Nordic Regionalism. Politics, Administration and Regional Development*. Aalborg: Aalborg University Press (pp. 201–25).

Halkier, H. (2010). 'Tourism knowledge dynamics'. In P. Cooke, C.D. Laurentis, S. MacNeill, and C. Collinge (eds) *Platforms of Innovation: Dynamics of New Industrial Knowledge Flows.* London: Edward Elgar (pp. 233–50).

Halkier, H. and Therkelsen, A. (2013). 'Breaking out of tourism destination path dependency? Exploring the case of coastal tourism in North Jutland, Denmark'. *German Journal of Economic Geography* 57(1–2), 39–51.

Hall, C.M. and Williams, A. (2008). *Tourism and Innovation*. London: Routledge.

Hamzah, A. and Hampton, M.P. (2013). 'Resilience and non-linear change in island tourism'. *Tourism Geographies* 15(1), 43–67.

Hardervig, B. (2006). *Skagen ferieliv gennem 100 år*. Skagen: Skagen Turistforening.

Hartzog, P.B. (2005). Panarchy: Governance in the Network Age. [online] URL: http://panarchy.com/Members/PaulBHartzog/Papers/Panarchy%20-%20Governance%20in%20the%20Network%20Age.pdf (accessed on 4 April 2013).

Hassink, R. (2010). 'Regional resilience: a promising concept to explain differences in regional economic adaptability?' *Cambridge Journal of Regions, Economy and Society* 3(1), 45–58.

Haywood, K.M. (2006). 'Legitimising the TALC as a Theory of Development and Change'. In R.W. Butler (ed.) *The Tourism Area Life Cycle vol. 2: Conceptual and Theoretical Issues*. Clevedon, UK: Channel View (pp. 29–47).

Henriksen, P.F. and Halkier, H. (2009). 'From local promotion towards regional tourism policies: Knowledge processes and actor networks in North Jutland, Denmark'. *European Planning Studies* 17(10), 1445–62.

Hill, E., Wial, H., and Wolman, H. (2008). 'Exploring regional economic resilience'. *Working Paper, Institute of Urban and Regional Development*, Working Paper 2008-04. Berkeley, CA: University of California Berkeley.

Hillmer-Pegram, K.C. (2013). 'Understanding the resilience of dive tourism to complex change'. *Tourism Geographies* 16(4), 598–614.

Hjalager, A.M. (2010). 'A review of innovation research in tourism'. *Tourism Management* 31(1), 1–12.

Hjalager, A.M. and Jensen, S. (2001). 'Nordjylland – en turismeregion i Danmark'. *Nordregio Working Paper* 2001(11), 47–70.

Holling, C.S. (1973). 'Resilience and stability of ecological systems'. *Annual Review of Ecology and Systematics* 4, 1–23

Jørgensen, M.T. and Halkier, H. (2013). *Samarbejde, Vidensdynamikker og Turismeudvikling i Danske Kystferiebyer*. Aalborg: Institut for Kultur og Globale Studier, Aalborg Universitet.

Kvistgaard, P. (2006). *Problemer og magt i regional turismepolicy*. Aalborg: Aalborg Universitetsforlag.

Lagiewski, R.M. (2006). 'The application of the TALC model: A literature survey'. In R.W. Butler (ed.), *The Tourism Area Life Cycle vol. 1: Applications and Modifications*. Clevedon, UK: Channel View (pp. 27–50).

Lambert, E., Hunter, C., and Pierce, G.J. (2010). 'Sustainable whale-watching tourism and climate change: Towards a framework of resilience'. *Journal of Sustainable Tourism* 18(3), 409–27.

Larsen, R.K., Calgaro, E., and Thomalla, F. (2011). 'Global environmental change'. *Global Environmental Change* 21(2), 481–91.

Laursen, L.H. and Andersson, L. (2014). 'Differentiated decline in Danish outskirt areas'. *Tidsskrift for Kortlægning og Arealforvaltning* 119(46), 96–113.

Lebel, L., Anderies, J.M., Campbell, B., Folke, C., Hatfield-Dodds, S., Hughes, T.P., and Wilson, J. (2006). 'Governance and the capacity to manage resilience in regional social–ecological systems'. *Ecology and Society* 11(1), 19. [online] URL: www.ecolog-yandsociety.org/vol11/iss1/art19/ (accessed on 30 September 2014).

Lew, A.A. (1999). 'Tourism and the Southeast Asian crises of 1997 and 1998: A view from Singapore'. *Current Issues in Tourism* 2(4), 304–15.

Lew, A.A. (2014). 'Scale, change and resilience in community tourism planning'. *Tourism Geographies* 16(1), 14–22.

Luthe, T. and Wyss. R. (2014). 'Assessing and planning resilience in tourism'. *Tourism Management* 44, 161–3.

Luthe, T., Wyss, R., and Schuckert, M. (2012). 'Network governance and regional resilience to climate change: Empirical evidence from mountain tourism communities in the Swiss Gotthard region'. *Regional Environmental Change* 12(4), 839–54.

Ma, M. and Hassink, R. (2013). 'An evolutionary perspective on tourism area development'. *Annals of Tourism Research* 41, 89–109.

MacKinnon, D. and Derickson, K.D. (2013). 'From resilience to resourcefulness: A critique of resilience policy and activism'. *Progress in Human Geography* 37(2), 253–70.

MacKinnon, D., Cumbers, A., Pike, A., Birch, K., and McMaster R. (2009). 'Evolution in Economic Geography: Institutions, political economy, and adaptation'. *Economic Geography* 85(2), 129–50.

Martin, R. (2010). 'Roepke Lecture in Economic Geography – Rethinking regional path dependence: Beyond lock-in to evolution'. *Economic Geography* 86(1), 1–27.

Martin, R. (2012). 'Regional economic resilience, hysteresis and recessionary shocks'. *Journal of Economic Geography* 12(1), 1–32.

Martin, R. and Sunley, P. (2006). 'Path dependence and regional economic evolution'. *Journal of Economic Geography* 6(4), 395–437.

Martin, R. and Sunley, P. (2007). 'Complexity thinking and Evolutionary Economic Geography'. *Journal of Economic Geography* 7, 573–601.

Martin, R. and Sunley, P. (2012). 'Forms of emergence and the evolution of economic landscapes'. *Journal of Economic Behavior and Organization* 82(2–3), 338–51.

Martin, R. and Sunley, P. (2014). 'Towards a developmental turn in Evolutionary Economic Geography?' *Regional Studies* 49(5), 712–32.

Milne, S. and Ateljevic, I. (2001). 'Tourism, economic development and the global–local nexus: Theory embracing complexity'. *Tourism Geographies* 3(4), 369–93.

Montanari, A. (1995). 'The Mediterranean region: Europe's summer leisure space'. In A. Montanari and A.M. Williams (eds) *European Tourism: Regions, Spaces and Restructuring*. Chichester: John Wiley (pp. 41–65).

Naturstyrelsen. (2014). *Nationalpark Thy*. [online] URL: http://nationalparkthy.dk/ (accessed on 11 May 2015).

Nyberg, L. (1995). 'Scandinavia: Tourism in Europe's northern periphery'. In A. Montanari and A.M. Williams (eds) *European Tourism: Regions, Spaces and Restructuring*. Chichester: John Wiley (pp. 97–107).

Orchiston, C. (2013). 'Impacts of the Christchurch earthquakes on regional tourism activity: An empirical Investigation into tourism businesses in Christchurch and Canterbury'. Paper presented at the conference CAUTHE 2013: Tourism and Global Change: On the Edge of Something Big. Christchurch, New Zealand: Lincoln University (pp. 583–5).

Pendall, R., Foster, K.A., and Cowell, M. (2010). 'Resilience and regions: Building understanding of the metaphor'. *Cambridge Journal of Regions, Economy and Society* 3(1), 71–84.

Pike, A., Dawley, S., and Tomaney, J. (2010). 'Resilience, adaptation and adaptability'. *Cambridge Journal of Regions, Economy and Society* 3(1), 59–70.

Pizam, A. and Smith, G. (2000). 'Tourism and terrorism: a quantitative analysis of major terrorist acts and their impact on tourism destinations'. *Tourism Economics* 6(2), 123–38.

Realdania. (2014). Havbadet i Nørre Vorupør. [online] URL: https://realdania.dk/samlet-projektliste/havbadet-i-noerre-voruupoer (accessed on 11 May 2015).

Regeringen. (2014). *Vækstplan for dansk turisme.* København: Regeringen.

Sanz-Ibáñez, C. and Anton Clavé, S. (2014). 'The evolution of destinations: Towards an evolutionary and relational economic geography approach'. *Tourism Geographies* 16(4), 563–79.

Stafford-Smith, M. and Moran, M. (2008). 'The community-settlement nexus-drivers of "Viability" in remote areas'. *The Rangeland Journal* 30 (1), 123–35.

Turismens Udviklings Center. (2000). *Den tyske udfordring. Analyseresultater og anbefalinger.* København: Turismens Udviklings Center.

Tyrrell, T. and Johnston, R.J. (2008). 'Tourism sustainability, resiliency and dynamics: Towards a more comprehensive perspective'. *Tourism and Hospitality Research* 8(1), 14–24.

Vækstteam for Turisme og Oplevelsesøkonomi. (2013). *Anbefalinger.* København: Erhvervs- og Vækstministeriet.

VisitDenmark. (2007). *Kystferiestrategi i retning mod helårsturisme.* København: VisitDenmark.

VisitDenmark. (2008). *Turismens økonomiske betydning i Danmark.* København: VisitDenmark.

VisitDenmark. (2014). *Kyst- og naturturisme. Turismens økonomiske betydning i kystdanmark.* København: VisitDenmark.

VisitNordjylland.dk. (2008). *Årsberetning 2007. Nordjysk turisme står sammen og tænker stort.* Åbybro: VisitNordjylland.dk.

VisitNordjylland.dk. (2012). *Fyrtårn Nordjylland. Fortællinger om en nordjysk turisme i fremdrift.* Åbybro: VisitNordjylland.dk.

VisitNordjylland.dk. (2014). *Om VisitNordjylland.* Åbybro: VisitNordjylland.dk.

Vorupør Erhvervsforening (2014). *Havbadet taget i brug!* [online] URL: www.vorupor.dk /news/31/havbadet-taget-i-brug.html?page_id=289 (accessed on 11 May 2015).

Walker, B.H., Carpenter, S.R., and Rockstrom, J. (2012). 'Drivers, slow variables, "fast" variables, shocks, and resilience'. *Ecology and Society* 17(3), 30.

Interviews

Skagen

Ole Dal, Dals brugskunst, Director
Lisette Vind Ebbesen, Skagens Museum, Director
Maria Groes Eldh, Skagen Turistforening, Head of Information and Projects
Rikke Gandrup, Color Hotel Skagen, Director
Lars Illum, Kulturhus Kappelborg, Director
Mette Stenbroen, Stenbroen Guld og Ure, Director of Tourism

Lise-Lotte Stisager, Frederikshavn Kommune, Consultant,
Ane Bjerg Thomsen, Skagen By- og Egnsmuseum, Director

Klitmøller

Stig Andersen, Hotel Klitheden, Director
Ole Riis Christensen, Thy Turistforening, Director
Rasmus Fejerskov, Westwind, Director
Preben Holler, Klitmøller borger- og handelsstandsforening, Chairman
Henrik Jensen, Thisted Kommune, Business Consultant
Flemming Yde Larsen, Hillgaard A/S (Feriepartner Thy, Euro Spar and Strandgårdens Camping), Director
Erik Odder, Nordsø Akvariet, Director
Gunda Odgaard, Rederiet Gule Rev, Director
Thorkild Sodborg, Independent project consultant
Thorbjørn Steenholm, Nationalpark Thy, Project manager

3 Contested pathways towards tourism-destination sustainability in Whistler, British Columbia

An evolutionary governance model

Alison Gill and Peter W. Williams

Introduction

Since the late 1980s there has been a shift in many capitalist economies away from government as the key decision-maker towards a more neoliberal ideology that embraces wider stakeholder engagement, resulting in a blurring of governance responsibilities between private and public institutions (Painter 2000; Kemp *et al.* 2005). However, effecting real change in modes of governance that embody principles of sustainability is an oft-contested process as path-dependent forces, grounded in strategies that prioritize economic growth, act as resistant forces to more innovative approaches to governance that address a broader range of sustainability objectives. In a tourism context, destinations have increasingly been challenged by volatility in market demand, as well as escalating environmental and social costs. Many of them are acknowledging that, in the face of complex global-change forces, innovative governance policies and practices are needed to increase competitiveness and sustainability (Guia *et al.* 2006; Dwyer *et al.* 2009). As the Organization for Economic Cooperation and Development (OECD) (2012) observes, this requires a more collaborative approach that encourages policy development in conjunction with the tourism industry, as well as an emphasis on regional or local-level decision-making. To improve coordination between central and sub-national governments, mechanisms such as the development of tourism strategies, the use of contracts and the creation of joint committees are potential mechanisms. To enhance industry–government interface, the establishment of representative associations and destination management organizations (DMOs) that provide a forum for co-operation and policy debate are recommended.

While the evolution of tourism destinations has been a long-standing area of interest for tourism geographers, evolutionary economic geography (EEG) perspectives offer new opportunities for understanding the drivers of change over both space and time. In this chapter we present an EEG model that highlights catalysts and inhibitors of change to destination governance and apply it as a tool in understanding the contested pathways towards a sustainable future. We conceive this contestation as occurring between path-dependent forces, that embody lock-in to established economic, political and social institutions, and path-creation forces that through human agency and entrepreneurship challenge the status quo by introducing new approaches. The model draws upon both theoretical and empirical work from a range of disciplines employing evolutionary theory. It is introduced here as a heuristic device to assist in understanding the complexities of governance change in tourist destinations. We position it as a tool for identifying factors critical to understanding: a) whether or not past approaches to addressing a specific goal or issue remain appropriate in new contexts; and b) what catalysts are most apt to generate the momentum needed to alter governance trajectories in ways that more effectively reach desired outcomes. We draw examples from previous studies on path-dependent (Gill and Williams 2011) and path-creation (Gill and Williams 2014) aspects of Whistler's governance evolution to illustrate the EEG model's utility.

To frame the discussion we begin by offering a brief introduction to literature on the core theoretical and conceptual underpinnings of the model and its application, notably: EEG; governance and sustainability; and destination governance and sustainability. We then present the model of constraints and catalysts in the transition towards sustainability in destination community governance. The model is not intended as a process model per se, but rather one that focuses attention on key constructs that underlie change. In the subsequent section we apply this model to the resort community of Whistler, British Columbia, drawing upon our long-term empirical research in this destination. We discuss each of the component parts of the model separately – notably: path dependence; path creation; and the contested terrain of destination governance – first by elaborating on conceptual issues and subsequently relating these to Whistler's experience. We conclude the chapter with a summary of the key findings and reflections on the utility of applying an EEG approach to the understanding of the transformation of destination governance towards more sustainable approaches.

Theoretical and conceptual foundations of the model

Evolutionary economic geography

Theories developed in evolutionary economics are finding application across a wide range of social science disciplines (e.g. geography, political science, history, sociology) as well as business and management studies. Interpretations by geographers have added a spatial dimension to the understanding of the evolution of places and their economic landscapes (e.g. Boschma and Martin 2007; Essletzbichler and Rigby 2007; MacKinnon *et al.* 2009; Pike *et al.* 2009; Martin 2010). In integrating evolutionary economic approaches into geography, MacKinnon *et al.* (2009) advocate adopting political economy approaches that embrace both evolutionary and institutional concepts in order to relate change and innovation to social relations amongst groups, thus raising questions regarding such issues as social agency and power. This is especially appropriate for examining governance and the capacity of traditional institutional frameworks and management processes to adapt to changing economic, environmental and political, social, demographic and political realities (Van Assche *et al.* 2014).

A central concept in evolutionary approaches is 'path dependence', a term that can be summarized as essentially meaning 'history matters' (David 1985, 1994). The term implies evolution that is characterized by positive feedbacks and self-reinforcing dynamics that begin with a chance event but result in inertia, stability and irreversibility (Pierson 2000; Meyer and Schubert 2007). This concept has become prominent amongst geographers examining new ways of conceptualizing the evolution of regional economies (Martin and Sunley 2006). The notion of 'lock-in' is a core aspect of path dependence and refers to a range of structural, cognitive and political elements that serve to maintain commitment to the established path (Grabher 1993; Hassink 2010).

More recently Garud and Karnøe (2001) introduced the notion of path creation. This offers a distinctive lens for understanding evolutionary processes by focusing on human agency and the role of entrepreneurs operating under real-time influence. Human agents both individually and collectively are seen as engaging in 'mindful deviation' from existing paths, with their actions understood within a real-time context. This differs from the post hoc perspective of path dependency that emphasizes how institutional functions stabilize behaviour, whereas path creation focuses on 'creative destruction' of the effects of lock-in and the role of innovation in creating new pathways (Garud and Karnøe 2001; Garud *et al.* 2010).

The recent widespread adoption and adaptation of evolutionary economic approaches across many disciplines has resulted in varying perspectives on how these two approaches are related. For example, Gáspár (2011: 94) considers this relationship with respect to futures studies and sees the interaction of path dependency and path creation as 'the bonds that tie the present to the past and to the future'. Schienstock (2007), in a study of techno-economic change in Finland, suggests that path creation offers a better understanding of recent institutional change than path-dependency approaches.

Recent studies increasingly recognize the complexity of understanding evolutionary processes. Within geography, Martin (2010) argues that David's (1985) original concept of lock-in is restrictive and narrow. He draws upon recent work in historical sociology and political science to rethink the application of path dependence in the context of institutional evolution, emphasizing change rather than continuity. Along this line of thinking, Strambach (2010) has proposed the idea of 'path plasticity', which suggests a broader interpretation of path dependence that is more flexible and can accommodate innovations. Strambach and Halkier (2013) and Halkier and Therkelsen (2013) have applied this perspective in a tourism context to offer a more nuanced understanding of path dependency. Meyer and Schubert (2007), in science, technology and innovation studies, propose an integrated model of path constitution that includes both path dependence and creation as components of a more elaborate understanding of path evolution.

Governance and sustainability

The relationship between sustainability and governance is central to the constructs of this chapter. Kemp *et al.* (2005: 13) see these two concepts, which entered common usage in the 1990s, as being 'children of a similar history and parentage'. Jordan (2008) views sustainable development and governance as being highly ambiguous and contested terms. For the purposes of this chapter, we view governance very generally as 'the formation of rules and decision-making procedures and the operation of social institutions guided by these rules' (Bosselmann *et al.* 2008: 4). We employ Meadowcroft's (2007: 299) definition of governance for sustainable development:

> [t]he processes of socio-political governance oriented towards the attainment of sustainable development. It encompasses public debate, political decision-making, policy formation and implementation, and complex interactions among public authorities, private business and civil society – in so far as these relate to steering societal development along more sustainable lines.

Farrell *et al.* (2005:143) characterize sustainable development as 'a political concept, replete with governance questions'. Sustainability poses specific challenges to governance that are different from other policy fields (Newig *et al.* 2007; Bosselmann *et al.* 2008). A major challenge in shifting to a sustainable trajectory is the conceptual and institutional separation of social and ecological systems that reinforces path dependence (Westley *et al.* 2011). To effect the creation of an ideal governance path would require major political, institutional and cognitive changes; indeed, it would require a changed worldview (Matutinović 2007) and a reformulating of the basics of democracy (Bosselmann *et al.* 2008). To at least move in that direction, Bosselmann *et al.* (2008) contend that governance for sustainability requires a shift towards ecological thinking. As proposed by Code (2006) this implies an approach that is responsive to local conditions and adaptive to changing conditions.

Given the complexities of sustainability, it is not surprising that the idea of co-evolution, drawn from generalized Darwinian theory, is emerging as the most appropriate way to examine its path (Kemp *et al.* 2005; Gowdy 2007; Matutinović 2007; Rammel *et al.* 2007). Expansion of the initial ecological-economics notion of co-evolutionary theories recognizes the interdependence of systems whereby a change in one system can effect change in other systems (Rammel *et al.* 2007; Schamp 2010). For example, there is a growing body of research on transition management (governance) conducted in the Netherlands. It offers a multilevel model of governance that adopts a co-evolutionary perspective to assist societies to gradually transform in a reflexive way. It employs evolutionary principles associated with processes of variation and selection to suggest how to move along a sustainability path (Kemp *et al.* 2007; Loorbach 2010). Although such models imply a process of 'societal self-steering' (Meadowcroft 2007), government is nevertheless central to coordination across the complexity of institutional and spatial scales (Dorcey 2004).

While multidisciplinary applications of evolutionary approaches have expanded conceptual understanding of evolutionary processes, there has been less clarity concerning methodological issues due to theoretical arguments that arise concerning the interpretation of original economics theory in other contexts.

Recent contributions address this issue. For instance, Sydow *et al.* (2012) present a methodology for understanding path constitution, and Dobusch and Kapeller (2013) offer other insights into various methods. While the details are beyond the scope of this paper, Dobusch and Kapeller (2013) suggest that, although various complementary methods are suited to examining path dependency, narrative case studies are the most appropriate tool for examining path creation.

Destination governance and sustainability

There are many destination governance models ranging from those that are corporate directed to those that are community focused (Flagestad and Hope 2001). Beritelli *et al.* (2007) emphasize the importance of context and the stage of a destination's development in determining the mode of governance. For example, there are distinct differences in the governance approaches applied in newer, comprehensively planned resorts, such as those established by large corporations in North American mountain destinations (Rothman 1998), compared with those in more organically evolved resort destinations, more frequently found in Europe (Murphy 2008; Laws *et al.* 2011). Ultimately the nature of destination governance reflects the varying coalitions, partnerships and discourses that emerge from the relative power of all actors within the dominant political regime (Gill 2007). As Horner (2000:13) states:

> resorts will evolve at the intersection of capital that is simultaneously local and global, public and private; consequently their form, function and image as marketed will be the outcome of the relative power of the actors representing these sources of capital.

Such complexity requires institutional arrangements in the form of policies, systems and processes that can legislate, plan and manage the destination to effectively coordinate the system. There is widespread acknowledgement that governance approaches in tourism destinations need to embrace principles of sustainability that meet the needs of both tourists and residents (Dinica 2009). However, as Bramwell (2011) observes, this is challenging due to having so many related policy decisions made in other policy domains at various scales. The result is a weak institutional setting for sustainable tourism policy development (Bramwell and Lane 2010). It is in this context that co-evolutionary approaches hold promise. As Ma and Hassink (2013: 99) observe, 'the co-evolutionary approach has its strength in analyzing heterogeneity and complexity at the micro and macro level, it can be useful to explain the evolution of tourism areas'. They illustrate this approach in their study of tourism development on the Gold Coast of Australia.

A number of different typologies of governance for tourism have been discussed. Hall (2011a) for example, distinguishes four basic types based on hierarchies, markets, networks and communities. Of relevance to the understanding of destination path-creation, a substantial body of research on innovation and destination networks has emerged (Nordin and Svensson 2005; Dredge 2006a; Guia *et al.* 2006;

Lazzeretti and Petrillo 2006; Beritelli *et al.* 2007; Baggio *et al.* 2010; Beaumont and Dredge 2010; Erkus-Osturk and Eraydin 2010; Pechlaner *et al.* 2010; Laws *et al.* 2011; Graci 2013). Further, an examination of the influence of entrepreneurs on destination governance suggests growing recognition of the importance of entrepreneurial reputation (Strobl and Peters 2013; Komppula 2014). Interest in examining the functioning of these more complex destination governance models has increased substantially over the past decade, especially in Europe (Bodega *et al.* 2004; Svensson *et al.* 2005, 2006; Keller and Bieger 2008;) and Australia (Dredge 2006a, 2006b; Beaumont and Dredge 2010; Ruhanen *et al.* 2010). In an Australian context Beaumont and Dredge (2010) identify three different approaches to local tourism governance. In their research, they identify these as being council-led networks, participant-led networks, and local tourism-organization-led networks, and consider the effects of each on sustainable tourism policy initiatives. Their findings highlight varying tensions and trade-offs between the different approaches with respect to such characteristics as legitimacy, efficiency, flexibility and responsiveness. Hall's (2011b) examination of policy learning and failure identifies the many challenges to establishing sustainable tourism governance. He concludes that, even though exogenous crisis events may result in policy shifts, there is no evidence to suggest a significant paradigm change due to the deeply entrenched existing growth paradigm.

A model of constraints and catalysts in transitioning towards sustainability in destination community governance

There is a growing recognition that, to remain competitive, destinations need to go beyond economic imperatives that prioritize economic growth and adopt more comprehensive and complex sustainability focused mandates supported by governance systems that engage stakeholders in a more meaningful manner. Bramwell and Lane (2011) contend that having theoretical frameworks suited to guiding such transformations are needed as they affect the issues and policy recommendations examined. In Figure 3.1 we present a generalized conceptual framework identifying the evolutionary forces shaping contestations over the character of governance systems, especially with respect to their focus and approach. While conceived in the context of Whistler's transition from growth-dependence towards a more sustainable future, we recognize that globally other types of transitional models can exist depending on the contextual conditions of the political, social and entrepreneurial environment of places, as well as on the level of maturity of the destination. However, the framework is intended as a heuristic device to guide the understanding of factors underlying change. Path-dependence and path-creation forces shape the character of governance systems and the nature of overall path constitution. We conceive contestation as occurring between path-dependent forces that embody lock-in to established economic, political and social institutions, and path-creation forces that, through human agency and entrepreneurship, challenge the status quo by introducing new approaches.

The terrain of destination governance is where differences in values, objectives and priorities are contested through various mechanisms. Kenny and Meadowcroft

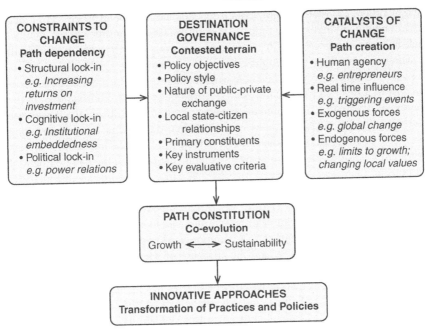

Figure 3.1 A model of constraints and catalysts in destination community governance transition towards sustainability.

(1999) contend that sustainable development is often defined around the core value of opposition to economic growth. The outcome reflects the structure of power relations within the destination. A transition from a growth-dependent orientation of governance towards one that embraces principles of sustainability introduces innovative approaches to practices and policies that move the destination towards a more sustainable future. The model is not intended as a process model, but rather one that identifies key elements embodied within the process. As such it does not imply that transition to a sustainability-oriented governance approach follows a straightforward linear path or that path-creation processes might not be subsequently subsumed within a more powerful path-dependence regime.

Whistler's governance transition towards sustainability

The following discussion presents each of the main conceptual elements of the model (path dependence, path creation and destination governance) separately. For each component the conceptual elements are elaborated and subsequently related to Whistler's experience of destination governance transition.

Path dependence

Path-dependent factors reinforce the persistence of existing governance systems, creating inertia and resistance to change, referred to as 'lock-in'.

Pierson (2000: 251) conceptualizes path dependence as 'a social process grounded in a dynamic of increasing returns'. Grabher (1993) identifies three distinct lock-in components of path dependence: structural, cognitive and political, all of which act as self-reinforcing mechanisms. Structural lock-in is self-reinforcing because once a decision becomes embedded into institutional arrangements the cost of a reversal of decision is high (Strambach 2010). For example, in the context of destination development, the cost of initial start-up and fixed costs are a strong incentive to stick with the initial path in order to benefit from increasing returns over time. Further, the structural lock-in to increasing returns is also exhibited in various institutional arrangements that result in the development of supporting business and social networks that can enhance knowledge-sharing, learning capacity and trust formation. Such coordinating functions greatly enhance increasing returns (North 1990) and are especially important in the tourism sector due to its complex and interdependent structure.

Cognitive lock-in is regarded as a common worldview or mindset that relates to institutional embeddedness and the structure of social relationships that link people to institutional environments. As Matutinović (2007: 101) observes, the dominant worldview in market-based democracies has its ideological grounding in neoliberalism and globalism, and any challenges to this are likely to be con-flict ridden. He sees any radical shift towards sustainability-oriented governance as contingent on prior changes in the dominant worldview. Cognitive lock-in is closely related to political lock-in (Grabher 1993). Political lock-in exhibits 'thick institutional tissue' that includes networks such as political administrations, large enterprises and business support agencies (Strambach 2010). Cognitive and politi-cal lock-in also include other components that structure behaviour, such as norms, rules, and written and unwritten laws (Bosselmann *et al.* 2008). As such they serve to preserve existing traditional structures that, in the interests of continuity and retention of power, constrain rather that nurture innovations (Grabher 1993; Hassink 2010).

The recent shift of evolutionary theory research into the broader multi-disciplinary arena has led to new perspectives on path dependence and institutional change that emphasize not only change but also continuity (Martin 2010). Two mechanisms operating at the micro-level that impart slow change to path-dependent institutional evolution are 'layering' and 'conversion'. Layering implies the gradual addition of amendments, new rules and procedures to existing systems, whereas conversion, which involves a more radical reorientation of an institution's form or function, may result from either layering or external pressures or developments (Boas 2007; Martin 2010). These changes are embedded within a path-dependent structure and constitute what Strambach and Halkier (2013) refer to as 'path plasticity', although, over time a new distinctive path could emerge (Boas 2007).

Path dependence in Whistler

In many ways Whistler is distinctive from most resort destinations in that it is a comprehensively planned, purpose-built destination that was initially established as a 'resort municipality' about 40 years ago. Over that period it has evolved into a major year-round mountain-tourism destination, catering to domestic and international visitors. Functionally, it is a single-industry community, with the vast majority of its 10,000 residents dependent for employment and/or amenities on the tourism sector. Whistler's path dependence was determined by the political and regulatory system established at its inception. That system locked the resort-community's development into a defined land base that guided varying levels of controlled growth for over three decades (Gill and Williams 2011). An important component in locking-in investors was the notion of increasing returns. The magnitude of initial investment by the provincial government who developed the infrastructure to stimulate private investment required an intense focus on reaching a critical mass of development that would subsequently ensure continuing returns on investment. An example of this, used to attract mountain developers, was the 'lands for lifts policy', which granted the ski companies future rights to real-estate development in return for their substantial investment in installing lift infrastructure. Over time, as the resort became more successful, the value of these development rights greatly increased. Another element of structural lock-in was the establishment of a destination management organization to which all businesses were required to belong. This coordination of marketing efforts across all sectors of the tourism economy together with an official community plan that established the basis for a regulatory framework for land use and resort priorities were all driven by a growth imperative.

Governance approaches did evolve over time. Initially an elite 'growth machine' form of governance (Molotch 1976) changed to a growth-management approach, with greater stakeholder engagement (Gill 2000, 2007). This represented a 'conversion' process (Boas 2007), as it resulted from organized pressure from the electorate to address community needs. Eventually, amendments to the Official Community Plans created new policies and processes that represented layering. Nevertheless, power remained with the three key groups of decision-makers: the municipality, the mountain operator(s) and the provincial government, all of whom were committed to continued growth. Such cognitive and political lock-in to the growth imperative is widespread in neoliberal capitalist society. Interestingly, despite the fact that environmental quality and protection were quality of life values that were consistently highly ranked by most residents over many years, there was relatively limited contestation of the resort community's growth agenda. This situation may have existed because cutting-edge environmental management policies and programs employed by corporate and resort managers to protect the destination's environmental qualities and enhance market competeiveness converged well with the values of residents. In a way, their environmental activities helped reinforce a trust that residents had in the local government to make decisions that addressed their needs and values. As De Vries *et al.* (2014: 2) attest: '[t]rust is seen as a lubricant for cooperation, as an important mechanism for the course of decision-making processes'.

Most importantly, one of the growth management policies created by the local government and known as a 'bed unit limit' became an important construct heavily endowed with the symbolism of sound environmental management

(Gill 2007). Established to define an ultimate limit to resort growth, this annually monitored development indicator was based on an estimated capacity of the destination with respect to water and sewage – and by default environmental quality. We have often cited the following statement from a letter written by a resident to the local newspaper that captures the depth of this sense of trust in the municipality's stewardship of the environment – 'I have three beliefs in life: death, taxes, and the 52,500 bed unit limit' (Gill and Williams 2011). In this statement we see reflected the influence of structural (in the form of policy) and cognitive (in this resident's belief in the policy's efficacy) lock-in that served to embed support for the growth agenda. As discussed in the next section on path creation, it was the perceived breaching of this trust, when the local government proposed raising the long-established bed unit limit, that led to contestation over the growth agenda and served as a triggering agent to the introduction of new goals for governance.

Path creation

While a range of endogenous and exogenous forces act as critical change events that can trigger a change in path constitution (Sydow *et al.* 2012), the role of human agency is central to understanding the process of path creation (Garud and Karnøe 2001; Schienstock 2007). It is the process of 'mindful deviation' in the context of 'real-time influence' that serves as a core construct in understanding the role of human agency in path creation (Garud and Karnøe 2001). Mindful deviation requires that entrepreneurs deliberately seek to break away from established institutional structures and practice, and reframe their thinking and approach along new pathways. This, as Garud and Karnøe (2001: 2) express it, 'implies the ability to disembed from existing structures defining relevance and also the ability to mobilize a collective despite resistance and inertia that path creation efforts will likely encounter'.

Innovation and entrepreneurship are central constructs in path creation (Pham 2006–7). The same individuals do not necessarily perform these functions. Visionaries or inventors have an idea, but entrepreneurs are necessary to put these ideas into action. As Pham (2006–7: 11) states, 'entrepreneurs, as opposed to inventors, are the true path creators'. While individual human agency can be identified in entrepreneurial leadership roles, collective human agency is also necessary to support the development of a new path. With reference to the creation of a governance path towards sustainability, Kemp *et al.* (2005: 13) see it as being 'best viewed as a socially instituted process of adaptive change in which innovation is a necessary element'. The following examples from Whistler's experience in shifting its growth-oriented governance model to one based on principles of sustainability demonstrate how human agency and the effects of real-time influence are integrally entwined in shaping governance pathways.

Path creation towards sustainability in Whistler

In our research in Whistler, we characterized the first two decades of the resort's evolution as being locked in to pro-growth path-dependent forces (Gill and

Williams 2011). However, this does not negate the role of human agency in the initial path creation that led to Whistler's development as a new ski resort. Indeed, a small but influential group of local businessmen played a visionary role in drawing initial attention to Whistler's potential for hosting a Winter Olympic Games, as well as its appropriateness for development as a major mountain-tourism destination. Further, as discussed above, collective human agency was important in the contestation that led to conversion from a growth machine to a growth-management governance approach. While the last example demonstrates that human agency was a factor in effecting changes in Whistler's governance, it did not disembed the path from its growth imperative.

To understand how a new pathway towards sustainability came about, the notion of 'real time influence' is well illustrated in the Whistler story. As Garud and Karnøe (2001: 22) observe, '[t]ime becomes a resource that offers entrepreneurs options to strike at the right time and place'. Several real-time events provided triggers that pushed Whistler along a governance path towards sustainability. The first, an endogenous event occurred when, in 2000, the resort reached its long-established bed-unit development cap. This coincided with escalating house prices and a crisis with respect to availability of affordable housing for workers (Gill and Williams 2011), and represented a 'critical juncture' (Holden 2009). Although the resort managers had an excellent track record with respect to environmental management and had talked about sustainability they did not see a way to break the lock-in to their very successful growth model. The path to move beyond the constraints of a bed-cap limit to direct future development towards the destination's longer-term economic, environmental and economic goals arose as the result of encountering Karl-Henrik Robèrt, the charismatic visionary founder of The Natural Step (TNS), a not-for-profit international sustainability organization, who came to Whistler on vacation and informally engaged with some community leaders. This resulted in several entrepreneurial agents from the municipality, the mountain corporation and local business becoming early adopters of the TNS approach. In turn they championed the idea of creating an innovative, comprehensive integrated sustainability plan – the first of its kind for a resort destination. It took several years of intense community education and engagement to bring the community on board with the principles of TNS (the importance of which will be discussed in the next section). The importance of learning and knowledge creation is emphasized as an important component of moving towards sustainability (Kolleck *et al.* 2011). Indeed, learning is seen as an essential policy objective in establishing governance towards sustainability (Kemp *et al.* 2005; Hall 2011b).

The timing of the designation of Whistler as a host resort for the 2010 Winter Olympic Games was also critical to forwarding Whistler's path towards sustainability. This occurred in 2003, when the resort community had already embarked along the TNS pathway to developing its own sustainability vision and priorities. With the community now embedded in 'thinking sustainably', it provided the resort leaders with the 'social license to operate' needed to negotiate the resort's terms of engagement with the Olympic organizers. As the International Olympic

Committee had also recently adopted sustainability as its overriding goal for the Games, this reinforced the legitimacy of Whistler's agenda. It also helped them negotiate Olympic athlete housing development standards that were not only environmentally leading edge, but also appropriate for post-Games resident-restricted use. The outcome of this process was the provision of an affordable housing supply that satisfied the most pressing concern of Whistler's residents. In doing so it maintained its commitment to a sustainability path. These two examples illustrate Garud and Karnøe's (2001) observations on 'real time influence' that all actions have real-time consequences on the path in the making. They highlight the importance not only of individual human agency but also collective action, and reinforce recent research in destination governance that emphasizes the importance of entrepreneurs in destination governance (Beritelli 2011a, 2011b; Strobl and Peters 2013; Komppula 2014).

Contested terrain of destination governance

Governance is seen by Van Assche *et al.* (2014: 11) as a process 'wherein worlds collide, fight for pre-eminence, mutate, transform and recombine'. The complexity of stakeholders in resort destinations gives rise to distinctive arenas of contestation. Differences often arise because of the value differences between the tourism industry and the residents. The nature of such contestation is reflected in the extensive literature on residents' attitudes to the impacts of tourism on destination communities (see Nunkoo *et al.* 2013). In most case these conflicts have been contested in the arena of local politics and the outcomes reflect the relative power of the actors.

To create new paths means that 'entrepreneurs often need to change the endogenized social practice, regulations or institutions away from accepted, comfortable or optimal structure' (Stack and Gartland 2005: 421). As Van Assche *et al.* (2014) observe, shifting from one approach of governance to another is not easy and the shift to a sustainability-focused governance system is proving to be one of the most difficult systems to implement. This is largely because of the deep embeddedness of the tourism industry in the globalized neoliberal agenda, where sustainability is often positioned as oppositional to growth (Kenny and Meadowcroft 1999; Hall 2011a).

We adopt Pierre's (1999) defining characteristics of governance to distinguish between the traditional growth models that currently dominate virtually all resort governance approaches and the newly emerging governance structures such as co-evolutionary transitional models that are striving towards sustainability. Application of these characteristics assists in understanding the basic underlying nature of contestation around decision-making in resort destinations as they reveal the nature of policy objectives and style, the identification of stakeholders and their relationship to local government, and the tools and strategies employed. We label the two governance types simply as 'growth' (basically following Pierre's 'pro-growth' designation) and 'sustainability', which is a specific form of corporatist governance that is sometimes referred to as 'governance for sustainability' (Meadowcroft 2007). As shown in Table 3.1 there are significant ideological differences between the two modes of governance.

Table 3.1 Selected defining characteristics of growth- and sustainability-oriented governance models.

Models of destination governance		
Defining characteristics	*Sustainability*	*Growth*
Policy objectives	Distribution	Growth
Policy style	Ideological	Pragmatic
Nature of public–private exchange	Concerted	Interactive
Local state–citizen relationship	Inclusive	Exclusive
Primary constituency	Civic leaders	Business
Key instruments	Deliberations	Partnerships
Key evaluative criteria	Shared decision-making	Growth

Source: Adapted from Pierre (1999: 388) and Gill and Williams (2011).

Governance for sustainable development is frequently linked to the *good governance* literature (Dorcey 2004; Kemp *et al.* 2005; Stratford *et al.* 2007), which is not surprising considering that many of the principles of good governance are reflected in sustainability principles and practices. Despite its prescriptive and somewhat presumptuous connotations, the notion of 'good governance' is widely understood to include fundamental principles of participatory, responsive, consensus oriented, accountable, equitable, transparent and effective methods in making the best use of resources. The appropriate indicators of these attributes are place specific (Kemp *et al.* 2005). The two governance approaches are distinguishable first and foremost with respect to their policy style and objectives. Growth models focus on economic growth, whereas sustainability approaches seek more equitable distribution of benefits across not just economic but social and environmental domains according to the ideology of sustainability. Governance for sustainability is based on the idea of participatory local democracy that engages a wide range of stakeholders across both public and private sectors. It is characterized by 'civic leadership', which is: 'reflected in the capacity of a community to: identify, analyze, collaborate and solve pressing societal needs and issues through the efforts of broadly engaged citizen organizations' (Canmore 2014: paragraph 1).

Contested resort governance in Whistler

As discussed earlier, under a well-managed and fairly transparent growth-management governance approach that served both resort and community needs, Whistler became a model for many resort communities around the globe. While there was some contestation around issues of environmental quality and affordability of resident housing, broadening the discourse from environmental concerns to one of sustainability was an astute move on the part of local government that was widely supported. An important component of the process of change was a period of intensive 'community conditioning' to engage and educate the community in principles of sustainability. This resulted a few years later in the adoption of a high-level plan and policy document entitled *Whistler2020*, described as 'long-term, comprehensive, community-developed, community-implemented, and action-focused' (*Whistler2020* 2010). The governance decision-making process was guided by perspectives from 15 Task Force Groups composed of a wide range of stakeholders (including representatives of private and public institutions, as well as individual community members) from both within and beyond the community. Overriding filtering criteria relating to TNS sustainability principles and Whistler's community vision guided all decisions and recommended action. An interactive and informative website provided on-going progress reports to the broader community on the implementation of recommended task force priorities (Gill and Williams 2011). As such the decision-making process embodied co-evolutionary mechanisms well suited to the complexity of governance for sustainability in a resort destination.

The 'sustainability journey' (as it was referred to in Whistler) was strengthened over a seven-year period by the resort's focus on preparing to host the 2010 Winter Olympics that also had 'sustainability' as a core value. This essentially offered an incubating environment that offered a 'protective space' for Whistler's innovative new governance model to function. Research in sustainability transition management has characterized such protective spaces as a source of path-breaking innovation (Kemp *et al.* 1998; Smith and Raven 2012). In Whistler's case, engagement with the International Olympic Committee afforded legitimacy, resources and support for the resort's sustainability initiative. It served to bring global attention to Whistler's innovations whilst simultaneously engaging the community in fast-tracked action in addressing their greatest social need for affordable housing.

However, this protective space disappeared once the Games were over. Whistler's economy, buffered for a few years by infusions of money associated with the Olympics, felt the delayed impact of the global economic recession. With a shift in political power that favoured business interests over sustainability, many of the operational components of *Whistler2020* were compromised. The task forces were essentially abandoned, and funding for community engagement on sustainability issues was substantially cut in favour of advancing immediate and targeted economic development initiatives. As Bosselmann *et al.* (2008) observe, the dominant form of governance in the Western capitalist economy is representative democracy that favours short-term gains over long-term responsibility, because politicians' jobs depend on them meeting the immediate needs of the voters. The power of stakeholders to effect change in trajectories can be immediate when crises are on the horizon. A report in Whistler's local paper suggested that:

> [w]ith too many empty beds, too many struggling hotels and a business community desperate to keep the money flow going, the province's diamond in the crown is struggling mightily to reinvent itself for the new century . . . Doesn't look all that sustainable at this point does it?

> (Beaudry 2010: 33)

Economic challenges tend to occur frequently and are often felt immediately by stakeholders. As such they are often uppermost on the agendas of politicians. Because social and environmental concerns tend to have longer gestation periods, they often are less immediate in the minds of decision-makers and may be fleeting and/or lost from institutional memory unless there is a crisis imminent.

Despite the setback to Whistler's sustainability agenda, the *Whistler2020* policy still remains in place, although its implementation through task-force engagement is on the back burner. Such deviations are not uncommon in path-creation processes as Garud and Karnøe (2001: 20) assert: '[t]hose who attempt to create new paths have to realize that they are part of an emerging collective and that core ideas and objectives will modify as they pass from hand to hand and mind to mind'. Conversely, it may suggest that Whistler is not moving along a *new* governance path towards sustainability but rather that these aberrations represent path plasticity within the established path-dependent mode.

Conclusions

In this chapter we have presented a conceptual model of destination governance that draws upon evolutionary economic theory to assist in understanding the constraints and catalysts to governance change. The model is intended as a heuristic device that focuses attention through the distinct lenses of path dependence and path creation on the conceptual elements of these two constructs. Path-dependent forces constrain actors from making changes because of the benefits embedded in the increasing returns that result from conforming to various structural, cognitive and political forms of lock-in. Thus, an examination of these factors helps understand why systems do not change even if they do not represent optimal situations. However, challenges to the *status quo* can come from path-creation forces. These forces depend on innovation, especially through the role that entrepreneurs play in leading and operationalizing visions of new pathways. Thus, the focus for understanding these catalysts of change comes from examining attributes of human behaviour both individually and collectively. A path-creation perspective also places emphasis on understanding how entrepreneurs strategically use real-time influence in helping create new pathways. Time is also a factor in understanding how endogenous and exogenous forces can act as either triggering events or incubating elements in the creation of new pathways.

We have used the model presented in this chapter to understand the factors underlying the contested terrain of destination governance and the debate over shifting from dependence on growth as a core policy objective towards one based on shared decision-making that embodies the principles of sustainability. Though conceiving governance evolution towards sustainability as an on-going process, the paradigm is not a process model per se, although we do depict that the outcome of contestation will affect the overall character of path constitution. We further suggest as a result of contestation that innovation resulting in some form of transformation in practice and policy may well occur – although this may represent a form of path-dependent plasticity rather than a new path. As Meyer and

Schubert (2007: 267) observe, 'path creation is not a solitary act but requires a long process of continual path creating and stabilizing events'; thus, the success of path creation can only be established in a post hoc fashion.

To demonstrate the utility of the model used, examples are drawn from our longitudinal empirical research on Whistler, British Columbia – a mountain-resort destination that for over a decade has been internationally recognized for introducing innovations in sustainability planning and practice (Gill 2000; Gill and Williams 2011, 2014). Using an evolutionary economic geography perspective helped in understanding why Whistler was able to rapidly grow and evolve into a leading mountain-resort destination, while at the same time maintain remarkably uncontested support from the resident population for its growth imperative. Much of this can be attributed to the initial comprehensive planning of the resort and the early institutional lock-in to the notion of a 'resort community', whereby not only were all tourism businesses required to work collaboratively to market the destination through a destination management organization, but residents benefitted from growth through the significant provision of community amenities that enhanced quality of life. Whilst Whistler's governance approach evolved over time, through layering of new policies and a more significant change or 'conversion' to a growth-management approach, Whistler's governance approach remained growth-dependent until path-creation forces came into effect with the introduction of an integrated comprehensive sustainability plan that embodied a decision-making process based on co-evolutionary mechanisms engaging a broad range of stakeholders.

A path-creation lens focusing on human agency is appropriate and useful in understanding contesting governance spaces as sustainability at it roots requires a fundamental change in worldview (Kemp *et al.* 2005; Bosselmann *et al.* 2008; Hall 2011b). Thus, understanding values and how these can be changed is critical. Further, we note the importance of the 'community conditioning' phase that educated and engaged all stakeholders in the language and principles of sustainability. The importance of on-going learning is reinforced in the subsequent retreat in the post-2010 Winter Olympic period when, after a decade of widespread commitment to pursuing a sustainability path, Whistler's council and business community withdrew their support, reverting to an economic growth agenda, and on-going learning opportunities relating to sustainability were greatly reduced. Learning is seen as a critical component of governance towards sustainability (Stagl 2007; Bosselmann *et al.* 2008; Hall 2011a).

To retain a trajectory along a new path to sustainability, it is necessary for entrepreneurs to have not only vision, but also thick social capital and legitimacy in the form of a community social licence to operate (Williams *et al.* 2012). This is not a new idea, as William James (1880: 6) observed long ago: '[t]he community stagnates without the impulse of the individual. The impulse dies away without the sympathy of the community'. In destinations with an elected local government, this is an important factor to bear in mind, especially when seeking long-term strategic goals such as those necessary to implement sustainable policy and practices. Adopting a path-creation perspective focuses attention on these critical aspects of human agency.

In conclusion, understanding the transition to sustainability as a long-term co-evolutionary process is becoming increasingly recognized as an appropriate methodological framework (Kemp *et al.* 2007; Rammel *et al.* 2007; Ma and Hassink 2013). The model presented here focuses attention on the underlying agents of change and offers a research framework supported by an ever-increasing body of both theoretical and empirical contributions from a multi-disciplinary array of researchers to guide tourism researchers. The general model presented is broadly applicable and can be applied and adapted to examine many aspects of tourism governance at any scale from the local to the global, including at the corporate governance level. Further, elaboration and extension of the core evolutionary constructs offers opportunity to develop the model. In particular, within tourism studies, one could extend the destination model beyond the innovation stage to consider policy mobility and knowledge transfer to examine evolution within tourism regions.

References

Baggio, R., Scott, N., and Cooper, C. (2010). 'Improving tourism destination governance: A complexity science approach'. *Tourism Review* 65(4), 51–60.

Beaudry, M. (2010). 'Rethinking Garibaldi at Squamish – A 21st century perspective'. *Pique Newsmagazine*, 4 June. www.piquenewsmagazine.com/whistler/alta-states/Content?oid=2168165 (accessed on 25 July 2015).

Beaumont, N. and Dredge, D. (2010). 'Local tourism governance: A comparison of three network approaches'. *Journal of Sustainable Tourism* 18(1), 2–28.

Beritelli, P. (2011a). 'Cooperation among prominent actors in a tourist destination'. *Annals of Tourism Research* 38(2), 607–29.

Beritelli, P. (2011b). 'Tourist destination governance through local elites: Looking beyond the stakeholder level'. Cumulative post-doctoral thesis, Institute for Systematic Management and Public Governance, Centre for Tourism and Transport. St Gallen, Switzerland.

Beritelli, P., Bieger, T., and Laesser, C. (2007). 'Destination governance: Using corporate governance theories as a foundation for effective destination management'. *Journal of Travel Research* 20, 1–12.

Boas, T.C. (2007). 'Conceptualizing continuity and change: The composite-standard model of path dependence'. *Journal of Theoretical Politics* 19(1), 33–54.

Bodega, D., Cioccarelli, G., and Denicolai, S. (2004). 'Evolution of relationship structures in mountain tourism'. *Tourism Review* 59(3), 13–19.

Boschma, R. and Martin, R. (2007). 'Editorial: Constructing an evolutionary economic geography'. *Journal of Economic Geography* 7, 537–48.

Bosselmann, K., Engel, R., and Taylor, P. (2008). *Governance for Sustainability – Issues, Challenges, Successes*. Gland, Switzerland: IUCN.

Bramwell, B. (2011). 'Governance, the state and sustainable tourism: A political economy approach'. *Journal of Sustainable Tourism* 19(4–5), 459–77.

Bramwell, B. and Lane, B. (2010). 'Sustainable tourism and the evolving roles of government planning'. *Journal of Sustainable Tourism* 18(1), 1–5.

Bramwell, B. and Lane, B. (2011). 'Critical research on the governance of tourism and sustainability'. *Journal of Sustainable Tourism* 19(4–5), 411–21.

Canmore (2014). 'The town of Canmore: Civic leadership'. www.canmore.ca/Municipal-Sustainability/Civic-Leadership/ (accessed on 28 October 2014).

Code, L. (2006). *Ecological Thinking: The Politics of Epistemic Location.* Oxford: Oxford University Press.

David, P.A. (1985). 'Clio and the economics of QWERTY: The necessity of history'. *American Economic Review* 75, 332–7.

David, P.A. (1994). 'Why are institutions the "carriers of history"?: Path dependence and the evolution of conventions, organizations and institutions'. *Structural Change and Economic Dynamics* 5(2), 205–20.

De Vries, J.R., Roodbol-Mekkes, P., Beunen, R., Lokhors, A.M., and Aarts, N. (2014). 'Faking and forcing trust: The performance of trust and distrust in public policy'. *Land Use Policy* 38, 282–9.

Dinica, V. (2009). 'Governance for sustainable tourism: A comparison of international and Dutch visions'. *Journal of Sustainable Tourism* 17(5), 583–603.

Dobusch, L. and Kapeller, J. (2013). 'Breaking new paths: Theory and method in path dependence research'. *Schmalenbach Business Review* 65, 288–311.

Dorcey, A.H.J. (2004). 'Sustainability governance: surfing the waves of transformation'. In B. Mitchell (ed.) *Resource and Environmental Management in Canada: Addressing Conflict and Uncertainty.* Don Mills, ON: Oxford University Press (pp. 528–54).

Dredge, D. (2006a). 'Policy networks and the local organization of tourism'. *Tourism Management* 27, 269–80.

Dredge, D. (2006b). 'Networks, conflict and collaborative communities'. *Journal of Sustainable Tourism* 14(6), 562–81.

Dwyer, L., Edwards, D., Mistilis, N., Roman, C., and Scott, N. (2009). 'Destination and enterprise management for a tourism future'. *Tourism Management* 30, 63–74.

Erkus-Osturk, H. and Eraydin, A. (2010). 'Environmental governance for sustainable tourism development: Collaborative networks and organisation building in the Antalya region'. *Tourism Management* 31(1), 113–24.

Essletzbichler, J. and Rigby, D. (2007). 'Exploring economic geographies'. *Journal of Economic Geography* 7, 549–71.

Farrell, K., Kemp, R., Hinterberger, F., Rammel, C., and Ziegler, R. (2005). 'From *for* to governance for sustainable development in Europe'. *International Journal of Sustainable Development* 8(1/2), 127–50.

Flagestad, A. and Hope, C. (2001). 'Strategic success in winter sports destinations: A sustainable value creation perspective'. *Tourism Management* 22, 445–61.

Garud, R. and Karnøe, P. (2001). 'Path creation as a process of mindful deviation'. In R. Garud and P. Karnøe (eds) *Path Dependence and Creation.* Mahwah, NJ: Lawrence Erlbaum Associates (pp. 1–41).

Garud, R., Kumaraswamy, A., and Karnøe, P. (2010). 'Path dependence or path creation?' *Journal of Management Studies* 47(4), 760–74.

Gáspár, T. (2011). 'Path dependency and path creation in a strategic perspective'. *Journal of Futures Studies* 15(4), 93–108.

Gill, A.M. (2000). 'From growth machine to growth management: The dynamics of resort development in Whistler, British Columbia'. *Environment and Planning A* 32, 1083–1103.

Gill, A.M. (2007). 'The politics of bed units: The case of Whistler, British Columbia'. In T. Coles and A. Church (eds) *Tourism, Politics and Place.* London: Routledge (pp. 125–59).

Gill, A.M. and Williams, P.W. (2011). 'Rethinking resort growth: Understanding evolving governance strategies in Whistler, British Columbia'. *Journal of Sustainable Tourism* 19(4–5), 629–48.

Gill, A.M. and Williams, P.W. (2014). 'Mindful deviation in creating a governance path towards sustainability in resort destinations'. *Tourism Geographies* 16(4), 546–62.

Gowdy, J. (2007). 'Avoiding self-organized extinction: Towards a co-evolutionary economics of sustainability'. *International Journal of Sustainable Development and World Ecology* 14, 27–36.

Grabher, G. (1993). 'The weakness of strong ties: The lock-in of regional development in the Ruhr area'. In G. Grabher (ed.) *The Embedded Firm: On the Socio-Economics of Industrial Networks*. London: Routledge (pp. 255–77).

Graci, S. (2013). 'Collaboration and partnership development for sustainable tourism'. *Tourism Geographies* 15(1), 25–42.

Guia, J., Prats, L., and Comas, J. (2006). 'The destination as a local system of innovation: The role of relational networks'. In L. Lazzeretti and C. Petrillo (eds) *Tourism Local Systems and Networking*. Oxford: Elsevier (pp. 57–66).

Halkier, H. and Therkelsen, A. (2013). 'Exploring tourism destination path plasticity: The case of coastal tourism in North Jutland, Denmark'. *Zeitschrift für Wirtschaftsgeographie* 57(1–2), 39–51.

Hall, C.M. (2011a). 'A typology of governance and its implications for tourism policy analysis'. *Journal of Sustainable Tourism* 19(4–5), 437–57.

Hall, C.M. (2011b). 'Policy learning and policy failure in sustainable tourism governance: from first- and second-order to third-order change?' *Journal of Sustainable Tourism* 19(4–5), 649–71.

Hassink, R. (2010). 'Locked in decline? On the role of regional lock-ins in old industrial areas'. In R. Boschma and R. Martin (eds) *The Handbook of Evolutionary Economic Geography*. Cheltenham, UK: Edward Elgar (pp. 450–67).

Holden, A. (2009). 'The environment-tourism nexus: Influence of market ethics'. *Annals of Tourism Research* 36(3), 373–89.

Horner, G. (2000). 'Mountains of money: The corporate production of Whistler Resort'. MA thesis. The University of British Columbia.

James, W. (1880). 'Great men, great thoughts, and the environment'. *Atlantic Monthly*, October, 1880. www.uky.edu/~eushe2/Pajares/jgreatmen.html (accessed on 22 April 2014).

Jordan, A. (2008). 'The governance of sustainable development: Taking stock and looking forwards'. *Environment and Planning C: Government and Policy* 26(1), 17–33.

Keller, P. and Bieger, T. (eds) (2008). *Real Estate and Destination Development in Tourism*. Berlin: Erich Schmidt Verlag.

Kemp, R., Schot, J.W., and Hoogma, R. (1998). 'Regime shifts to sustainability through processes of niche formation: the approach of strategic niche management'. *Technology Analysis and Strategic Management* 10, 175–95.

Kemp, R., Loorbach, D., and Rotmans, J. (2007). 'Transition management as a model for managing processes of co-evolution towards sustainable development'. *International Journal of Sustainable Development and World Ecology* 14, 1–15.

Kemp, R., Parto, S., and Gibson, R. (2005). 'Governance for sustainable development: moving from theory to practice'. *International Journal of Sustainable Development* 8(1/2), 12–30.

Kenny, M. and Meadowcroft, J. (1999). *Planning Sustainability: The Implications of Sustainability for Public Planning Policy*. London: Routledge.

Kolleck, N., de Haan, G., and Fischbach, R. (2011). 'Social networks for path creation: Education for sustainable development matters'. *Journal of Futures Studies* 15(4), 77–92.

Komppula, R. (2014). 'The role of individual entrepreneurs in the development of competitiveness for a rural tourism destination – A case study'. *Tourism Management* 40, 361–71.

Laws, E., Richins, H., Agrusa, J., and Scott, N. (eds) (2011). *Tourism Destination Governance: Practice, Theory and Issues.* Wallingford, UK: CABI.

Lazzeretti, L. and Petrillo, C.L. (eds) (2006). *Tourism Local Systems and Networking.* Oxford: Elsevier.

Loorbach, D. (2010). 'Transition management for sustainable development : A prescriptive, complexity-based governance framework'. *Governance: An International Journal of Policy Administration and Institutions* 23(1), 161–83.

Ma, M. and Hassink, R. (2013). 'An evolutionary perspective on tourism area development'. *Annals of Tourism Research* 41, 89–109.

MacKinnon, D., Cumbers, A., Pike, A., Birch, K., and McMaster, R. (2009). 'Evolution in economic geography: Institutions, political economy and adaptation'. *Economic Geography* 85(2), 129–50.

Martin, R. (2010). 'Roepke lecture in economic geography-rethinking regional path dependence: Beyond lock-in to evolution'. *Economic Geography* 86(1), 1–27.

Martin, R. and Sunley, P. (2006). 'Path dependence and regional economic evolution'. *Journal of Economic Geography* 6, 395–437.

Matutinović , I. (2007). 'Worldviews, institutions and sustainability: An introduction to a co-evolutionary perspective'. *International Journal of Sustainable Development and World Ecology* 14(1), 92–102.

Meadowcroft , J. (2007). 'Who is in charge here? Governance for sustainable development in a complex world'. *Journal of Environmental Policy and Planning* 9(3–4), 299–314.

Meyer, U. and Schubert, C. (2007). 'Integrating path dependency and path creation in a general understanding of path constitution: The role of agency and institutions in the stabilisation of technical institutions'. *Science, Technology and Innovation Studies* 3, 23–44.

Molotch, H. (1976). 'The city as a growth machine'. *American Journal of Sociology* 82, 309–30.

Murphy, P.E. (2008). *The Business of Resort Management.* Oxford: Elsevier.

Newig, J., Voß, J.-P., and Monstadt, J. (2007). 'Editorial: Governance for sustainable development in the face of ambivalence: Uncertainty and distributed power – an introduction'. *Journal of Environmental Policy and Planning* 9(3–4), 185–92.

Nordin, S. and Svensson, B. (2005). 'The significance of governance in innovative tourism destinations'. In P. Keller and T. Bieger (eds) *Innovation in Tourism: Creating Customer Value.* St Gallen: AIEST (pp. 159–70).

North, D.C. (1990). *Institutions, Institutional Change and Economic Performance.* Cambridge: Cambridge University Press.

Nunkoo, R., Smith, S., and Ramkissoond, H. (2013). 'Residents' attitudes to tourism: A longitudinal study of 140 articles from 1984 to 2010'. *Journal of Sustainable Tourism* 21(1), 5–25.

OECD. (2012). 'Tourism governance in OECD countries'. In *OECD Tourism Trends and Policies 2012.* Paris: OECD (pp. 13–54).

Painter, J. (2000). 'State and governance'. In E. Sheppard and T. Barnes (eds) *A Companion to Economic Geography.* Oxford: Blackwell (pp. 359–76).

Pechlaner, H., Raich, F., and Beritelli, P. (2010). 'Editorial: Destination governance'. *Tourism Review* 65(4), 3.

Pham, X. (2006–7). 'Five principles of path creation'. *Oeconomicus* VIII, 5–17.

Pierre, J. (1999). 'Models of urban governance: The institutional dimension of urban politics'. *Urban Affairs Review* 34(3), 372–96.

Pierson, P. (2000). 'Increasing returns, path dependence, and the study of politics'. *American Political Science Review* 94(2), 251–67.

Pike, A., Birch, K., Cumbers, A., MacKinnon, R., and McMaster, R. (2009). 'A geographical political economy of evolution in economic geography'. *Economic Geography* 85(2), 175–82.

Rammel, C. Stagl S., and Wilfing, H. (2007). 'Managing complex adaptive systems – A co-evolutionary perspective on natural resource management'. *Ecological Economics* 63, 9–21.

Rothman, H. (1998). *Devil's Bargain: Tourism in the Twentieth-Century American West.* Lawrence, KN: University Press of Kansas.

Ruhanen, L., Scott, N., Ritchie, B., and Tkaczynski, A. (2010). 'Governance: A review and synthesis of literature'. *Tourism Review* 65(4), 4–16.

Schamp, E.W. (2010). 'On the notion of co-evolution in economic geography'. In R. Boschma and R. Martin (eds) *The Handbook of Evolutionary Economic Geography.* Cheltenham, UK: Edward Elgar (pp. 432–49).

Schienstock, G. (2007). 'From path dependence to path creation: Finland on its way to the knowledge-based economy'. *Current Sociology* 55(1), 92–109.

Smith, A. and Raven, R. (2012). 'What is protective space? Reconsidering niches in transitions to sustainability'. *Research Policy* 41, 1025–36.

Stack, M. and Gartland, M.P. (2005). 'The repeal of prohibition and the resurgence of national breweries: Productive efficiency or path creation'. *Journal of Management History* 43(3), 420–32.

Stagl, S. (2007). 'Theoretical foundations of learning processes for sustainable development'. *International Journal of Sustainable Development and World Ecology* 14(1), 52–62.

Strambach, S. (2010). 'Path dependence and path plasticity. The co-evolution of institutions and innovation. The German customized business software industry'. In R. Boschma and R. Martin (eds) *The Handbook of Evolutionary Economic Geography.* Cheltenham, UK: Edward Elgar (pp. 406–31).

Strambach, S. and Halkier, H. (2013). 'Editorial – Reconceptualizing change: Path dependency, path plasticity and knowledge combination'. *Zeitschrift für Wirtschaftsgeographie* 57 (1–2), 1–14.

Stratford, E., Davidson, J., Griffith, R., Lockwood, M., and Curtis, A. (2007). *Sustainable Development and Good Governance: The 'Big Ideas' on Australian NRM.* Report #3 of the project 'Pathways to good practice in regional NRM governance'. Hobart: University of Tasmania.

Strobl, A. and Peters, M. (2013). 'Entrepreneurial reputation in destination networks'. *Annals of Tourism Research* 40, 59–82.

Svensson, B., Nordin, S., and Flagestad, A. (2005). 'A governance perspective on destination development – exploring partnerships, clusters and innovation systems'. *Tourism Review* 60, 32–7.

Svensson, B., Nordin, S., and Flagestad, A. (2006). 'Destination governance and contemporary development models'. In L. Lazzeretti and C. Petrillo (eds) *Tourism Local Systems and Networking.* Oxford: Elsevier (pp. 83–96).

Sydow, J., Windeler, A., Müller-Seitz, G., and Lange, K. (2012). 'Path constitution analysis: A methodology for understanding path dependence and path creation'. *Business Research* 5(2),155–76.

Van Assche K., Beunen, R., and Duineveld, M. (2014). *Evolutionary Governance Theory: An Introduction*. Cham, Switzerland: Springer.

Westley, F., Olsson, P., Folke, C., Homer-Dixon, T., Vredenburg, H., Loorbach, D., Thompson, J., Mans, N., Lambin, E., Sendzimir, J., Banerjee, B., Galaz, V., and van der Leeuw, S. (2011). 'Tipping toward sustainability: Emerging pathways of transformation'. *Ambio* 40, 762–80.

Whistler2020. (2010). 'Whistler 2020: Moving toward a sustainable future'. www.whistler 2020.ca (accessed on 27 July 2015).

Williams, P.W., Gill, A.M., Marcoux, J., and Xu, N. (2012). 'Nurturing "social license to operate" through corporate-civil society relationships in tourism destinations'. In C. Hsu and W. Gartner (eds) *The Routledge Handbook of Tourism Research*. London: Routledge (pp. 196–214).

4 Tourism area research and economic geography theories

Investigating the notions of co-evolution and regional innovation systems[1]

Robert Hassink and Mulan Ma

Introduction

Most of the theories of economic geography are focused on explaining the spatial patterns of manufacturing industries, and less on explaining these patterns for service industries, such as the tourism industry. However, a few geographers have been active in looking at the potential intersections between tourism geography and economic geography (Shaw and Williams 1994; Ioannides and Debbage 1998; Williams and Shaw 1998; Ioannides, 2006; Gibson 2009). While economic geography is the field of study that deals with the uneven distribution of general economic activities in space and time, tourism geography is concerned with the highly dynamic spatial tourism activities within and across destinations over time. Obviously, different characteristics of the manufacturing industry and the tourism industry lead to different economic landscapes in space (arguably, for instance, the tourism sector is more place bound). By contrast, however, the production of tourism-related services or products shares commonalities with other production sectors, such as manufacturing and producer services. For instance, the tourism industry uses similar input factors as the manufacturing industry, such as natural resources, capital, labour, technology, and management. In this respect, tourism is not only a resource-based industry, but also inherently represents a market-based grouping of economic activities. In this context, tourism geographers have derived some theoretical notes from economic geography and vice versa (Ioannides and Debbage 1998). One of the main reasons behind the increasing popularity of theoretical economic geography concepts in tourism studies is the increasing importance of innovation and evolution in the sector, areas that have been theorized much earlier in economic geography. Innovation, a concept that has long been in vogue in economic geography, has recently attracted much attention in tourism research and tourism geography (Hall and Williams 2008; Hjalager 2010a).

Innovation and evolution are the main focus of this chapter. There are two theoretical avenues in economic geography that could be used to bridge to tourism studies, the first being the evolutionary economic geography paradigm (Boschma and Martin 2010), while the other relates to the so-called territorial innovation models, such as clusters, industrial districts, learning regions, and regional innovation systems (Moulaert and Sekia 2003). From the former we have selected co-evolution as a promising notion for tourism studies and from the latter, regional innovation systems, as we see great potential in combining both into a useful theoretical ensemble to explore and explain the evolution of tourism areas. There are several definitions of co-evolution and hence there are some misunderstandings around the concept. Drawing upon Essletzbichler's (2012) definition, we define co-evolution in this chapter as the systematic embeddedness of firms and industries in an institutional environment, at several spatial scales. Tourism regional innovation systems are defined as territories:

> where a group of agents interact among themselves, supported by ancillary or auxiliary industries and external agents. They all generate relational assets and establish links with their macro-environment allowing collective learning and common knowledge, both critical in determining the innovation capacity of the system.
>
> (Prats *et al.* 2008: 182)

The aim of this chapter is, therefore, to deepen and explore the links between economic geography and tourism studies by focusing on two key notions, namely co-evolution and regional innovation systems. We are convinced that they can play a key explanatory role in understanding and explaining the development of tourist destinations through time. The chapter is structured as follows. The next section briefly introduces the broader theoretical framework of evolutionary economic geography and examines its potential relevance to the study of tourism. In the third section, co-evolution is presented in the context of tourism area development, with tourism regional innovation systems discussed in the section after that. The final section presents some conclusions and avenues for future research.

Tourism areas and evolutionary economic geography

In the economic geography literature, there has been a cultural turn, a learning turn, a relational turn, and most recently an evolutionary turn (Scott 2000), the latter being this chapter's main focus. Evolutionary economic geography (EEG) was inspired by an evolutionary turn in economics that is currently attracting increasing attention, mainly from European economic geographers, who seek to employ theoretical notions such as variation, selection, novelty, co-evolution, path dependence, lock-ins, and routines in the realm of economic geography (Martin and Sunley 2006, 2007; Boschma and Martin 2010; Martin 2010; Hassink *et al.* 2014). This perspective analyses and explains 'the processes by which the economic landscape – the spatial organization of economic production, circulation, exchange, distribution and consumption – is transformed from within over time' (Boschma and Martin 2010: 6). Furthermore, it critically analyses which of these theoretical notions from evolutionary economics are useful for tackling key questions in economic geography, such as '[W]hy is it that some regional economies become locked into development paths that lose dynamism, whilst other regional economies seem able to avoid this danger?' (Martin and Sunley 2006: 395).

There are three major theoretical and conceptual frameworks for EEG (Boschma and Martin 2010: 6). The first theoretical foundation is Generalized Darwinism, including concepts from modern evolutionary biology such as variety, novelty, selection, retention, mutation, adaptation, and co-evolution. Complexity theory, which concerns the aspects of complex 'far-from-equilibrium' adaptive systems, is considered as the second theoretical base. It consists of various notions, including emergence, self-organization, adaptation and hysteresis (Martin and Sunley 2007). The third theoretical framework is based on the path-dependence theory, which has been prominently discussed in economic geography (Martin and Sunley 2006; Hassink 2010; Martin 2010). It emphasizes the concepts of contingency, self-reinforcement, and dynamics, and includes the notions of 'lock-in', branching, and path creation.

Evolutionary economic geographers aim to study the path-dependent dynamics underlying uneven economic development in space and time. In particular, they analyse and explain the geography of firm dynamics and the rise and fall of technologies, industries, and networks in different territories (Martin and Sunley 2006). They also take into account the role of institutions (MacKinnon *et al.* 2009; Hassink *et al.* 2014), particularly from a co-evolutionary perspective (Schamp 2010).

Recent research approaches have applied the theories of economic geography (especially EEG) to the evolution of tourism areas. For example, Papatheodorou (2004), in a study of resort evolution, provided a new understanding of core-periphery patterns at different spatial scales as evolutionary outcomes of path-dependent dynamics; and Russell and Faulkner (2004) used the chaos perspective to examine the evolutionary process and to understand the complex and dynamic relationships between various stakeholders in tourism areas. More recently there have been several promising attempts to link tourism issues more strongly to evolutionary ideas in economic geography (Brouder and Eriksson 2013; Brouder 2014; Ma and Hassink 2013, 2014). Brouder and Ioannides (2014) see three advantages of using EEG in tourism area research: first, it sees economic issues in a broad perspective; second, it is spatially sensitive, as it stresses local embeddedness, multiple scales, and long-term gradual developments; and third, it focuses on innovation as the engine of economic development. In similar but slightly broader terms, Sanz-Ibáñez and Anton Clavé (2014) identify three fundamental pillars of local tourism destinations that can be related to both evolutionary and relational economic geography: 1. human agency (collective action and interaction of stakeholders, enabled by the generation and application of knowledge); 2. contextuality (social, economic, environmental and political structures and market trends at global and local levels); and 3. path dependence (historical trajectory of the area as a result of events and decisions made in the past). The potential contribution of EEG may hence offer new theoretical and empirical perspectives for tourism geographers dealing with questions of tourism area development in different geographical contexts. Moreover, some tourism researchers working with the tourism area life-cycle model (Butler 1980), until now the main model explaining tourism area development through time, have begun to employ notions of EEG, such as path dependence and co-evolution, to compensate for some of the weaknesses of this model (Ma and Hassink 2013, 2014). In these publications a path-dependence model for tourism area development was also developed (Ma and Hassink 2013, 2014). In this contribution the focus will hence be on the potential of co-evolution, as one evolutionary notion, for analysing and explaining tourism area development.

Co-evolution

The term 'co-evolution' was originally used in biology and refers to a situation in which 'two evolving populations coevolve if and only if they both have a significant causal impact on each other's ability to persist' (Murmann 2003: 210). Co-evolutionary theories indicate that organizational populations are mutually interdependent and have a reciprocal influence on each other. Nelson (1994) applied this approach in economics to understand the co-evolving and co-adapting process among knowledge, technology, organizations, institutions and industry. Quite recently, this approach has been further introduced into evolutionary economic geography. Although co-evolution is regarded as a key concept in EEG, it has often been misunderstood (Schamp 2010). For many economists co-evolution has to do with different populations, such as industries, who adapt themselves to each other. For many economic geographers co-evolution strongly refers to the systematic embeddedness of firms and industries in an institutional environment, at several spatial scales (Essletzbichler 2012). For them, institutions are actually regarded as the differentiating characteristic of co-evolution. In this context Essletzbichler (2012: 191) states that, in the research by many economists,

> space is simply filled by firms or technologies with no further explanatory role provided for place in explaining the evolution of industries or technologies . . . Rather than separating institutional from evolutionary economic geographies and examine . . . co-evolution . . . at the intersection of the two approaches . . . the co-evolution of economic entities and institutions at multiple scales should be at the center of EEG.

Ter Wal and Boschma (2011: 930) also endorse this view in the following statement:

> Further refinement of the theoretical framework is particularly necessary with respect to the role of institutions . . . [m]any research challenges remain in how an institutional set-up – at the level of cities, regions or nations – develops over time as new industries emerge and others decline.

Recently, in tourism research a few papers have been published with co-evolution in their title. However, the authors imply slightly different things in their use of the term 'co-evolution' (Brouder and Ioannides 2014; García-Cabrera and Durán-Herrera 2014; Brouder and Fullerton 2015). Brouder and Fullerton (2015) analyse co-evolution of new paths next to the dominant tourism path with the example of the Niagara region in Canada. In their view 'co-evolution . . . highlights the heterodox nature of the tourism economy within the regional economy' (Brouder and Fullerton 2015: 7). The new wine region of Niagara is seen as an alternative path to the traditional tourist development associated with the famous Niagara Falls. Brouder and Fullerton (2015) stress the potential for multiple paths in a tourism area to co-evolve (see Martin and Sunley, 2006, who also raise issues concerning the existence of different paths within a region, but in more general terms). Co-evolution in this sense can either refer to different tourism paths within a region or to several regional economic paths including tourism. In Brouder and Fullerton's (2015) study, co-evolving paths also show the intra-regional diversity, since the wine sector is located in a distinct sub-region. Co-evolving paths make the regional economy more sustainable and less dependent on dominant regional brands. Here there are clear links to the concept of related variety, which stresses that related sectors in a region positively affect knowledge spillovers, externalities and hence growth (Frenken *et al.* 2007). The changes in the Niagara region are slowly evolving, organic, and mostly endogenous. As Brouder and Fullerton (2015: 15) observe, '[t]he development of tourism in the Niagara region will only be sustainable if it is understood, not as a traditional cascade effect from Niagara Falls to the more peripheral communities, but as a co-evolving, community-driven endeavour'. The institutional part of co-evolution is not stressed in their paper, as it strongly focuses on different industrial paths.

In contrast, García-Cabrera and Durán-Herrera (2014: 81) stress 'the bi-directional influence between firms' managerial decisions and the institutional environment'. On the basis of the reaction of Spanish tourism firms during the recent economic crisis, they draw some conclusions on co-evolution and its importance for the tourism industry in general and tourism destination evolution in particular. Tourism firms may either take the institutional environment as given or try to influence and lobby the institutional environment (García-Cabrera and Durán-Herrera 2014). In the latter truly co-evolutionary case, they become institutional entrepreneurs. As shown in Figure 4.1, García-Cabrera and Durán-Herrera (2014: 82) assert that '[c]o-evolution shows how tourism firms act as institutional entrepreneurs and contribute to shaping the institutional environment that affects them'.

As shown in Figure 4.2, Ma and Hassink (2013) have proposed a co-evolutionary approach towards tourism area development, which displays the interactions among various tourism sectors, governments and the dynamics of the institutional systems within which tourism products are embedded.

This co-evolutionary approach also strengthens the heterogeneity and complexity of tourism area development, containing various possible evolutionary pathways occurring at multiple levels within a destination. It also emphasizes that the scales and scopes of interactions vary in different phases of path-dependent processes of tourism areas. For example, in the emerging phase of a tourism area, tourism attractions may be dominant and have strong interactions with other

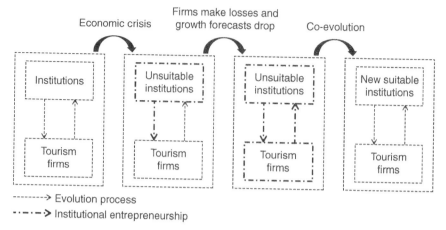

Figure 4.1 Co-evolution in tourism areas.

Source: García-Cabrera and Durán-Herrera (2014), reproduced with permission.

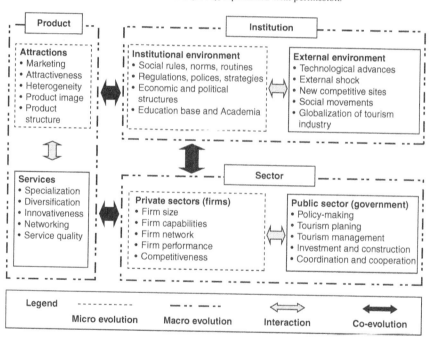

Figure 4.2 The co-evolutionary process of tourism area development.

Source: Ma and Hassink (2013), reproduced with permission.

elements, while tourism sectors are small-scale and largely dependent on the development of tourism attractions. In the development and maturity phase of a tourism area, dominant sectors, products and institutions co-exist and have strong interactions with each other (Ma and Hassink 2013). All in all, co-evolution either refers to the mutual interrelations between industries in a region or to the interrelations between firms and industries and their institutional environment at several spatial scales. It is particularly the second meaning that shows clear links to the innovation system approach to which we turn now.

Tourism regional innovation systems

In general, regional innovation systems can be regarded as an applied theoretical concept in economic geography that is strongly related to co-evolution and has interesting application potentials for research on tourism area development. Cooke *et al.* (1998: 1581) define regional innovation systems as those, 'in which firms and other organisations [such as research institutes, universities, innovation support agencies, chambers of commerce, banks, government departments] are systematically engaged in interactive learning through an institutional milieu characterised by embeddedness'. The concept can be seen as part of a broader group of territorial innovation models, to which clusters and learning regions also belong (Moulaert and Sekia 2003). Innovation has become the key focus of local and regional development polices due to the increasing importance both of the knowledge economy in general and of the regional level, with regard to diffusion-oriented innovation support policies (Fritsch and Stephan 2005). The regional level is more and more seen as the level that offers the greatest prospect for devising governance structures to foster learning in the knowledge-based economy, due to four mechanisms, namely: knowledge spillovers, spin-offs, intra-regional labour mobility, and networks (Cooke and Morgan 1998; Boschma 2008).

Partly supported by national and supranational support programs and encouraged by strong institutional set-ups found in successful regional economies such as Silicon Valley in the USA, Baden-Württemberg in Germany and Emilia-Romagna in Italy, many regions in industrialized countries have been setting up science parks, technopoles, technological financial aid schemes, innovation support agencies, community colleges and initiatives to support clustering of industries since the second half of the 1980s. The central aim of these policies is to support regional endogenous potential by encouraging the diffusion of new technologies. Since the mid-1990s, these policies have been influenced by theoretical and conceptual ideas, namely the above-mentioned territorial innovation models, such as regional innovation systems, the learning region, and clusters. However, recently it has been increasingly doubted whether lessons can be learned from successful regional economies in order to create 'Silicon Somewheres' (Hospers 2006). Furthermore, the scale issue - that is the role of the regional level vis-à-vis the national and supranational level in supporting innovations - has been critically evaluated recently (Fromhold-Eisebith 2007), and some authors question the assumed independence of regional systems from national influences that seem to be predominant (Bathelt and Depner 2003). Also, complaints have become louder about regional innovation policies becoming too standardized (Tödtling and Trippl 2005). Finally, different empirical definitions regarding spatial boundaries of regions and regional innovation systems make it difficult to provide clear policy advice (Doloreux and Parto 2005).

The basis of regional innovation systems are regional networks and interdependencies between firms and organizations such as research institutes, financial service providers, technology transfer agencies or regional governments, as well as institutions in terms of norms, rules, routines and conventions (Cooke *et al.* 1998; Asheim *et al.* 2011). The systemic dimension of a regional innovation system results from the coupling of three subsystems leading to synergy effects of enhanced regional innovation capacities, namely: the financial subsystem, the cultural setting and milieu in regions, and third, interactive learning (Cooke *et al.* 1997). The regional innovation system approach relates to evolutionary thinking in two ways (Uyarra 2010; Iammarino 2005): first of all, it is a dynamic approach. By drawing on different case studies, Cooke (2004) illustrates that regional innovation systems change over time. Second, and more importantly, the regional innovation system approach clearly emphasizes *co-evolutionary processes*. Cooke *et al.* (1998) argue for mutual interdependencies between institutions, organizations and firms. On the one hand, organizations and firms are claimed to be embedded in institutional settings, which regulate economic interactions. On the other hand, organizations and firms impact upon institutions in two ways: they are able to reinforce institutions by reproducing established behaviour and introduce new sets of practices, which challenge the existing institutional context.

Due to multiple systemic intra- and inter-regional linkages, regional innovation systems are potentially flexible and capable of adjustments. However, institutions and organizations are seen as rather reluctant to change and transformation can turn out to be a slow and lengthy process (Boschma 2008). This can lead to *lock-in* situations (Hassink 2010). In such cases, institutional and organizational set-ups of regions do not match the demands of new markets or technologies any longer. Both the co-evolution of institutions and organizations and their relative stabilities become problematic for regional growth because they reinforce an economic or technological path that is already outdated. The regional innovation system approach, therefore, is well suited to analyse regional lock-ins, because they result from strong systemic relations between the institutional, organizational and policy levels (Cooke *et al.* 1998). Because of these relations policy measures to combat lock-ins have to simultaneously consider changes within the economic and institutional environment. Tödtling and Trippl (2005) suggest, for instance, the creation of knowledge networks including new industries and technologies, as well as renewing the educational and scientific infrastructures of the region. Boschma (2008) argues to diversify and broaden the regional economic base to allow for multiple development paths that are not selective towards particular regions or sectors. To achieve highly flexible institutions and organizations, regional innovation systems should also promote rather loose systemic relations and a culture that supports openness and willingness to change (Cooke *et al.* 1998). Policy should focus on related variety in order 'to broaden and diversify the regional economic base' and, at the same time, on 'building on region-specific resources and extra-regional connections' (Boschma 2008: 328).

In tourism research, there has been an increasing interest in different forms of innovation, which has been well documented by Hjalager (2010a). Although the tourism sector has been innovative throughout its history, in classical theories of innovation in economics, the manufacturing industry has always been used as an example. Halkier *et al.* (2014) also observe the growing pressure on tourist destinations to become more innovative, given the increasing number of destinations to choose from and the growing number of experienced and demanding tourists. Hjalager (2010a) observes three driving forces of innovation in the tourism sector, the Schumpeterian approach (where entrepreneurs are major contributors to innovation), the technology-push vs demand-pull paradigm, as well as territorial innovation models (Moulaert and Sekia 2003). Moreover, some authors stress the role of interrelations between different sectors. For example, Hjalager (2010a) suggests that spill-back and spill-over effects to supplying industries, such as cosmetic manufacturing vis-à-vis wellness tourism, partly compensate for the lack of innovativeness in the core tourism sector. This related variety has recently also been discussed by James and Halkier (2014) in relation to local food production and tourism in northern Denmark.

The relationship between governance, policy and innovation in the tourism sector has also been taken up recently in the tourism-related literature. As Rodríguez *et al.* (2014: 77) observe, there is a 'persistent isolation of tourism from innovation policy and innovation systems discourses'. It is only recently in Spain that they have observed a rare case of tourism funded as part of a national innovation program. Rodríguez *et al.* (2014) stress the importance of the multi-level policy perspective for tourism. They also stress the importance of focusing on removing barriers to innovation in tourism areas, such as risk aversion, resistance to change, over-hierarchical structures, red tape, and short-term thinking. They state that:

> Such barriers contribute to the suggestion that tourism firms tend to be late adopters, 'gap-fillers' and imitators . . . This clearly raises further questions about the extent to which broad top-down initiated innovation policies can . . . be translated into effective measures to remove barriers to innovation in individual tourism clusters, destinations, and firms.
>
> (Rodríguez *et al.* 2014: 80)

The Spanish example also shows that a broad group of actors need to be included: the more diverse the actors are in policy development and implementation, the more successful the implementation and the outcomes of the policies (Rodríguez *et al.* 2014). Rodríguez *et al.* (2014: 90) clearly link these policy and governance issues to the innovation system approach, noting that: 'tourism policies are more likely to be effective when grounded in an understanding of tourism innovation systems . . . that account for the different sub-sectoral demands on tourism businesses'. A systematic approach is needed in order to overcome barriers, because many of them are interrelated. Some barriers are general, some barriers are specific to the tourism sector, some specific to the kind of region (e.g. peripheral regions; see Tödtling and Trippl 2005). Since there are no quick-fix solutions, Rodríguez *et al.* (2014) conclude that we need differentiated innovation policies and a hybrid combination of top-down and bottom-up approaches.

In addition to this more general literature on innovation policy and tourism, there are also some explicit attempts to link regional innovation systems to the tourism sector (Carson *et al.* 2014). Regional tourism innovation systems can be regarded as both spatial and sectoral systems, and hence have similarities to tourism clusters. Hjalager (2010b) is one of the few scholars who empirically applied the regional innovation system to tourism by examining the Sea Trout Funen Initiative in Denmark from an innovation-system perspective. According to her, 'tourism is . . . an economic activity with many special features that do not necessarily resemble those focused on by the majority of innovation research into manufacturing industries' (Hjalager 2010b: 193). The main distinct feature is: tourism is more strongly linked to spatial localities than most producers and service providers (see also Rodríguez *et al.* 2014: 78).

In a conceptual paper, Prats *et al.* (2008: 182) present a so-called tourism local innovation system which is:

> settled on a particular territory where a group of agents interact among themselves, supported by ancillary or auxiliary industries and external agents. They all generate relational assets and establish links with their macro-environment allowing collective learning and common knowledge, both critical in determining the innovation capacity of the system.

They also refer to tourism regional innovation systems, in the case of an integration of several local systems in a larger entity. Interestingly, Prats *et al.* (2008) refer to clusters and industrial districts as two territorial innovation models (Moulaert and Sekia 2003), but they do not refer to the innovation-system literature in building up their model of tourism local innovation systems. According to Prats *et al.* (2008), cluster and industrial district concepts stress factors also important in tourism destinations, namely proximity, inter-connectedness and a large variety of participants. Local institutions, social capital, common culture and language help to support the diffusion of tacit knowledge. They only stress the positive sides of social capital, proximity and local institutions (positive lock-ins), but neglect the potential negative sides (path dependence and negative lock-ins). In contrast to many papers on regional innovation systems, they stress that tourism local innovation systems do not have precise physical or political boundaries. Tourism local innovation systems consist of four main building blocks: tourism agents, relational elements, the macro-environment and outcomes (Figure 4.3). Concerning tourism agents, they distinguish between private firms (such as hotels and restaurants, but also cleaning and laundry services), R&D centres (universities, polytechnics, public research establishments, consultancy companies and vocational schools), the local community (individual citizens or citizen groups, such as NGOs), public administration (all public actors affecting tourism), as well as auxiliary agents and external agents (such as tour operators). The relational structure of elements

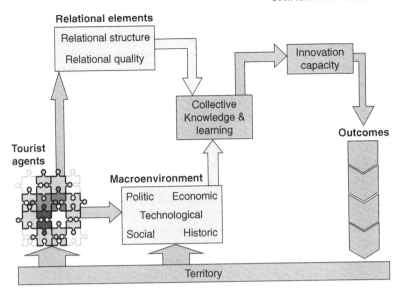

Figure 4.3 Tourism local innovation model.

Source: Prats *et al.* (2008), reproduced with permission.

can be restricted to internal connections or open to outside agents, and is further characterized by the degree of connectedness (poorly, richly), and the relational quality of ties (strong, frequent and trustful vs weak and sporadic, with little trust). Together with the relational elements, the macro-environment affects collective knowledge and learning, and hence innovativeness and outcomes.

Prats *et al.* (2008) explicitly see the model of tourism local innovation systems as a way to analyse the evolution of tourism destinations and to assess their innovation capacity. They also develop the model in order to find out which relational network structure is favourable to innovation in tourism destinations.

Carson *et al.* (2014: 457) in their empirical study on Burra, a small town in rural South Australia, stress the importance of networking, collaboration and interactive knowledge exchange as 'key requirements for converting tourism destinations into tourism innovation systems'. They also discuss the boundaries of systems acknowledging that the question of: '[a]t what scale regional innovation systems should ideally occur . . . has remained a contested issue' (Carson *et al.* 2014: 458). This issue is particularly important in peripheral regions, which often consist of large areas, in which local systems might work separately next to each other. Particularly in peripheral regions it is important to know which local systems work together, in order to achieve critical mass and economies of scale for destination marketing. The question is whether administrative borders are the right ones to understand innovation processes in tourism destinations. Intra-regional competition between local tourism areas might also lead to resistance to regional marketing bodies. Carson *et al.* (2014) use social network analysis to investigate internal connectivity between actors. The culture of operating in isolation was seen as one of the main reasons for low connectivity and low competitiveness (Carson *et al.* 2014). Local tourism systems had few aspirations and capabilities to form, together with adjacent local systems, a tourism regional innovation system. Barriers to inter-local co-operation are, among others: a local culture of operating in isolation; an excessive reliance on public sector leadership; and a lack in terms of the ability to benefit from new knowledge brought in by migrants. Carson *et al.* (2014) analysed the network and collaboration behaviour of a local tourism system to understand its contribution to a tourism regional innovation system. Local sub-systems clearly need to be taken into account in the analysis of tourism regional innovation systems.

Overall, interesting work has been done recently on innovation systems at the local and regional level in relation to tourism area development. Although the innovation system is presented as an evolutionary concept (Prats *et al.* 2008), often not more than lip service is paid to the evolutionary element of innovation systems (see also Rodríguez *et al.* 2014). The stress on social network analysis for instance, shows that in fact the view of innovation systems is relatively static and focuses on the relations within systems and their impact on innovativeness and competitiveness. In our view the notion of co-evolution is the missing link between the innovation system approach in tourism studies and the increasing interest in the evolution of tourism areas. Similar to regional economies in general and the regional innovation systems discussed above, tourism areas are complicated systems containing various products, sectors and institutions and their mutual interactions.

Conclusions

This chapter discussed recent conceptual debates in economic geography around innovation and evolution and their potential contribution to tourism geography. In doing so there was a strong focus on the notion of co-evolution derived from the paradigm of evolutionary economic geography, focusing on how, over time, the spatial economy transforms itself through irreversible and dynamic processes from within. The relationship between co-evolution and regional innovation systems has been recently introduced into tourism studies as tourism regional innovation systems. These concepts provide examples of theoretical notes from economic geography with potentially interesting explanatory power in tourism geography.

We have pointed out that the notion of co-evolution can be used both to deepen the links between EEG and tourism studies in general, and to strengthen the concept of tourism regional innovation systems in particular. The co-evolutionary perspective highlights the co-evolutionary processes occurring between tourism sectors, tourism products and institutions at multiple levels within a tourism area. With the help of such a perspective, it becomes clear that the evolution of tourism areas is a complicated, multiple-level co-evolution rather than a simple curve with different stages.

In the tourism literature, there are some explicit attempts to link regional innovation systems to the tourism sector and even to the evolution of tourism destinations. In our view the notion of co-evolution is the missing link between the innovation system approach in tourism studies and the increasing interest in the evolution of tourism areas. As the regional innovation system approach clearly emphasizes *co-evolutionary processes*, regional innovation systems can be regarded as an applied theoretical concept in economic geography that is strongly related to co-evolution and has interesting application potentials for research on tourism area development. Interesting work has been done recently on innovation systems at the local and regional level in relation to tourism area development. More significantly, a combination of the co-evolutionary approach and regional innovation systems could be used to analyse the generation of variability and divergence within and between the component entities of the destination.

Interesting research questions for future research that can be derived from the co-evolutionary perspective on tourism regional innovation systems include: Can the notion of 'localized learning' or 'adaptive capability' in economic geography be used to explain the co-evolution of tourism areas? To what extent do the heterogeneity and diversity of tourism products and sectors impact the co-evolution of tourism areas? Which are the causes and which are the effects in the interrelated links between tourism products, sectors and institutions? What kind of mismatches can be identified between tourism firms and their institutional environment at several scales? To what extent are mismatches caused by critical events or moments (see also Chapter 5)? How do the key actors in tourism regional innovation systems react to critical events and moments? Do critical events or moments function as catalysts for change in tourism evolutionary paths or do they lead to negative lock-ins and institutional hysteresis? Are there differences between tourism areas concerning the speed of reaction to critical events and moments and how can these differences be explained? In future research, more empirical case-study research is needed to apply and explore the co-evolutionary perspective on tourism regional innovation systems.

Note

1 This chapter draws from an article published earlier in *Annals of Tourism Research* (Ma and Hassink 2013), from the publishers of which we have received the permission to reprint some parts. This work was supported by the National Science Foundation of China (No. 41401145).

References

Asheim, B. T., Smith, H. L., and Oughton, C. (2011). 'Regional innovation systems: theory, empirics and policy'. *Regional Studies* 45(7), 875–91.

Bathelt, H. and Depner, H. (2003). 'Innovation, Institution und Region: Zur Diskussion über nationale und regionale Innovationssysteme'. *Erdkunde* 57(2), 126–43.

Boschma, R. (2008). 'Regional innovation policy'. In B. Nooteboom and E. Stam (eds) *Micro-foundations for Innovation Policy*. Amsterdam: Amsterdam University Press (pp. 315–41).

Boschma, R. and Martin, R. (2010). 'The aims and scope of evolutionary economic geography'. In R. Boschma and R. Martin (eds) *Handbook of Evolutionary Economic Geography*. Cheltenham: Edward Elgar (pp. 3–39).

Brouder, P. (2014). 'Evolutionary economic geography: a new path for tourism studies?' *Tourism Geographies* 16(1), 2–7.

Brouder, P. and Eriksson, R. H. (2013). 'Tourism evolution: On the synergies of tourism studies and evolutionary economic geography'. *Annals of Tourism Research* 43, 370–89.

Brouder, P. and Fullerton, C. (2015). 'Exploring heterogeneous tourism development paths: Cascade effect or co-evolution in Niagara?' *Scandinavian Journal of Hospitality and Tourism* 15(1–2), 152–66.

Brouder, P. and Ioannides, D. (2014). 'Urban tourism and evolutionary economic geography: Complexity and co-evolution in contested spaces'. *Urban Forum* 25(4), 419–30.

Butler, R. W. (1980). 'The concept of a tourist area cycle of evolution: Implications for management of resources'. *Canadian Geographer* 24(1), 5–12.

Carson, D. A., Carson, D. B., and Hodge, H. (2014). 'Understanding local innovation systems in peripheral tourism destinations'. *Tourism Geographies* 16(3), 457–73.

Cooke, P. (2004). 'Introduction: Regional innovation systems – an evolutionary approach'. In P. Cooke, M. Heidenreich, and H.-J. Braczyk (eds) *Regional Innovation Systems. The Role of Governance in a Globalized World*. London: Routledge (pp. 1–18).

Cooke P. and Morgan, K. (1998). *The Associational Economy: Firms, Regions, and Innovation*. Oxford: Oxford University Press.

Cooke, P., Uranga, M. G., and Etxebarria, G. (1997). 'Regional innovation systems: Institutional and organisational dimensions'. *Research Policy* 26(4–5), 475–91.

Cooke, P., Uranga, M. G., and Etxebarria, G. (1998). 'Regional systems of innovation: An evolutionary perspective'. *Environment and Planning A* 30(9), 1563–84.

Doloreux, D. and Parto, S. (2005). 'Regional innovation systems: Current discourse and unresolved issues'. *Technology in Society* 27(2), 133–53.

Essletzbichler, J. (2012). 'Evolutionary economic geographies'. In T. Barnes, J. Peck, and E. Sheppard (eds) *The Wiley-Blackwell Companion to Economic Geography*. Chichester: Wiley-Blackwell (pp. 183–98).

Frenken, K., van Oort, F. G., and Verburg, T. (2007). 'Related variety, unrelated variety and regional economic growth'. *Regional Studies* 41(5), 685–97.

Fritsch, M. and Stephan, A. (2005). 'Regionalization of innovation policy: Introduction to the special issue'. *Research Policy* 34(8), 1123–7.

Fromhold-Eisebith, M. (2007). 'Bridging scales in innovation policies: How to link regional, national and international innovation systems'. *European Planning Studies* 15(2), 217–33.

García-Cabrera, A. M. and Durán-Herrera, J. J. (2014). 'Does the tourism industry co-evolve?' *Annals of Tourism Research* 47, 81–3.

Gibson, C. (2009). 'Geographies of tourism: Critical research on capitalism and local livelihoods'. *Progress in Human Geography* 33(4), 527–34.

Halkier, H., Kozak, M., and Svensson, B. (2014). 'Innovation and tourism destination development'. *European Planning Studies* 22(8), 1547–50.

Hall, C. M. and Williams, A. M. (2008). *Tourism and Innovation*. London: Routledge.

Hassink, R. (2010). 'Locked in decline? On the role of regional lock-ins in old industrial areas'. In R. Boschma and R. Martin (eds) *Handbook of Evolutionary Economic Geography*. Cheltenham: Edward Elgar (pp. 450–68).

Hassink, R., Klaerding, C., and Marques, P. (2014). 'Advancing evolutionary economic geography by engaged pluralism'. *Regional Studies* 48(7), 1295–307.

Hjalager, A. M. (2010a). 'A review of innovation research in tourism'. *Tourism Management* 31(1), 1–12.

Hjalager, A. M. (2010b). 'Regional innovation systems: The case of angling tourism'. *Tourism Geographies* 12(2), 192–216.

Hospers, G.-J. (2006). 'Silicon somewhere? Assessing the usefulness of best practices in regional policy'. *Policy Studies* 27(1), 1–15.

Iammarino, S. (2005). 'An evolutionary integrated view of regional systems of innovation: Concepts, measures and historical perspectives'. *European Planning Studies* 13(4), 497–519.

Ioannides, D. (2006). 'Commentary: The economic geography of the tourist industry: Ten years of progress in research and an agenda for the future'. *Tourism Geographies* 8(1), 76–86.

Ioannides, D. and Debbage, K. (1998). *The Economic Geography of the Tourist Industry: A Supply-Side Analysis*. London: Routledge.

James, L. and Halkier, H. (2014). 'Regional development platforms and related variety: Exploring the changing practices of food tourism in North Jutland, Denmark'. *European Urban and Regional Studies*. doi: 10.1177/0969776414557293. [online] URL: http://eur.sagepub.com/content/early/2014/12/09/0969776414557293.abstract (accessed on 10 December 2014).

Ma, M. and Hassink, R. (2013). 'An evolutionary perspective on tourism area development'. *Annals of Tourism Research* 41, 89–109.

Ma, M. and Hassink, R. (2014). 'Path dependence and tourism area development: The case of Guilin, China'. *Tourism Geographies* 16(4), 580–97.

MacKinnon, D., Cumbers, A., Pike, A., Birch, K., and McMaster, R. (2009). 'Evolution in economic geography: Institutions, political economy and adaptation'. *Economic Geography* 85(2), 129–50.

Martin, R. (2010). 'Roepke lecture in economic geography—Rethinking regional path dependence: Beyond lock-in to evolution'. *Economic Geography* 86(1), 1–27.

Martin, R. and Sunley, P. (2006). 'Path dependence and regional economic evolution'. *Journal of Economic Geography* 6(4), 395–438.

Martin, R. and Sunley, P. (2007). 'Complexity thinking and evolutionary economic geography'. *Journal of Economic Geography* 7(5), 573–602.

Moulaert, F. and Sekia, F. (2003). 'Territorial innovation models: A critical survey'. *Regional Studies* 37(3), 289–302.

Murmann, J. P. (2003). *Knowledge and Competitive Advantage: The Coevolution of Firms, Technology, and National Institutions*. Cambridge: Cambridge University Press.

Nelson, R. R. (1994). 'The co-evolution of technology, industrial structure, and supporting institution'. *Industrial and Corporate Change* 3(1), 47–63.

Papatheodorou, A. (2004). 'Exploring the evolution of tourism resorts'. *Annals of Tourism Research* 31(1), 219–37.

Prats, L., Guia, J., and Molina, F. X. (2008). 'How tourism destinations evolve: The notion of tourism local innovation system'. *Tourism and Hospitality Research* 8(3), 178–91.

Rodríguez, I., Williams, A. M., and Hall, C. M. (2014). 'Tourism innovation policy: Implementation and outcomes'. *Annals of Tourism Research* 49, 76–93.

Russell, R. and Faulkner, B. (2004). 'Entrepreneurship, chaos and the tourism area lifecycle'. *Annals of Tourism Research* 31(3), 556–79.

Sanz-Ibáñez, C. and Anton Clavé, S. A. (2014). 'The evolution of destinations: towards an evolutionary and relational economic geography approach'. *Tourism Geographies* 16(4), 563–79.

Schamp, E. W. (2010). 'On the notion of co-evolution in economic geography'. In R. Boschma and R. Martin (eds) *Handbook of Evolutionary Economic Geography*. Cheltenham: Edward Elgar (pp. 432–49).

Scott, A. J. (2000). 'Economic geography: The great half-century'. *Cambridge Journal of Economics* 24(4), 483–504.

Shaw, G. and Williams, A. M. (1994). *Critical Issues in Tourism: A Geographical Perspective*. Oxford: Blackwell.

Ter Wal, A. L. J. and Boschma, R. A. (2011). 'Co-evolution of firms, industries and networks in space'. *Regional Studies* 45(7), 919–33.

Tödtling, F. and Trippl, M. (2005). 'One size fits all? Towards a differentiated regional innovation policy approach'. *Research Policy* 34(8), 1203–19.

Uyarra, E. (2010). 'What is evolutionary about "regional systems of innovation"? Implications for regional policy'. *Journal of Evolutionary Economics* 20(1), 115–37.

Williams, A. M. and Shaw, G. (1998). *Tourism & Economic Development: Western European Experiences* (3rd edn). Chichester: Wiley.

5 Moments as catalysts for change in the evolutionary paths of tourism destinations

Cinta Sanz-Ibáñez, Julie Wilson and Salvador Anton Clavé

Introduction

Studies on the evolution of destinations are well established (e.g. Butler 2006a, 2006b, 2014), although research focused on analysing how and why destinations change over time as well as the long-term effects of leading policies and agency of the processes of change are arguably more scarce (Saarinen 2004). Even less researched are the specific moments at which destinations' economic paths are forced to shift direction, be this through the creation of new paths or the appearance of a more subtle incremental change over time. Indeed, as Gale and Botterill (2005: 159) argue in a critique of traditional life-cycle approaches, 'the critical incidents that mark the transition from one stage to the next [in destination evolution] are poorly defined and often difficult to substantiate empirically'. This chapter focuses on the potential for *moments* as a conceptual framework in examining how destinations evolve over time and as a viable alternative to traditional life-cycle-based models.

Interpretation of this field of research as representing a *path metaphor* may hold some answers in this respect. Here we use the term 'path metaphor' in a collective sense to refer to the range of concepts framed by the idea of economic paths, such as path dependence, path shaping, path creation or path plasticity. This metaphor has been increasingly employed by regional economists and economic geographers when analysing the long-term dynamics of regions and industries (Boschma and Martin 2010) and, more recently, of tourism destinations (Brouder 2014; Sanz-Ibáñez and Anton Clavé 2014). Related to moments as key components of the evolutionary path of a destination, evolutionary approaches to tourism have mainly focused the attention on studying responses given by destination stakeholders to incidents along the lines of triggering events, critical events or shocks with a notable impact – either positive or negative – on destinations' trajectories (e.g. Ritchie *et al.* 2013). Nevertheless, recent developments in urban social geography such as the cultural political economy approach (Ribera-Fumaz 2009; Sum and Jessop 2013) have started to examine the root causes of urban socio-economic change through a new lens, including cultural aspects, policies and agencies (Moulaert *et al.* 2007), which should also be fruitful when analysing the dynamics of destinations. Drawing upon this work we define *moments* as path-shaping evolutionary inflection points that cause a destination's path (trajectory) to shift in direction and focus.

This chapter examines the role and nature of such moments in the tourism evolution process, in terms of how paths are shaped by their occurrence(s). Focusing in the first instance on the context of moments in evolutionary economic geography (EEG) via a review of previous research, the chapter then proposes a conceptual framework for understanding the moments as inflection points in path shaping via the main discourses associated with their effects on tourism destinations. In order to illustrate the framework's potential for understanding how destinations change over time, a key moment in the evolution of Catalonia's central Costa Daurada – the opening of the PortAventura theme park in the mid-1990s – is examined by applying the conceptual framework relating to moments in interpreting this key event. Finally, the chapter offers some useful directions for future research and draws some conclusions on the capacity and potential for the framework's application in tourism destination contexts.

The path metaphor in tourism evolutionary approaches

In the context of tourism geography, a fledging yet promising line of research has recently begun to focus on the translation of recent economic geography approaches – hitherto used to analyse the evolution of industrial districts, clusters and other localized forms of specialization (Boschma and Frenken 2006; Boschma and Martin 2007, 2010) – to increase understanding of how and why tourism destinations evolve over time (Brouder 2014; Sanz-Ibáñez and Anton Clavé 2014).

The work published so far presents some seminal reflections and exploratory case studies that are generally sound in theoretical and empirical terms, while highlighting the potential of applying notions such as co-evolution (Ma and Hassink 2013; Randelli *et al.* 2014; Brouder and Fullerton, 2015), resilience (Lew 2013; Ioannides and Alebaki 2014; Mariotti and Zirulia 2014), survival (Brouder and Eriksson 2013), complexity (Meekes 2014), path dependence (Bramwell and Cox 2009; Ma and Hassink 2013, 2014; Williams 2013), path creation (Gill and Williams 2011, 2014) or path plasticity (Anton Clavé and Wilson 2016; Halkier and Therkelsen 2013).

The path metaphor – encompassing the path-dependence concept, as well as the different notions therein that represent diverse alternative evolutionary trajectories such as path creation and path plasticity – has been the most recurrent within EEG. This established analogy between paths and evolutionary processes assumes that destinations are constantly in-the-making, permitting an approach which displays distinctive powerful forms of interpreting the nuanced, local-specific dynamics of tourist places over time. Indeed, the analogy emphasizes the significant role of both stakeholder agency and selective/spontaneous incidents in unlocking tourism places from stagnation and avoiding decline. This presents an opportunity with which to address these issues from a non-deterministic perspective – a common criticism of traditional life-cycle approaches – which may help to focus on analysing the evolving qualities *of* tourist places (Equipe MIT 2002) instead of the analysis of tourism *in* places (e.g. Plog 1973; Butler 1980; Prideaux 2004).

The domain of the path metaphor can be used to understand the unexpected ways in which destinations can depart from their historical legacies and structures in the same sense that Bramwell (2011) mentions the concept of path shaping. First, it includes the translation of the path-dependence concept, directly associated with place dependence (Martin and Sunley 2006). This notion, following the work of Ma and Hassink (2013, 2014) in the tourism context, emphasizes the role of history – that is, pre-existing conditions, as well as the past events and decisions – and geography – understood as the contextual specificities of each destination in social, economic and environmental terms – in influencing development paths. However, path dependence is not only a force constraining destination dynamics that leads to political, cognitive or functional lock-in processes (see, for instance, the extensive debate on this issue in Bathelt and Glückler 2003; Grabher 2005; Hassink 2005; Martin 2010). Nor is it a force that generates inevitable downgrading or down-scaling effects or even path destruction in tourism places, which would suppose the complete abandonment of the tourism activity. Instead, breaking with existing dependent paths can enable the definition of new pathways of development by transforming the current model of tourism, improving destination competitiveness and sustainability and/or enhancing the performance of firms, which might ultimately be associated with growth and upgrading or up-scaling processes (Gereffi 1999).

Along these lines, and without underestimating the central role of path dependence as a useful mechanism to explain change and the configuration of evolutionary trajectories (Strambach and Halkier 2013), there are other powerful notions that might elucidate the well-documented emergent, continually transforming and essentially contingent nature of destinations' evolutionary trajectories (Agarwal 2012). For instance, Gill and Williams (2011, 2014) took the notion of path creation (Garud and Karnøe 2001) as an explanatory framework for both the deliberated and agency-driven processes adopted in the case of Whistler, British Columbia, to increase the sustainability of the resort while adopting a highly responsive global strategy. Alternatively, Halkier and Therkelsen (2013), from a path-plasticity perspective (Strambach 2010; Strambach and Halkier 2013;), emphasized the possibility of incremental innovations within established institutional settings as sources of readjustment enabling destinations to remain dynamic in the long run.

Complementarily, other tourism geographers studying the long-term dynamics of mature destinations labelled such effects with diverse terminologics that might also be taken into account in building up the path metaphor. This is the case of Agarwal (2002) when applying the concept of restructuring to destination change processes or Anton Clavé (2012), who categorized three different types of destinations according to the (re)development strategies implemented by decision-makers: the *reactives*, who adopted policies of renewal, differentiation, heritage preservation, image improvement and maintenance of tourism activity; the *creatives*, who made innovative use of potential attractions and value innovation processes generated by their own residents and visitors; and finally, the *transitives*, who intensified their residential functions by incorporating more permanent urban services and making a transition towards the urban condition (Harvey 1989) as fully fledged urban places, having previously evolved only as tourism resorts (see also Anton Clavé and Wilson 2016).

In parallel, similar proposals emphasizing the role of (pro)active policy intervention and institutions as a tool to favour regional resilience and develop new growth and development pathways have emerged recently within the field of EEG that could be applied to tourism places. Asheim *et al.* (2013), for example, introduced the notions of *path renewal*, a process characterized by regional branching into new technological trajectories, and *path extension*, associated with the strengthening of existing industries by incremental process innovations geared to securing higher productivity. Others have analysed processes of downgrading/ downscaling of destinations or even the abandonment of tourism as an industrial activity (Baum 1998). In this vein, Clivaz *et al.* (2014) introduce the concept of *abyss* to describe the total collapse of the tourism sector in a place without any economic alternative. Using the concept of *tourist capital of resorts*, the latter authors also discuss how collective agency can even suppose a metamorphic dynamic in relation to the conversion of resorts into urban places (op. cit.). In addition, in a third dimension of their threefold typology (beyond the possible outcomes of abyss and metamorphosis), Clivaz *et al.* (2014) refer to *relay* as the capacity of a resort to keep its touristic attractiveness. All in all, based on Martin and Sunley's (2006: 408) claims, we argue that the path metaphor might be regarded as a heuristic approach,

> wherein the process of economic evolution could be understood as an ongoing, never-ending interplay of path dependence, path creation, [path plasticity] and path destruction that occurs as actors in different arenas reproduce, mindfully deviate from, and transform existing socio-economic-technological structures, socio-economic practices and development paths.

In the context of the research conducted under the umbrella of the 'path metaphor', the specific catalysts for change – that is, the incidents, events or decisions with an impact on destinations' evolutionary trajectories – have generated a significant body of research using different but related terminologies. Baggio and Sainaghi (2011), employing a complex systems lens, pointed out the effects of natural or anthropogenic, external or internal triggering events in challenging existing structures and the current states of destinations and even move them to a new (non-permanent) order. Similarly, Ritchie *et al.* (2013) emphasized the spillover effects of crisis-related events – either crises, which they consider are caused by lack of management and anticipation, or disasters, which can only be responded to in retrospect – and demonstrated that such disaster events have not only negative outcomes, which may be the most salient, but also positive ones such as incentives to innovate and anticipate future similar situations. In the same vein, Mariotti and Zirulia (2014) explored adaptive (or evolutionary) resilience as enacted by public and private strategies in a local tourism destination to respond to a negative shock. Hall (2010), dealing with the notion of crisis events, also raises more pertinent insights into this issue.

However, above all, it seems the literature on specific catalysts for change is mostly oriented towards analysing critical, external and unexpected shocks or events – such as natural disasters or economic crises – while leaving an uncovered gap, which concerns those moments beyond the natural environment and general economic trends, principally social and cultural ones. Such an issue is reflected increasingly in urban social geography (Moulaert *et al.* 2007; Ribera-Fumaz 2009, on cultural political economy; Bianchi 2012; Sum and Jessop 2013;), where there is a gradual engagement with the ideas of path dependence and path creation and concern for *inter alia* the analysis of selective moments in urban socio-economic change (Moulaert *et al.* 2007), policy intervention, institutional change and key agencies, causing initially dependent economic paths to shift in a different direction. These new approaches are opening up new avenues in the tourism research agenda (Bramwell 2011; Mosedale 2011).

To address these issues, we put forward the notion of 'moments', conceived of as given points in time (and space) signalling shifts in the development pathways of tourism places. We argue that analysis of such moments over the course of destination evolution is a useful endeavour *in addition* to studying a given evolutionary trajectory, life cycle or simply the end results of path-plasticity/creation processes in action. This might be useful in answering more nuanced questions, for example the one raised by Randelli *et al.* (2014: 277) in a rural tourism context when asking: 'in an evolutionary scenario, who [is it that] drives the change?'. This is clearly an important question in EEG, and we might add to this 'who' the question of *what* drives the change, and *when, where* and *how*. In encompassing this complex vision of triggers for change in evolution and their resultant impacts, the term 'moments' is seen to be more holistic and multi-faceted than other, more traditional terminologies. The following section will unravel the thinking behind this new conceptual framework that we propose.

Moments in path-shaping trajectories

The aim of this section is to debate how the concept of *moments* might be useful as a heuristic device in understanding how destinations evolve as places. The starting point for advancing this concept was the question of whether more attention should be paid to what happens at (and between) the key points of change in the evolutionary trajectory of a destination. Synonymous with these key points in this sense, moments are proposed as path-shaping evolutionary inflection points that cause a particular path (trajectory) to shift in direction and focus, rather like a join-the-dots exercise. In this sense, the moments idea is conceived as a response to the tendency to only focus on the impact of one key moment (e.g. a shock) in destination evolution, when perhaps it would be pertinent to conceptualize and contextualize the various moments or path shifts of any given destination, considering the role and the components of the before, during and after each moment in their evolutionary trajectory. This will be discussed and illustrated later in the chapter when analysing the whole course of one of the key moments of the evolution of the central Costa Daurada tourism destination where the PortAventura theme park is located.

Moments as evolutionary inflection points

In differential calculus, an inflection point is a point on a curve at which the curvature or concavity changes sign from plus to minus or from minus to plus. In considering evolution as path shaping (Jessop 2008; Bramwell 2011), or even in terms of the impacts and shifts that might take place caused by the onset of a given moment, the inflection-point analogy is a useful one.

The moments concept is, of course, imbued with multiple meanings and displays considerable complexity. Clearly, however, each moment is entirely unique in terms of its characteristics, in that there are a multitude of parameters that they might display and catalytic or transformative functions that they might perform. Their complex nature also depends on whether they constitute primarily a causative trigger or a consequential impact, suggesting that many moments might be binary in nature. Consider, for example, whether some moments are path-creating, while others are path-plastic in nature, according to their eventual effects. In terms of their impacts (or outcomes), these effects might either be instantaneous, like switching a light on or off (creation), or more gradual/incremental, like a huge ocean liner changing course slowly but surely and then regaining speed (plasticity), hereby suggesting that there are many dimensions to consider.

Attention will now be turned to the discourses surrounding the moment and the range of parameters and characteristics that such moments might display. Having established that moments are probably much more than snapshots of particular significant points in time, we argue that it is also possible to identify different types of moments depending on their characteristics, range, scale and orientation. For instance, they might be the result of a planned initiative or spontaneous, or driven by a top-down or bottom-up process, be regulatory or resource-based or endogenous or exogenous. Finally, they could engender different types of change in relation to 'pre-lock-in' or 'pre-moment' conditions – recuperation, abandonment, reinforcement, renewal, extension or transition, for example.

The intensity of the moment may also be important, as observed above, with some being path-creating (more radical) and others path-plastic (more incremental). What seems to remain clear is that the understanding and narrating of moments requires local context specificity to prevail. Moulaert *et al.* (2007: 196) observe (with reference to path dependence and cultural political economy approaches) a 'tendency to overlook the fact that development is deeply historical, place-specific and embedded within specific and concrete institutional settings'. They also advocate use of social innovation approaches which, they argue, give 'fuller consideration to the path-dependent and context-bounded nature of urban development strategies' (2007: 197; see also Sum and Jessop 2013), providing further justification for a more in-depth, nuanced reading of evolutionary trajectories by zoning in on particular moments therein.

Discourses of the moments in the path metaphor

Figure 5.1 provides a visualization of the kinds of discourses that might be associated with the path metaphor in relation to a given moment; it should be read and understood sequentially from left to right in a timeline manner. Starting on the far left, there is the *pre-moment scape* (taking a conceptual cue from Williams, 2013, on scapes and flows; and Van der Duim's notion of tourismscapes, 2007; see also Van der Duim *et al.* 2012). This is the contextual domain in which everything that might have a bearing on the subsequent nature of the moment is considered; be they pre-conditioning factors and situations, prior economic, social, environmental, political and cultural conditions (and tendencies) and indeed, pre-cursor/prior moments (which might be termed secondary or peripheral moments). Also present are the underlying contextual 'impetus' narratives (at different scales), which relate to the origins of a given moment and which shape the discourses associated with the subsequent shift in path. These narratives may be hegemonic or alternative in nature; top-down or more grassroots; and the extent of their influence will ultimately depend on their degree of place embeddedness in the local context.

Next, our conceptual framework anticipates that, at some point within the space-and-time context of the pre-moment scape, there will be a *trigger* incident of some kind. The second column from the left in Figure 5.1 deals with these triggers and sets out what form they might take in relation to a given moment. Butler (2014: 218) terms them 'key agents of change in a resort that affect the transition process from one stage of development to another' and argues that these have not been dealt with to any real extent in tourism research. He also states that it would be of great value to destinations if it were possible to identify and anticipate situations and events which might act as triggers to such unrest and stage change in the life cycle (Butler, citing Gale and Botterill 2005).

For the purposes of our framework, the main dichotomy in relation to the nature of triggers is whether they are spontaneous or selective (taking a cue from Moulaert *et al.* 2007). As outlined above, most previous conceptualizations have only really dealt with the spontaneous kind, in terms of critical shock-type events, although such spontaneous triggers need not be so radical in nature. In terms of spontaneous triggers, these may relate to environmental, fiscal or physical factors or even, to a lesser extent, unexpected and/or unpredictable outcomes of social, cultural or political processes. Spontaneous triggers may also be external or internal, endogenous or exogenous, and occur at different scales (local/regional/national/international/global). They may be more structural or relate to agency and anthropogenic factors, while they may also be catalytic and stimulatory or incapacitating and debilitating in the first instance.

Selective triggers, by contrast, do not depend on a shock occurrence (although arguably they may emerge in response to a prior moment based on a spontaneous trigger). More likely to be based on decisions made, they may relate to

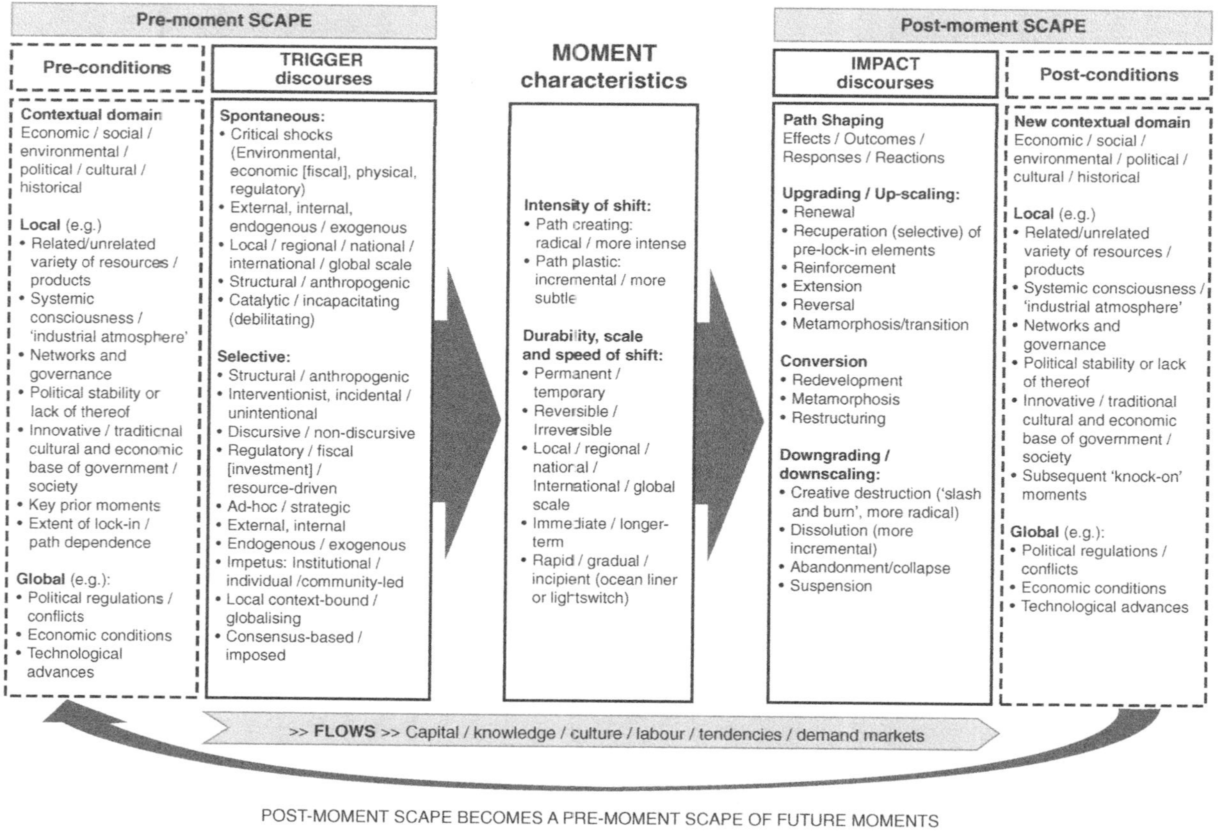

Pre-moment SCAPE

Pre-conditions

Contextual domain:
Economic / social / environmental / political / cultural / historical

Local (e.g.)
- Related/unrelated variety of resources / products
- Systemic consciousness / 'industrial atmosphere'
- Networks and governance
- Political stability or lack thereof
- Innovative / traditional cultural and economic base of government / society
- Key prior moments
- Extent of lock-in / path dependence

Global (e.g.):
- Political regulations / conflicts
- Economic conditions
- Technological advances

TRIGGER discourses

Spontaneous:
- Critical shocks (Environmental, economic [fiscal], physical, regulatory)
- External, internal, endogenous / exogenous
- Local / regional / national / international / global scale
- Structural / anthropogenic
- Catalytic / incapacitating (debilitating)

Selective:
- Structural / anthropogenic
- Interventionist, incidental / unintentional
- Discursive / non-discursive
- Regulatory / fiscal [investment] / resource-driven
- Ad-hoc / strategic
- External, internal
- Endogenous / exogenous
- Impetus: Institutional / individual /community-led
- Local context-bound / globalising
- Consensus-based / imposed

MOMENT characteristics

Intensity of shift:
- Path creating: radical / more intense
- Path plastic: incremental / more subtle

Durability, scale and speed of shift:
- Permanent / temporary
- Reversible / Irreversible
- Local / regional / national / International / global scale
- Immediate / longer-term
- Rapid / gradual / incipient (ocean liner or light switch)

Post-moment SCAPE

IMPACT discourses

Path Shaping
Effects / Outcomes / Responses / Reactions

Upgrading / Up-scaling:
- Renewal
- Recuperation (selective) of pre-lock-in elements
- Reinforcement
- Extension
- Reversal
- Metamorphosis/transition

Conversion
- Redevelopment
- Metamorphosis
- Restructuring

Downgrading / downscaling:
- Creative destruction ('slash and burn', more radical)
- Dissolution (more incremental)
- Abandonment/collapse
- Suspension

Post-conditions

New contextual domain
Economic / social / environmental / political / cultural / historical

Local (e.g.)
- Related/unrelated variety of resources / products
- Systemic consciousness / 'industrial atmosphere'
- Networks and governance
- Political stability or lack of thereof
- Innovative / traditional cultural and economic base of government / society
- Subsequent 'knock-on' moments

Global (e.g.):
- Political regulations / conflicts
- Economic conditions
- Technological advances

>> FLOWS >> Capital / knowledge / culture / labour / tendencies / demand markets

POST-MOMENT SCAPE BECOMES A PRE-MOMENT SCAPE OF FUTURE MOMENTS

Figure 5.1 Discourses of the moments in tourism destination evolution.

structural factors or be agency driven and more anthropogenic in nature. Furthermore, despite being selective (hence intentional) they might still take on an interventionist orientation or perhaps be more incidental or unintentional (albeit selective). The underlying stimuli for selective triggers might be regulatory and investment driven or possibly resource driven. In terms of policy-related selective moments, their impetus may be *ad hoc* and responsive or more strategic, coming from endogenous or exogenous forces. In terms of originators, the moment may be triggered selectively on an institutional level or be individual and/or community led, while triggers may also be embedded in the local context or have a more globalizing effect. Finally, selective triggers may be generated from consensus or having been imposed from the top down, while the kind of industrial diversification, or variety, they might trigger may be related or unrelated to the existing economic base (Frenken *et al.* 2007).

The central column in Figure 5.1 relates to the characteristics and dimensions of the actual *moment* in which the shift in path is caused. The elements that might come into play at this point in the process are mostly related to the specific characteristics of the inflection point; the moment in which the path shifts in direction in response to a given trigger or triggers. Among the most important characteristics are the durability, scale and speed of the moment in which the shift takes place – ranging from instantaneous/immediate to prolonged/longer term; from macro to micro scale (global to local); and rapid, gradual or incipient (returning to the metaphor of the light switch and the ocean liner discussed above). By extension, the moment may represent a permanent or temporary catalyst for change (note that this refers to the nature of the actual point of change, rather than the permanence or otherwise of the subsequent effects that stem from it – which is discussed later). There is also the question of whether the moment sets a reversible or irreversible process in motion, as well as whether the scope of the moment is radical or incremental (and this latter point would determine whether a moment might be described as path creating or path plastic). Similarly, the relative intensity of the shift is also a necessary consideration, in terms of whether the moment represents a more subtle or more intense shift in direction.

The second column from the right in Figure 5.1 deals with discourses surrounding the *impacts* that the moment generates once it has happened. If we were to think about impacts as underlying narratives of moments in path evolution, we might talk about such impacts as consequential processes leading to path-shaping effects and, indeed, to new processes. In conceptualizing the narratives of these impacts as outcomes of a moment (or moments), again one might distinguish between a number of different characteristics and associated discourses of change. To begin with, there is the question of whether the resultant impacts have an overall stabilizing or destabilizing effect post-moment and also whether this results in the shaping of a single path or multiple paths in parallel. Beyond this, there would appear to be a dichotomy of impacts – those relating to upgrading/up-scaling effects and those relating to downgrading/downscaling effects.

Firstly, possible upgrading and upscaling discourses may centre on processes of renewal, the (selective or forced) recuperation of pre-lock-in economic activities, reinforcement of existing industrial bases, extension of successful elements, reversal of problematic elements, transition (which may involve a shift to either related or unrelated variety of the economic base) and, of course, innovation in its many possible manifestations. Conversely, downgrading and/or downscaling impact discourses may stem from processes of creative destruction (possibly in a 'slash and burn', more radical manner following a major shock), dissolution (a more incremental effect), complete abandonment of existing elements and ,finally, the (temporary) suspension of economic elements that have undergone stagnation. Ultimately, redevelopment, metamorphosis and restructuring could also represent new paths, not only for tourism in the destination but for the destination as a fully fledged place in its own right (see Anton Clavé and Wilson 2016; Anton Clavé 2012; Clivaz *et al.* 2014).

The final column of the table (on the far right-hand side) is that of the *post-moment scape*. This phase relates essentially to longer-term outcomes, which may represent a new context(s); new economic landscapes evidenced by a clearly identifiable shift in path. There may be subsequent 'knock-on' moments to come in the future and these will depend not only on the nature of the prior moment (or moments) which shaped them, but also on the geographical and historical local specificity of the place in question. The future paths that permeate the post-moment scape may also be based on hegemonic narratives or alternative narratives. Just like in earlier phases, new processes may stem from top-down or grassroots initiatives or stimuli, and the direction they take will depend on their degree of place embeddedness and whether the resultant variety of flows will be related or unrelated to earlier economic, political, social, cultural and environmental situations. In this sense, the post-moment scape effectively becomes the pre-moment scape of future moments.

Finally, running beneath the framework are the *flows*, which pass through the entire process in a fluid manner, not necessarily in a linear sense, and which almost certainly will contribute to sending the path-shaping process in one direction or another.

It is argued that these different phases as represented by the columns in the framework, as well as the underlying flows, amount to a more nuanced and complex manner of understanding the evolution of (tourism) places. Moreover, there is scope for this conceptual framework – developed in the context of tourism destinations – to be adapted and applied to other economic landscapes and contexts that have been theorized via the path metaphor, with the aim of understanding what happens in path-shaping terms between two given points of an evolutionary trajectory. To illustrate the capacity of this framework to explain path-shaping processes centred on a given moment, the moments framework will now be applied to a specific case – the opening of the PortAventura theme park in Catalonia, on the Western Mediterranean coast.

Exploring discourses of moments

Anton Clavé (2010) states that, since its opening in 1995, the PortAventura theme park has played a key role in the development of the Costa Daurada tourism region, situated in Southern Catalonia. The two towns in which the Park is located (Salou and Vila-seca) form part of one of the most visited destinations in the Mediterranean. In 2013, between them they received more than 2.1 million visitors staying in regulated accommodation that generated more than 9.1 million overnights, as well as the capacity of almost 30,000 second homes. More than a half million people live in the surrounding area of the theme park, making it the second most dynamic economic cluster in Catalonia after the metropolitan area of Barcelona. The area is home to prominent chemical industries, port operations, tourism and food industry corporations and activities, and two medium-sized cities, Tarragona and Reus. There are about 50,000 permanent residents in Salou and Vila-seca which, until the late 1980s, counted as the same municipality.

The PortAventura theme park was developed in collaboration with both Vila-seca and Salou, as well as regional public agents. Both towns considered PortAventura (currently receiving around 3.5 million visitors per year) as the ideal promoter of a new image for the combined destination and as a tool for the reorganization of the destination's urban structure (Anton Clavé 2005). The setting of the Park was planned in the 1980s and its development was afforded the benefits of a law as regards the concession of available land (more than 825 ha) and possibilities for its expansion.

In applying the moments idea to this case, a chronology of events and the tangible results of the strategies of management, cooperation and development, promoted both by the public and by the private sectors, will be explained briefly in order to illustrate how the opening of PortAventura might be understood as a key moment in the path shaping of the central Costa Daurada as a tourism destination.

Figure 5.2 illustrates that, even though the Park opened in 1995, the pre-conditioning contextual domain in which the PortAventura inauguration takes place, the *pre-moment scape*, can be traced back to the beginning of the 1980s. Studies clearly reveal a lock-in situation for tourism activity in the area during the 1980s (Anton Clavé 1997a). One of the main reasons was the loss of appeal and competitiveness of the destination faced with the emergence of other newer, alternative coastal resorts, as well as the new range of demand trends and tourism motivations seen in the 1980s. Other local problems exacerbating the lack of competitiveness for the tourism sector in the area included the close proximity of a large-scale and intensive petrochemical industry and the extension of the industrial and commercial Port of Tarragona. Add to this the considerable pollution associated with the Port that affected the beach and the water-supply problems for the whole area, which influenced negatively the quality of life of the local population as well as the day-to-day economic activities of the many industries located in the area.

Nevertheless, thanks to a collective envisioning of the conditions underlying these social, economic, cultural and environmental tendencies, several actions and strategies were undertaken, both to ensure the economic viability of the area (including a major water transfer from the nearby river Ebro, about 80 km south of the area) and, in the specific case of the tourism industry, to rejuvenate the tourism product in the area. During the 1980s, with healthier municipal public finances, a promising economic outlook and greater collaboration between private

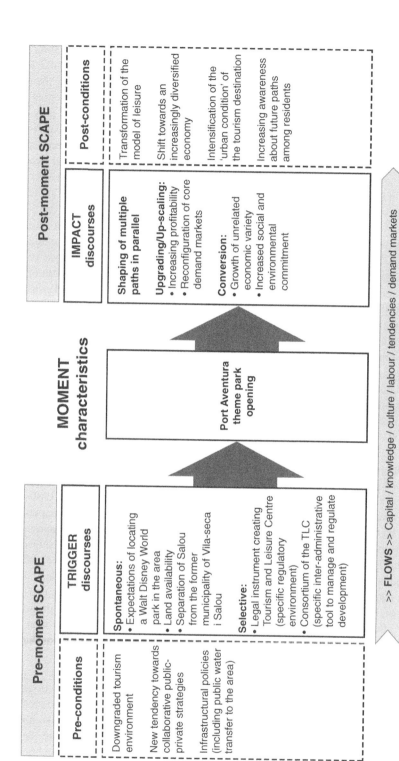

Pre-moment SCAPE

Post-moment SCAPE

MOMENT characteristics

Pre-conditions

Downgraded tourism environment

New tendency towards collaborative public-private strategies

Infrastructural policies (including public water transfer to the area)

TRIGGER discourses

Spontaneous:
- Expectations of locating a Walt Disney World park in the area
- Land availability
- Separation of Salou from the former municipality of Vila-seca i Salou

Selective:
- Legal instrument creating Tourism and Leisure Centre (specific regulatory environment)
- Consortium of the TLC (specific inter-administrative tool to manage and regulate development)

Port Aventura theme park opening

IMPACT discourses

Shaping of multiple paths in parallel

Upgrading/Up-scaling:
- Increasing profitability
- Reconfiguration of core demand markets

Conversion:
- Growth of unrelated economic variety
- Increased social and environmental commitment

Post-conditions

Transformation of the model of leisure

Shift towards an increasingly diversified economy

Intensification of the 'urban condition' of the tourism destination

Increasing awareness about future paths among residents

>> **FLOWS** >> Capital / knowledge / culture / labour / tendencies / demand markets

Figure 5.2 PortAventura as a moment in the evolution of the central Costa Daurada.

initiative and the municipal institution, initiatives were taken within the tourism sector with the aim of promoting new hotel developments and the creation of recreational facilities as means of renewing the destination's amenities (Ros Santasusana 2012). These initial actions were accompanied by urban restructuring and public infrastructural improvements. These might be understood as prior actions trying to generate some path plasticity to combat the rigidity of the existing pathway that was heading towards a lock-in situation. In fact, an increasing level of public involvement can be identified since the 1980s, years before PortAventura was even planned.

The moments conceptual framework anticipates the existence of trigger incidents that were spontaneous and/or selective – that is, not dependent on a shock occurrence, but related to structural factors or agency driven. Among the spontaneous factors in this case were Walt Disney World's plans to create a theme park in Catalonia during the 1980s, before eventually deciding to locate their European park in Paris. Local and regional stakeholders considered the area to be a serious candidate for the location of the European Disney park and the decision of the company to locate it in Paris stimulated the idea that having a top tourism attraction could be a catalyst for releasing the place from its lock-in. Also, there was enough well-located land available and ready for developing a new concept of recreational and tourist activity, which stemmed from a conflictive process of negotiating the new urban plan for the area during the 1980s. Due to this, the approval of the plan was delayed and the more than 825-ha area where the future Park would be located remained available without any specific development purpose designated. Finally, coinciding chronologically with the decision to situate the Park in the area, the separation of Salou, the richest and more tourism-oriented part of the former municipality of Vila-seca i Salou, and the 1989 creation of two new local administrations also represented a strong trigger. Although spontaneous, in the sense that these factors were not driven with a theme park development objective in mind, all of three were triggers that created the conditions, following a process of incidental intervention, both endogenous and exogenous in impetus, that left a specific environment ready for the creation of PortAventura (see also Campa and Veses 2012; Oliveras 2012; and Ros Santasusana 2012 for more detail).

In terms of selective triggers, there was the political will on the part of the Catalan Government and of the local municipal administrations of Vila-seca (and after the separation, Salou) to respond to the need to transform an outdated model of tourism and leisure that was hegemonic in Catalonia during the 1980s. This political will also led to the implementation of a novel legal framework for both Spain and Europe, which gave an incentive to develop and regulate a theme park in a manner that, at that time, was relatively groundbreaking (Anton Clavé 1997b). Besides the theme park, hotels, residences, shopping centres, and golf and other sport areas were also envisaged, as well as the creation of the Vila-seca i Salou Tourism and Leisure Centre Consortium, an inter-administrative tool developed as a response to the separation of Salou in order to manage and regulate the development of the Park and the complementary commercial, recreational, sporting, hotel and residential activities that were planned around it (Fuentes and Rodríguez 2012).

On 2 May 1995, PortAventura in its present guise was officially opened to the general public. This event can be understood as a symbolic representation of the actual *moment* in which the shift in path took place for the central Costa Daurada. The characteristics and dimensions of the Park are the direct result of and the response to the spontaneous and selective triggers which had played a prior role. Additionally, we must mention the initial choice of the US company Anheuser Busch as the developer of the project in 1989, plus the several setbacks and challenges such as the separation of Salou, the negotiations with landowners and also the strategies of new players that entered as new developers between 1989 and 1995, such as the Grand Tibidabo corporation, the utilities company FECSA, the Catalan savings bank (La Caixa) and the British group Pearson. Furthermore, there was the new legal framework enacted to determine the development course of the project. Since then, PortAventura has been undergoing a phase of expansion which is heading in the direction of transforming the initial Park into a larger tourism and leisure complex by developing new concepts and generating wider opportunities for the economy of the area, as well as conditioning the whole urban and spatial pattern of the local and regional area where the Park is located.

New players have since entered into the management of the project, most notably Universal Studios (between 1998 and 2004), the Italian group Bonomi (part of Invest Industrial and currently the main stakeholder; in 2009) and the US investment fund KKR (in 2013). New attractions have been developed within the Park since 1998, including a new waterpark, four 500-room hotels, a Beach Club located on the sea front, three golf courses, with 45 holes, and a Convention Centre. The most important factors in the case of PortAventura as a key moment in the recent path-shaping of Salou and Vila-seca, as well as in Catalonia in general, are its durability (around a 20-year span of creating new conditions for tourism development activity), scale (both local and regional) and speed (a sustained and long-term gradual process of creating innovations and adding new components to the tourism and leisure value chain generated in the area). This represents an ongoing catalyst for change that has set an irreversible incremental process in motion, which can be described as path plastic and whose impacts, as we will see in the next section, led to the upgrading/upscaling of the whole area and also foster destinations' transformation into fully fledged urban places, rather than just resorts.

As Campa and Veses (2012) describe, the Costa Daurada (as well as both Vila-seca and Salou therein and, indeed, the whole of Catalonia), has not been unaffected by the large influx of visitors to PortAventura over the past 20 years. The most relevant *impacts* are of course related to the upgrading/upscaling in the tourism sector, including the reconfiguration of the dominant demand markets to the area and the increasing quality of supply markets and, as a consequence, the increasing profitability of the industry. Other than this, PortAventura has generated diverse and multiple paths in parallel, according to the characteristics and prior path-dependency of each specific place which falls under the influence of the Park. In fact, differences can be observed and differential co-evolution processes are visible between the two different municipalities where the Park is located and also in comparison with other local destinations and surrounding places that fall under the Park's sphere of influence. The two core municipalities are dependent on their respective public and private strategies held by institutions and stakeholders to take advantage of and respond to the opportunities created by the Park development and, as such, their current situations are not the same, even if the path-shaping moment for both of them was exactly the same. For example, it has been documented that Vila-seca constitutes an example of the implementation of a successful public–private partnership, enabling the creation of a cluster of high quality hotels (Duro 2012). As a result, in 2013 Vila-seca had a RevPar (revenue per available room) of almost 80€ during the summer period, achieving sixth position in a ranking of the 53 more outstanding coastal tourism destinations in Spain, while Salou's RevPar was only 63.35€, achieving twenty-third position in the same ranking.

More generally, the PortAventura project has clearly stimulated the economy of Southern Catalonia by not only boosting the creation of new hotels or new shopping and recreational activities in the area and shifting the demand profile towards a more affluent and family-oriented appeal, but it has also accelerated the development of major transport infrastructure (new dual-carriageways, a new terminal at Reus airport and the AVE high-speed train link, among others), as well as the expansion of new, unrelated activities and technical and knowledge services, plus new commodity suppliers, linked to the development of the Park. In the latter sense, the Park has also been committed to an initiative creating the University School of Tourism and Leisure at the Rovira i Virgili University (now the Faculty of Tourism and Geography) and the Tourism Observatory of the Costa Daurada, launched at the beginning of the 2000s. PortAventura has managed to achieve a level of brand and product visibility only attainable by very few projects, and even some of its iconic rides, for example Dragon Khan, have become a part of everyday parlance, part of the symbolic effects of theme parks as quality tags for specific places, as analysed by Zukin (1991).

More specifically, environmental concerns have been taken into account already by Park managers, and the Park has been a champion of corporate environmental awareness. An Environmental Committee was set up from the outset and the good practices implemented have filtered through the rest of the company, the rest of the industry and even to other industrial sectors that realize the importance of a clean and unpolluted environment in order the ensure the quality of life of the resident population and the wellbeing of visitors. Additionally, PortAventura has become a company that promotes actions related with its immediate social environment (see Campa and Veses 2012 for examples).

PortAventura is arguably a key component of the new economic landscape of Southern Catalonia in terms of shaping the *post-moment scape* in the destination. First, it should be emphasized that PortAventura has brought about a major change in the Costa Daurada's leisure and tourism model, and to a lesser extent (but equally noteworthy) in that of the rest of Catalonia and even that of Spain. Future paths of the area are visibly shaped by the characteristics and dimensions of the post-moment path shaped by PortAventura, which in turn is modelling the geographical and historical local specificity of the place. The moments conceptual framework maintains that future paths may be based on hegemonic narratives or alternative narratives and new processes both from the top-down or at grass-roots levels, with the aim of configuring new moments triggered themselves by the creation of PortAventura. In this sense, future achievements will depend (as with the configuration of PortAventura's current scape) on the dimensions, characteristics and scale of new events yet to occur and on the discussion and debate held by society directly or through their political representatives. The current shift towards an increasingly diversified economy, the intensification of the urban and residential function of the tourism destination and the increasing awareness about future possible paths among residents are new components of the post-moment scape created directly by the opening of PortAventura. With regard to this, for instance, new social debate in the area is of utmost interest. In particular, the question of how and to what extent new entertainment developments proposed for the wider entertainment complex where PortAventura is located (which include casino-based gaming and other shopping and hotel developments) fit or not with the currently hegemonic narrative of the place as a tourist destination for family holidays, having adopted PortAventura as an iconic symbol (see Anton Clavé and Baron Yelles 2015). Results will depend in this case (as will results related to other industrial sectors in the area) on the degree of place embeddedness of the new projects and, as stated in earlier sections, on the resultant variety of flows and their relationships with earlier economic, political, social, cultural and environmental situations. In this sense, the post-moment scape created by PortAventura becomes the pre-moment scape of future moments.

Flows running beneath the entire process illustrate that evolution is not just based on the dimensions and characteristics of processes but, fundamentally, on the inherent policies, instruments, initiatives and programmes that both private and public stakeholders develop in the context of one specific moment. Flows include culture, knowledge, capital, labour, demand markets, global players, tactical approaches, social debates and political short and long termism. One fundamental issue here, thus, is that the transformation of destinations stems from responses by local systems to the needs brought about by global market changes, having many implications for the management of destinations as multi-sectorial regional and local spaces.

All in all, the case of PortAventura highlights the usefulness of analysing how flows materialize in specific contextual scapes, and the question of how moments are triggered (and become triggers themselves) is fundamental in helping to explain the development of moments whose impacts will shape the future of one specific destination. Depending on the nature of the place, the power of such flows and the dimension, characteristics, range and scale of the moment, they can have clear effects, due to their direct and indirect impacts, on the path shaping of the destination and even on the creation of a new unrelated (and perhaps more urban) variety, as Clivaz *et al.* (2014) or Anton Clavé (2012) argue, when affirming that resorts do not always necessarily remain as resorts forever.

Conclusions

In this chapter we have presented a conceptual framework of moments that draws upon EEG approaches in order to aid understanding of how the trajectory of a given place (in this case, a destination) is shaped, within a geographical and historical conjuncture, via the specific events that affect their dynamics. The framework is intended as a heuristic device that focuses attention on moments as complex, context-bound processes that include several marked elements therein: pre- and post-scapes, triggers and impacts.

We argue that the moments concept has scope to go beyond the domain of other constructs such as, for example, the Tourism Area Life Cycle (TALC), which, as Gale and Botterill (2005) note, is a resort model and hence less applicable to urban industrial and rural areas that have turned to tourism for the purposes of economic (re)development or to restructured resorts. As it is derived in a non-deterministic vein and not limited to being a resort 'model' in any sense, the moments conceptual framework has the potential to address various shortcomings of the TALC by, for example, not defining the shape of a 'global' evolutionary curve as applicable to all tourism places and, instead, allowing analysis of individual places according to their own specific trajectories and key moments therein. Furthermore, the moments framework allows analysis of the evolution of tourism destinations *as places*, rather than focusing on the evolution of tourism *in* destinations, as the TALC does. Indeed, in principle the framework could be applied to any place and any industrial sector, and so it is more flexible and transferable not only as a theoretical concept, but also as a planning tool for understanding how and why places transform.

All in all, we have used the conceptual framework presented in this chapter to understand what might trigger key moments in the evolutionary path-shaping of places, as well as the associated how, why, when and where of the idea. As a result, upgrading, conversion and downgrading impacts have been identified, entrenching the moments idea within various conceptual notions. Some of these originally developed from outside the EEG domain, but nonetheless have considerable utility in understanding the trigger effects of a given evolutionary path, path dependence, contextuality and human agency (Sanz-Ibáñez and Anton Clavé 2014) in terms of tourism performance evolution, but also in terms of the transformation of (tourism) places.

Furthermore, path-shaping impacts can unfold as path creation or path plasticity, which in turn creates new conditions defining the post-moment scape that, in a long-term approach, may become the new pre-moment scape when new triggers of change start to act and new decisions are taken by stakeholders in the place. The dimension, scope, range and characteristics of flows of capital, knowledge, culture, labour, tendencies and demand markets will determine the specific response, or the characteristic moment of a given destination to the triggers that emerge in any historically given scape. In this sense, geography matters – as the role of spatial scale, historical embeddedness and political advocacy are key – as well as the relationship to pre-lock-in conditions, that is, inertial movement such as recuperation, abandonment, reinforcement, corrective, compensatory and resilience-building responses play a central role (plus, future research on this topic might also bear in mind the possibility that path-shaping moments in some circumstances may have the effect of actually reinforcing prior path-dependence).

We have argued that triggers and impacts are grounded in contextual environments that we term pre- and post-condition scapes, which, following Moulaert *et al.* (2007: 203), 'challenge established governance, discourse and projects and the extent to which they can lead to further and wider alternative social action'. This is obviously affected by the specific historical and geographical context of any local destination at any given moment, according to the inertia effects of its own past and present conditions. In this sense, we highlight the key role that a certain moment can have in the shaping of markedly (even if subtly) different paths for different destinations. This allows recognition of the co-evolutionary nature of long-term destination transformation change and how past decisions affect the capacity of response and influence for the future with regard to a specific key moment in the path shaping process.

Additionally, the conceptual framework presented in this chapter allows the integration of several perspectives that are supported by an increasing body of both theoretical and empirical multi-disciplinary research on the evolution of destinations from the outside the core of EEG (and even including some conventional life-cycle-related analysis). Moreover, the framework holds resonance with recent developments in urban social geography such as the cultural political economy approach (Ribera-Fumaz 2009; Sum and Jessop 2013) to theorizing pathways in urban development. This is of utmost interest insofar as one of the very foundations of the moments framework is the recognition of the 'urbanizing' nature of many forms of tourism developments and destinations or, at least, the path towards a fledging urban condition of many tourism places (Anton Clavé 2012). In this vein, we support the interpretation by Clivaz *et al.* (2014: 21) of the different resort trajectories as uneven; and engaging differently constituted touristic capital, as well as the conversion of this capital into other forms of capital, seems an important step for a more thorough analysis and explanation of what happens to tourist resorts over a long period.

To demonstrate the utility of moments as an idea, we have drawn upon longitudinal empirical research undertaken on the effects of having situated the PortAventura theme park in a specific location on the central Costa Daurada destination and how this moment might be understood over the course of two whole decades of introducing innovations, development of changes and creation of unrelated paths in the planning and everyday reality of area, with a focus on the role of local and global stakeholders therein. This case demonstrates that a moments lens is appropriate and useful in understanding how change is produced instead of only evaluating the end results of path-plasticity or path-creation trajectories. It also demonstrates that a focus on positive moments as well as on negative, critical shocks may be applied.

In conclusion, beyond its specific application in this chapter, the moments conceptual framework is arguably broadly transferable, being adaptable to examine any aspect of tourism destination dynamics at any scale from the local to the global and at any period of time, allowing an integrated understanding of the succession of moments that can shape the trajectory of a destination. We maintain that the basic premises of the framework proposed here offer the opportunity to develop this idea according to the needs of other industrial and activity contexts, in terms of future research potential. The direction in which this idea shifts the debate on tourism evolution will be of interest within both EEG and tourism geographies.

Acknowledgements

The research presented in this chapter was undertaken within the GLOBALTUR [CSO2011-23004/GEOG] and MOVETUR [CS02014-51785-R] projects, financed by the Spanish Ministry of Science and Innovation. The authors sincerely thank the editors of the book for their thorough revisions and constructive comments on earlier versions of this chapter.

References

Agarwal, S. (2002). 'Restructuring seaside tourism. The resort lifecycle'. *Annals of Tourism Research* 29(1), 25–55.

Agarwal, S. (2012). 'Relational spatiality and resort restructuring'. *Annals of Tourism Research* 39(1), 134–54.

Anton Clavé, S. (1997a). *Diferenciació i reestructuració de l'espai turístic. Processos i tendències al litoral de Tarragona*. Tarragona: El Mèdol.

Anton Clavé, S. (1997b). 'The PortAventura theme park and the restructuring of coastal tourist areas in Catalonia'. *European Urban and Regional Studies* 4(3), 255–67.

Anton Clavé, S. (2005). *Parques Temáticos. Más Allá del Ocio*. Barcelona: Ariel.

Anton Clavé, S. (2010). 'Leisure parks and destination redevelopment: The case of PortAventura, Catalonia'. *Journal of Policy Research in Tourism, Leisure and Events* 2(1), 66–78.

Anton Clavé, S. (2012). 'Rethinking mass tourism, space and place'. In J. Wilson (ed.) *Routledge Handbook of Tourism Geographies: New Perspectives on Space, Place and Tourism*. London: Routledge (pp. 217–24).

Anton Clavé, S. and Baron Yelles, N. (2015). 'Néolibéralisme, mondialisation de l'industrie du jeu et création d'espace urbain. Réflexion à partir de la stratégie globale de Las Vegas Sands Corporation'. In N. Fabry, V. Picon-Lefebre, and P. Benjamin (eds) *Quand le Tourism Fait la Ville. Formes, Modèles, Pratiques*. Paris: L'Oeil D'Or, Collection 'critiques et cités' (pp. 25–40).

Anton Clavé, S. and Wilson, J. (2016). 'The evolution of coastal tourism destinations: a path plasticity perspective on tourism urbanisation'. *Journal of Sustainable Tourism*, doi: 10.1080/09669582.2016.1177063.

Asheim, B., Bugge, M. M., Coenen, L., and Herstad, S. (2013). *What Does Evolutionary Economic Geography Bring to the Policy Table? Reconceptualising Regional Innovation Systems* (No. 5). Lund: CIRCLE Electronic Working Paper Series.

Baggio, R. and Sainaghi, R. (2011). 'Complex and chaotic tourism systems: Towards a quantitative approach'. *International Journal of Contemporary Hospitality Management* 23(6), 840–61.

Bathelt, H. and Glückler, J. (2003). 'Toward a relational economic geography'. *Journal of Economic Geography* 3, 117–44.

Baum, T. (1998). 'Taking the exit route: Extending the tourism area life cycle model'. *Current Issues in Tourism* 1(2), 167–75.

Bianchi, R. (2012). 'A Radical Departure: A critique of the critical turn in tourism studies'. In J. Wilson (ed.) *Routledge Handbook of Tourism Geographies: New Perspectives on Space, Place and Tourism*. London: Routledge (pp. 46–54).

Boschma, R. and Frenken, K. (2006). 'Why is economic geography not an evolutionary science? Towards an evolutionary economic geography'. *Journal of Economic Geography* 6(3), 273–302.

Boschma, R. and Martin, R. (2007). 'Constructing an evolutionary economic geography'. *Journal of Economic Geography* 7(5), 537–48.

Boschma, R. and Martin, R. (eds) (2010). *The Handbook of Evolutionary Economic Geography*. Cheltenham, UK: Edward Elgar.

Bramwell, B. (2011). 'Governance, the state and sustainable tourism: a political economy approach'. *Journal of Sustainable Tourism* 19(4–5), 459–77.

Bramwell, B. and Cox, V. (2009). 'Stage and path dependence approaches to the evolution of a national park tourism partnership'. *Journal of Sustainable Tourism* 17(2), 191–206.

Brouder, P. (2014). 'Evolutionary economic geography and tourism studies: Extant studies and future research directions'. *Tourism Geographies* 16(4), 540–45.

Brouder, P. and Eriksson, R. H. (2013). 'Staying power: What influences micro-firm survival in tourism?' *Tourism Geographies* 15(1), 125–44.

Brouder, P. and Fullerton, C. (2015). 'Exploring heterogeneous tourism development paths: Cascade effect or co-evolution in Niagara?' *Scandinavian Journal of Hospitality and Tourism* 15(1–2), 152–66.

Butler, R. W. (1980). 'The concept of a tourist area cycle of evolution: Implications for management of resources'. *The Canadian Geographer* 24(1), 5–12.

Butler, R. W. (2006a). *The Tourism Area Life Cycle Vol. 2: Conceptual and Theoretical Issues*. Clevedon, UK: Channel View Publications.

Butler, R. W. (2006b). *The Tourism Area Life Cycle Vol. 1: Applications and Modifications*. Clevedon, UK: Channel View Publications.

Butler, R. W. (2014). 'Coastal tourist resorts: History, development and models'. *ACE: Architecture, City and Environment [Arquitectura, Ciudad Y Entorno]* 9(25), 203–28.

Campa, F. and Veses, V. (2012). 'Leadership, differentiation and social responsibility. The role of PortAventura'. In S. Anton Clavé (ed.) *10 Lessons on Tourism. The Challenge of Reinventing Destinations*. Barcelona: Planeta (pp. 397–411).

Clivaz, C., Crevoisier, O., Kebir, L., Nahrath, S., and Stock, M. (2014). *Resort Development and Touristic Capital of Place* (No. 5). Neuchâtel: Maison d'Analyse des Processus Sociaux (p. 25).

Duro, J. A. (2012). 'The transformation of the hotel development model'. In S. Anton Clavé (ed.) *10 Lessons on Tourism. The Challenge of Reinventing Destinations*. Barcelona: Planeta (pp. 381–96).

Equipe MIT. (2002). *Tourismes I. Lieux Communs. [Tourisms I. Common Places.]* Collection Mappemonde. Paris: Belin (p. 320).

Frenken, K., Van Oort, F., and Verburg, T. (2007). 'Related variety, unrelated variety and regional economic growth'. *Regional Studies* 41(5), 685–97.

Fuentes, J. R. and Rodríguez, M. (2012). 'Administrative innovation in the management of strategic local projects. The case of the Tourism and Leisure Centre Consortium as a unique element of territorial revitalisation and a model for overcoming projects'. In S. Anton Clavé (ed.) *10 Lessons on Tourism. The Challenge of Reinventing Destinations*. Barcelona: Planeta (pp. 309–23).

Gale, T. and Botterill, D. (2005). 'A realist agenda for tourist studies, or why destination areas really rise and fall in popularity'. *Tourist Studies* 5(2), 151–74.

Garud, R. and Karnøe, P. (2001). 'Path creation as a process of mindful deviation'. In R. Garud and P. Karnøe (eds)*Path Dependence and Creation*. Mahwah, NJ: Lawrence Erlbaum Associates (pp. 1–41).

Gereffi, G. (1999). 'International trade and industrial upgrading in the apparel commodity chain'. *Journal of International Economics* 48, 37–70.

Gill, A. M. and Williams, P. W. (2011). 'Rethinking resort growth: Understanding evolving governance strategies in Whistler, British Columbia'. *Journal of Sustainable Tourism* 19(4–5), 629–48.

Gill, A. M. and Williams, P. W. (2014). 'Mindful deviation in creating a governance path towards sustainability in resort destinations'. *Tourism Geographies* 16(4), 546–62.

Grabher, G. (2005). 'Switching ties, recombining teams: Avoiding lock-in through project organization?' In G. Fuchs and P. Shapira (eds) *Rethinking Regional Innovation and Change: Path Dependency or Regional Breakthrough*. Boston: Springer (pp. 63–84).

Halkier, H. and Therkelsen, A. (2013). 'Exploring tourism destination path plasticity. The case of coastal tourism in North Jutland, Denmark'. *Zeitschrift für Wirtschaftsgeographie* 57(1–2), 39–51.

Hall, C. M. (2010). 'Crisis events in tourism: Subjects of crisis in tourism'. *Current Issues in Tourism* 13(5), 401–17.

Harvey, D. (1989). *The Urban Experience*. Baltimore: Johns Hopkins University Press.

Hassink, R. (2005). 'How to unlock regional economies from path dependency? From learning region to learning cluster'. *European Planning Studies* 13(4), 521–35.

Ioannides, D. and Alebaki, M. (2014). *Resilience Thinking: A Drive for Innovative Approaches in Tourism?*, presented at the International workshop of the RSA Research Network on Tourism and Regional Development: 'Evolution and transformation in tourism destinations: Revitalisation through innovation?'. Vila-seca, Spain, February.

Jessop, B. (2008). *State Power. A Strategic-Relational Approach*. Cambridge, UK: Polity Press.

Lew, A. A. (2013). 'Scale, change and resilience in community tourism planning'. *Tourism Geographies* 16(1), 14–22.

Ma, M. and Hassink, R. (2013). 'An evolutionary perspective on tourism area development'. *Annals of Tourism Research* 41, 89–109.

Ma, M. and Hassink, R. (2014). 'Path dependence and tourism area development: The case of Guilin, China'. *Tourism Geographies* 16(4), 580–97.

Mariotti, A. and Zirulia, L. (2014). *Getting Out of the Quagmire. Public and Private Strategies in Rimini after the 1989 Mucilage Crisis*, presented at the International workshop of the RSA Research Network on Tourism and Regional Development: 'Evolution and transformation in tourism destinations: Revitalisation through innovation?'. Vila-seca, Spain, February.

Martin, R. (2010). 'Roepke lecture in economic geography – rethinking regional path dependence: Beyond lock-in to evolution'. *Economic Geography* 86(1), 1–27.

Martin, R. and Sunley, P. (2006). 'Path dependence and regional economic evolution'. *Journal of Economic Geography* 6, 395–437.

Meekes, J. (2014). *Regional Development and Leisure in Fryslân: A Complex Adaptive Systems Perspective through Evolutionary Economic Geography*, presented at the Association of American Geographers 2014 Annual Meeting. Tampa, USA, April.

Mosedale, J. (2011). 'Thinking outside the box. Alternative political economies in tourism'. In J. Mosedale (ed.) *Political Economy of Tourism. A Critical Perspective*. London: Routledge (pp. 93–108).

Moulaert, F., Martinelli, F., Gonzalez, S., and Swyngedouw, E. (2007). 'Introduction: Social innovation and governance in European cities: Urban development between path dependency and radical innovation'. *European Urban and Regional Studies* 14, 195–209.

Oliveras, J. (2012). 'Urban planning for tourism and territorial management'. In S. Anton Clavé (ed.) *10 Lessons on Tourism. The Challenge of Reinventing Destinations*. Barcelona: Planeta (pp. 267–90).

Plog, S. C. (1973). 'Why destination areas rise and fall in popularity'. *Cornell Hotel and Restaurant Administration Quarterly* 13, 6–13.

Prideaux, B. (2004). The resort development spectrum: The case of the Gold Coast, Australia. *Tourism Geographies* 6(1), 26–58.

Randelli, F., Romei, P., and Tortora, M. (2014). 'An evolutionary approach to the study of rural tourism: The case of Tuscany'. *Land Use Policy* 38, 276–81.

Ribera-Fumaz, R. (2009). 'From urban political economy to cultural political economy: Rethinking culture and economy in and beyond the urban'. *Progress in Human Geography* 33(4), 447–65.

Ritchie, B. W., Crotts, J. C., Zehrer, A., and Volsky, G. T. (2013). 'Understanding the effects of a tourism crisis: The impact of the BP oil spill on regional lodging demand'. *Journal of Travel Research* 53(1), 12–25.

Ros Santasusana, J. (2012). 'Collaboration and consensus policies between administrations and the private sector'. In S. Anton Clavé (ed.) *10 Lessons on Tourism. The Challenge of Reinventing Destinations*. Barcelona: Planeta (pp. 291–308).

Saarinen, J. (2004). '"Destinations in change": The transformation process of tourist destinations'. *Tourist Studies* 4(2), 161–79.

Sanz-Ibáñez, C. and Anton Clavé, S. (2014). 'The evolution of destinations: Towards an evolutionary and relational economic geography approach'. *Tourism Geographies* 16(4), 563–79.

Strambach, S. (2010). 'Path dependence and path plasticity: the co-evolution of institutions and innovation – the German customized business software industry'. In R. Boschma and R. Martin (eds) *The Handbook of Evolutionary Economic Geography*. Cheltenham, UK: Edward Elgar (pp. 406–31).

Strambach, S. and Halkier, H. (2013). 'Conceptualising change. Path dependency, path plasticity and knowledge combination'. *Zeitschrift für Wirtschaftsgeographie* 57(1–2), 1–14.

Sum, N. L. and Jessop, B. (2013). *Towards a Cultural Political Economy: Putting Culture in its Place in Political Economy*. Cheltenham, UK: Edward Elgar Publishing.

Van der Duim, R. (2007). 'Tourismscapes: An actor-network perspective'. *Annals of Tourism Research* 34(4), 961–76.

Van der Duim, R., Ren, C., and Thór Jóhannesson, G. (2012). *Actor-Network Theory and Tourism: Ordering, Materiality and Multiplicity*. London: Routledge.

Williams, A. M. (2013). 'Mobilities and sustainable tourism: Path-creating or path-dependent relationships?' *Journal of Sustainable Tourism* 21(4), 511–31.

Zukin, S. (1991). 'Disney World: The power of facade/the facade of power'. In S. Zukin (ed.) *Landscapes of Power: From Detroit to Disney World*. Berkeley, CA: University of California Press (pp. 217–50).

6 Path dependence in remote area tourism development

Why institutional legacies matter

Doris Anna Carson and Dean Bradley Carson

Introduction

Central Australia – also known as the 'Red Centre' – has been one of Australia's most iconic tourism destinations, with major attractions such as Uluru (Ayers Rock), Kata Tjuta (the Olgas) and Watarrka (Kings Canyon) featuring prominently in national and international tourism-promotion campaigns for decades. Yet, much time has passed since the Red Centre's tourism heydays in the 1990s, when it was a 'must-see' destination on tourist itineraries in Australia and annual visitor numbers were at around half a million tourists. Tourism in Central Australia has been facing an unprecedented crisis over the past few years, coming off a decade-long decline in visitor numbers, increasing disinvestment of external tourism and transport operators, and a lack of new and innovative tourism products that could rejuvenate an increasingly tired destination image (Carson *et al.* 2012). Drawing on recent debates in evolutionary economic geography (EEG) (MacKinnon *et al.* 2009; Martin 2010, 2012; Hassink *et al.* 2014), this chapter traces the development path of tourism in Central Australia to investigate the extent to which path dependence and negative lock-in may have contributed to the failure to pursue change even as the crisis has deepened.

Tourism destinations in remote and sparsely populated areas are subject to quite distinct development constraints, including small and fragmented local industry players, distance to markets and decision-makers, and dependence on external investors (Keller 1987; Hall 2007; Müller and Jansson 2007). They are, therefore, likely to evolve in different ways compared with destinations in urban or even other (less remote) peripheral areas that are within easy access from major population centres. This chapter discusses how historic institutional legacies and entrenched political approaches to economic development in remote peripheries may impact on the nature of tourism development and consequently shape the adaptability of local tourism systems. In doing so, we are using theoretical insights from the literature on resource dependence and the 'staples thesis', which add a useful explanatory layer to the analysis of regional economic-development trajectories in remote peripheries (Halseth *et al.* 2014), including those involving tourism development (Schmallegger and Carson 2010). This chapter supports recent calls for a more integrated approach towards EEG research that considers the role of place-dependent institutions, the wider political economy and the multi-level relations between firms, organizations and institutions in shaping regional economies (MacKinnon *et al.* 2009; Barnes and Sheppard 2010; Hassink *et al.* 2014).

Reconnecting EEG with institutional, political and relational perspectives

Economic geographers have long been interested in understanding how the economic landscape evolves over time and what processes lead to regional economic change and development. Drawing on various evolutionary concepts used in biology, economics and political studies, there has been an increasing focus since the mid-2000s on establishing EEG as a new paradigm to advance the study of regional economic change and develop stronger epistemological and methodological foundations for empiric research. As a relatively new and still-emerging paradigm, the definition of scope and focus within EEG is far from being complete, and there are on-going debates about the range of theoretical concepts and frameworks that could be valuable to apply in EEG research to provide a more comprehensive evolutionary perspective on regional economic change (Hassink *et al.* 2014; Martin and Sunley 2015).

In particular, there have been debates about whether or not to separate EEG from institutional and political economy approaches to economic geography (Boschma and Frenken 2009; Essletzbichler 2009; MacKinnon *et al.* 2009; Barnes and Sheppard 2010; Oosterlynck 2012). Some leading scholars in the field (Boschma and Frenken 2006, 2009; Boschma and Martin 2007; Essletzbichler and Rigby 2007) have described the emergence of, and changes within, economic industries across regions primarily as the result of the industrial dynamics of firms and their organizational routines at the micro level. This micro-level evolutionary approach has largely been influenced by a range of imported theoretical frameworks, such as Generalized Darwinism, complexity theory and Nelson and Winter's (1982) theory of the role of firms in evolutionary change, which tend to prioritize analysis of micro-level processes of selection, self-adaptation and learning over broader (meso- or macro-scale) socio-political and institutional forces (Hassink *et al.* 2014). While advocates of this firm-focused approach consider territorial institutions important in the process of legitimising or conditioning firm behaviour, they do not see them as determinants of industrial dynamics. Instead, they argue that firms and organizations develop their routines in path-dependent, idiosyncratic ways which are not necessarily bound to specific territories and their institutional environments. They further suggest that institutions are more likely to co-evolve with industrial dynamics, particularly as firms, government agencies and consumers engage in collective action to adapt or establish new institutions (Boschma and Frenken 2009; Essletzbichler 2009).

Other authors have criticized this strong focus on micro-level firm dynamics within EEG as too narrow, suggesting that it fails to understand how broader political, socio-cultural and institutional structures influence the behaviour of firms at the micro-level (MacKinnon *et al.* 2009; Barnes and Sheppard 2010;

Oosterlynck 2012; Hassink *et al.* 2014). From their perspective, institutions (i.e. the formal and informal rules, regulations, norms, habits and conventions that guide human behaviour on both individual and collective scales), as well as 'bigger picture' systemic structures, such as modes of regulation and governance and dominant regimes of capital accumulation, have a crucial impact on industrial dynamics at the micro-level (Martin and Sunley 2015). Related to this perspective are recent relational approaches towards economic geography research (Bathelt and Glückler 2011, 2014) that consider firms and organizations embedded within wider networks of social relations and institutions.

Relational economic geography emphasizes the importance of interactions and interdependencies between multiple actors and institutions operating on multiple (local, regional, national and global) scales, meaning that places and their economies evolve not only as a result of locally specific actors and institutions, but also from relations that link them to wider processes and structures of consumption, labour division, governance and so on (Coe *et al.* 2004; MacKinnon *et al.* 2009; Hassink *et al.* 2014). Thus, there seems to be an increasing recognition that EEG needs to more explicitly incorporate broader institutional perspectives from multiple scales to understand the interdependencies between firm behaviour and institutions and to explain uneven economic development at the regional level (Barnes and Sheppard 2010; Hassink *et al.* 2014; Martin and Sunley 2015).

Central to all of these approaches remains the idea of path dependence (Martin 2010, 2012), which in its broadest sense implies that 'history matters' in shaping economic development trajectories. This means that early decisions and development inevitably influence how actors and organizations respond to changing circumstances in subsequent stages of development. In the initial interpretation of path dependence (which Martin, 2010, referred to as the standard or 'canonical' model of path dependence), the core idea is that 'progressive lock-in to a self-reproducing stable state or configuration' is an almost unavoidable outcome (Martin 2010: 180). While this scenario may have positive outcomes (for example, increased knowledge and innovation potential due to increased levels of specialization), the concept of lock-in has mostly been used to explain why certain (usually declining) regional economies fail to diversify and rejuvenate as they become over-attached to a particular industry, market or technology. Essentially, these economies become 'stuck in established practices, ideas, and networks of embeddedness that no longer yield increasing returns and may even induce negative externalities' (Martin and Sunley 2006: 416). According to Grabher (1993), such lock-in can occur in multiple inter-connected ways, including functional lock-in (through rigid ties and networks that impede the formation of alternative connections), cognitive lock-in (through entrenched shared visions and ideas, common practices and accepted norms) and political lock-in (through rigid political-administrative systems, embedded power structures and governance approaches).

The idea of lock-in has more recently been challenged by evolutionary economic geographers, arguing that lock-in is only one of many possible outcomes of path dependence. In fact, Martin (2010) pointed out that the standard path-dependence model focuses too much on 'continuity' (doing more of the same) rather than evolution, and therefore does not allow for the consideration of alternative pathways that evolve through continuous and incremental change. From this perspective, path-dependent development trajectories may evolve through processes such as 'layering' (adding new actors, institutions or relations to the system), 'delayering' (removing such system components), 'conversion' (changing the function or purpose of existing components) or 'recombination' (combining old and new components), thus leading to new path creation (Martin 2010: 188). Conversely, new paths may arise out of exogenous shocks and crisis events, or in the most extreme cases as a result of path destruction when excessive lock-in has caused the regional economy to fail and requires the abandonment of traditional paths in search of new development (Martin and Sunley 2006). Nevertheless, the capacity to adopt new paths, as well as the nature of alternative paths that are available, continue to depend primarily on what has gone before.

Path dependence in remote resource peripheries

Considerations of path dependence, path destruction and path creation are important in the process of establishing new industries, particularly in cases where those new industries are substantially different from old industries. The emergence of tourism in remote peripheries that have traditionally relied on primary resource extraction could be considered as one such scenario. Tourism in remote areas is often introduced as a new economic activity at times when traditional resource industries are declining and economic diversification and rejuvenation are urgently needed. This phenomenon has been observed in many developed countries, including the USA, Canada, Australia, New Zealand and parts of northern Scandinavia, and a relatively large body of literature has emerged since the 1980s, discussing the issues and challenges involved in remote area tourism development (see, for example, Keller 1987; Hohl and Tisdell 1995; Hall 2007; Müller and Jansson 2007; George *et al.* 2009; Koster 2010). Yet, there has been relatively little systematic examination of how the concepts of path dependence and path creation apply in the context of a transition or diversification from resource to tourism industries, and how the various structural, political, institutional and socio-cultural legacies of resource-based economies influence development paths in tourism (Schmallegger and Carson 2010; Carson and Carson 2011). Moreover, the tourism literature has been criticized in recent years for an increasing number of research studies on tourism development (including historical perspectives on destination lifecycles) that have examined tourism in isolation from the broader political and socio-economic environment (Hall 2007; Müller and Jansson 2007). Some authors have, therefore, argued that evolutionary research perspectives in tourism geography need to more explicitly recognize the broader historic, institutional, political and relational context that gives rise to tourism pathways and influences the way tourism systems develop (see, for example, Bramwell 2011; Brouder and Eriksson 2013; Sanz-Ibáñez and Anton Clavé 2014).

Staples thesis and path dependence

A relatively large body of literature has emerged over the past century around the notion of resource dependence and its impacts on regional development dynamics in peripheral economies, and these insights are useful in understanding tourism pathways in remote areas. In particular, the Canadian 'staples thesis' of economic growth has proven to be a valuable tool in explaining regional development paths in remote areas of Canada, the USA and Australia (Barnes *et al.* 2001; Huskey 2006; Markey *et al.* 2006; Wellstead 2008; Carson 2011; Argent 2013; Halseth *et al.* 2014). The staples thesis emerged in the early twentieth century from the writings of Harold A. Innis (1933), who – albeit using different terminology – essentially argued that a long-term dependence on exporting minimally processed natural resource commodities (i.e. 'the staples') to external core centres leads to a form of lock-in that poses substantial barriers to self-sustaining regional development. As summarized by Halseth *et al.* (2014: 358), regional economies in such resource peripheries can 'become "locked-in" as the social, economic, labour, investment, institutional, and infrastructure elements of established resource economies drive thinking and decision making'. This situation came to be known as the 'staples trap', meaning that resource economies struggle to diversify and continue to focus on staples industries even when those industries no longer generate sufficient income (Watkins 1963; Wellstead 2008).

The specific geographical characteristics of resource peripheries, including the abundance of natural resources, sparse and small local populations, and the absence of other strong local industries, generate a particular type of political economy that becomes 'addicted' to resource export (Freudenburg 1992; Howlett and Brownsey 2008; Halseth *et al.* 2014). Centralized (national or provincial) governments base their economic development strategies on bulk resource export industries (e.g. mining, forestry, and more recently also energy), along with large-scale infrastructure investment projects aimed at fast economic growth, and a focus on attracting major external investors who are able to co-finance such developments. Large sunk costs involved in these developments require certain levels of government patronage to protect those favoured industries from the vagaries of external markets, as well as from other, potentially competing interests. Monopolistic use of infrastructure and technologies, as well as regulatory exemptions and financial incentives for external investors have been common ways to prop up staples industries that are simply 'too big to fail' (Howlett and Brownsey 2008; Halseth *et al.* 2014). This commonly leads to an entrenched export mentality among governments, which continues to favour resource export over alternative forms of economic development, and under which competing interests (e.g. environmental, Indigenous) become subordinate to staples exploitation (Howlett and Brownsey 2008; Wellstead 2008). Development and growth become highly localized (e.g. within a particular mill or mining town) and rarely produce meaningful spillover effects on a broader regional level, particularly as resource income is often reinvested straight back into supporting the dominant resource industry instead of encouraging alternative development. As a result, limited socio-economic diversification has been a common experience in resource peripheries, demonstrated by the emergence of isolated, single-industry towns that are highly vulnerable to 'boom and bust' cycles – synonymous with rapid growth during periods of strong resource demand followed by catastrophic decline (through disinvestment, unemployment and outmigration) when external markets collapse (Barnes *et al.* 2001).

Continuous reliance on government and external players for investment and decision-making can stifle the formation of endogenous entrepreneurial spirit and leadership capabilities, leading to an embedded culture of dependency in the periphery and an inability to drive alternative development in times of resource bust (Watkins 1963; Wellstead 2008). Local entrepreneurship is particularly constrained by limited opportunities for economic linkages, as required technologies, labour and knowledge tend to be imported from external sources rather than developed internally (Gunton 2003). In fact, there is often minimal complementary business development in supply-and-processing industries in the periphery as external players control the various stages of the commodity value chain. Typically, the few local businesses that do manage to become contractors for the dominant resource company (e.g. businesses in transport, construction or various trades), or businesses servicing the needs of the working population (e.g. retail and hospitality operators), are themselves highly dependent on the prosperity of the resource industry, and come and go with boom-and-bust cycles.

In terms of connectivity and relations, the common tendency in resource communities is to look to external sources of investment and knowledge, yet leave the connection seeking and management to higher-level (usually government) agencies that have the required financial means and political clout. At the same time, internal networking capabilities (for example, among small local firms and community organizations) become truncated as there is no real need for business or community collaboration and knowledge sharing as long as resource industries provide guaranteed income and employment (Markey *et al.* 2006). Similarly, local knowledge and capacity building is often not high on community agendas during boom times, as high-paid (but low-skilled) jobs are plentiful and there is little need for local training and higher education (Marshall *et al.* 2007). Serious attempts at economic diversification and local capacity-building usually start in times of economic decline, when the periphery is drained of economic and human capital. However, in many cases such attempts are of a temporary nature, as local communities hope for the resources boom to return and quickly abandon alternative development strategies once the staples industries have recovered (Carson and Carson 2011).

Halseth and colleagues (2014) recently discussed whether such resource path-dependence in remote peripheries, as described by the Innisian staples trap, is in fact comparable with a situation of lock-in, or whether regional development paths show signs of transition and emergence, including shifts in established patterns of development and the implementation of new dynamics and processes that reshape the economic landscape. Using northern British Columbia as an example, Halseth and colleagues (2014) argued that, although recent changes and transitions are noticeable in terms of the nature of the staple, the scale of development, the location of investors and markets, and the consideration of local (specifically Indigenous) interests, the fundamental dependency relationships with external sources of capital and decision-making had not changed. Continuity featured strongly in the region's development path, and staples production had remained 'strongly entrenched and supported by both the region's as well as the province's prevailing staples paradigm' (Halseth *et al.* 2014: 358). Hence, while the region may not be affected by a 'lock-in' in the strictest sense of the word (i.e. not able to change a particular industrial development path), the regional system has clearly become 'trapped' in a continuous cycle of staples development in which one staple (e.g. forestry or coal mining) is simply replaced by another (e.g. oil, gas or hydrology) – yet with very similar structural, political and institutional development constraints.

Tourism as just another staple? The case of Central Australia

In our research in Central Australia (Schmallegger and Carson 2010), we found that the staples trap can also affect the development of non-staples industries such as tourism. In essence, our argument was that the territorial political economy and institutional environment had become so focused on 'big ticket' resource projects, high-volume export markets and large-scale external investors, that tourism in Central Australia – in the absence of a 'real' natural staples commodity – was turned into a staples substitute. This has made tourism subject to similar industry characteristics, external dependency relationships, vulnerability to boom-and-bust cycles and truncated local development that are commonly seen in more classic staples industries. The remainder of this chapter revisits the case of tourism in Central Australia and outlines the main historic, political and institutional forces and processes that have led to this form of path dependence.

Central Australia is a large and sparsely populated desert region (approx. 550,000 km[1] with a resident population of just under 40,000, about one-third of them Indigenous) and is located in the southern part of the Northern Territory (NT) (Figure 6.1). Its main population centre is Alice Springs (approx. 30,000 residents), with the remaining population spread across several small townships, Indigenous communities and pastoral stations. The region is very remote and a long way from any of the larger Australian cities, with only one major highway connecting Alice Springs to Darwin (the capital of the NT, about 1,500 km to the north) and Adelaide (the capital of South Australia, about 1,500 km to the south). The socio-economic development path of the region is closely linked to the specific historic, political and economic role of the NT as a whole. As one of Australia's remote frontiers, the NT was settled by European colonizers in the second half of the nineteenth century to establish a transport and communication line from Adelaide to Darwin in order to connect the Australian mainland with international centres (in particular Great Britain). This was accompanied by increasing mining exploration and pastoral settlement, along with a growing military presence in the north to protect Australia from foreign invasion. Initially a colony of the state of South Australia, the NT was handed over to the Commonwealth in

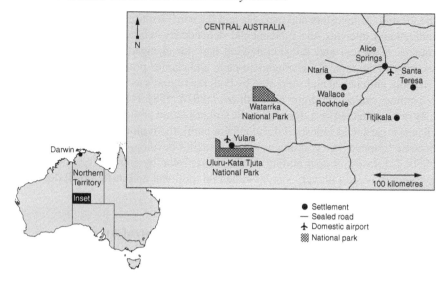

Figure 6.1 Map of Central Australia.

1911 and remained under federal control until the late 1970s. During that time, its role as a strategic defence base and resource frontier for the south consolidated, and several large-scale investments in defence, transport and mining infrastructure (particularly uranium mining) emerged across the NT. In 1978, the NT was finally granted self-government with state-like political and administrative structures. Subsequent NT governments have since been keen to prove that the NT – despite its disadvantaged physical and socio-economic environment (i.e. isolation from Australian core centres, harsh climate, sparse populations and a large share of 'disadvantaged' Indigenous people) – is a viable de-facto state that can sustain a strong economy and a growing population.

Governmental development priorities have since been 'concentrated on interventionist development policies to pursue rapid economic and population growth' (Pforr 2001: 278). As part of this rationale, 'major projects' based around large-scale infrastructure investments have become embedded as the cornerstones of government development agendas, with the Department of the Chief Minister maintaining a major projects office responsible for the recruitment of large-scale resource and construction investments (Northern Territory Government 2014). Such projects have been a popular vehicle to not only lure influential, multi-/national corporations to the NT, but to boost the population by attracting large (albeit short-term) cohorts of external workers (Carson *et al.* 2010; Taylor and Carson 2014).

Examples of past major projects have primarily included investments in the resources sector (e.g. the establishment of instant mining towns and more recently off-shore gas developments), as well as the transport sector (e.g. the construction of deep-water port facilities in Darwin and the 'Ghan' railway connection between Adelaide and Darwin). Yet tourism-related developments have also found their way onto the major project list, starting with the government-funded construction of the Yulara resort town near Uluru in 1983, and culminating in the development of a multi-billion dollar waterfront tourism precinct in Darwin in the mid-2000s (Carson *et al.* 2010).

The major project approach to tourism dates back to the early years of self-government, when then Chief Minister Everingham declared tourism as one of the NT's investment priorities (Pforr 2001) because it was repeatedly touted as the fastest growing private sector industry and job creator. Central Australia in particular benefited from the new tourism boom starting in the 1980s and became the centre of attention for large-scale tourism infrastructure investment and marketing. Until then, the region had been reliant on pastoralism and transport services, yet without the presence of a major investment industry. Tourism had largely been small-scale and uncoordinated up until the 1970s, with several accommodation and bus tour operators providing basic tourist services, often as a secondary source of income (Berzins 2007). The construction of the Yulara resort town – a state-of-the-art tourist complex with multiple accommodation facilities, restaurants, shops and staff housing – gave rise to the era of mass tourism in Central Australia. Annual tourist numbers at Uluru increased from roughly 50,000 in the mid-1970s to around 350,000 in the mid-1990s (McKercher and du Cros 1998; Chlanda 2004). Alice Springs (approx. 450 km to the east of Yulara) also benefited from the boom and experienced an increase in large-scale tourism infrastructure, with several international brand hotels, a casino and an international-standard golf course being established during the 1980s. Another tourist resort was constructed at Watarrka national park (approx. 300 km north-east of Yulara), which completed the popular Red Centre tourist itinerary triangle (from Alice Springs to Yulara or vice versa, with a stopover at Watarrka). Official visitor statistics collected by Tourism Research Australia (TRA) since 1999 suggest that leisure tourist numbers to the Red Centre (including Alice Springs, with its surrounding MacDonnell Ranges, Yulara and Watarrka) peaked at around 500,000 visitors in 1999–2000 (TRA 2013).

Tourism in Central Australia has been compared with staples development because the way tourism was commercialized from the 1980s onwards is reminiscent of the dominant value chains in staples export industries (Schmallegger and Carson 2010). Tourism became one of the NT's three major export industries (along with mining and pastoralism), and the NT government started to invest increasing resources into external marketing to boost visitor numbers. Since the 1980s, the NT government has continued to register the highest per capita (both in terms of residents and tourists) tourism budget of all states and territories in Australia (Berzins 2007), with the majority of funds being used for promotion, especially to prestigious (yet volatile) overseas 'export markets'. According to TRA data, over 60 per cent of annual leisure tourists to Central Australia have come from overseas. This means that Central Australia has attracted the highest proportion of international tourists for any regional tourism destination in the country – a remarkable feat considering the lack of direct international flights into the region. The predominant tourism experience has remained close to a somewhat 'unprocessed' bulk commodity, meaning that it has relied on relatively superficial exploitation of the region's scenic appeal (sightseeing around the national parks) for the mass market, with little diversification into complementary activities and products that could engage visitors in in-depth encounters with local people. As a result, homogenous short-term sightseeing itineraries, high visitor turnover, and extremely low repeat visitor rates have dominated tourist mobilities in Central Australia, and these mobilities have remained largely unchanged since the 1980s (McKercher and du Cros 1998; Schmallegger and Carson 2010).

The continuous need to 'chase' external investors has been a common feature of NT tourism over the past decades, and this has been evident in the NT government's repeated attempts to sell off the government-funded Yulara resort to private investors after construction. The resort was finally sold in 1997 to the General Property Trust Group, a real-estate investment trust headquartered in Sydney and listed on the Australian stock exchange. Voyages Hotels & Resorts, a subsidiary of the General Property Trust, subsequently became the main operator of Yulara, as well as the resorts at Kings Canyon and in Alice Springs. Privatization of the Yulara resort was preceded by the NT government's decision in the early 1990s to build a new domestic airport at Yulara to boost visitor numbers to the resort through direct interstate flights. By that time, the resort had become a huge financial liability (and a recurring election issue) for the NT government, which was desperate to increase the resort's profitability and make it more attractive to potential buyers. The construction of Yulara airport was heavily criticized by tourism stakeholders in Alice Springs, as they saw more and more tourists (who would have normally travelled via Alice Springs) bypass the town. To date, there remains ongoing resentment in Alice Springs about the government's decision to protect its 'too big to fail' Yulara investment at the expense of tourism in Alice Springs. Critics argue that the airport at Yulara has essentially concentrated tourism in a company-run single-industry town and curtailed tourism benefits for the surrounding region (Chlanda 2014).

Apart from the big accommodation operators, other major external stakeholders, most notably the various airlines and interstate bus tour providers servicing Alice Springs and Yulara, have been dominant players in the Central Australian tourism system. Local linkages in the form of small (and also Indigenous) tourism operators have only been tangentially involved. For example, small-scale and family-owned tourism businesses (which are so common in many other rural tourism destinations) have been scarce, particularly in the accommodation and restaurant sectors, which have been dominated by multi-/national hotel chains (Schmallegger and Carson 2010). In addition, much of the complementary small business development (e.g. pubs, cafés, souvenir shops, art galleries and guided tour operations) has remained dependent on high visitor volumes being generated through the marketing and investment efforts of the government and the big-industry players. This became obvious at the peak of the recent tourism crisis, when several small operators (including, for example, the Indigenous 'flagship' tourism operator at Uluru) had to suspend or close down operations due to a lack of incoming cash flow (Fitzgerald 2012; Horn 2012).

To illustrate the tourism crisis in a nutshell: leisure visitor numbers to Central Australia collapsed by over 40 per cent between 2000 and 2012 (TRA 2013), with particular strong declines during 2008–2012 when the global financial crisis (GFC) and the simultaneously high Australian dollar kept many international sightseeing tourists away from the region. In Alice Springs, the number of accommodation establishments and visitor beds declined by more than a quarter in the ten-year period 2002–2011 (ABS 2012a), and hospitality employment (in accommodation and restaurants) declined by around 20 per cent (or 200 jobs) during the same period (while the remaining workforce shrank by only 5 per cent) (ABS 2012b). This decline might well have been more severe had it not been offset by an influx of business visitors (primarily non-resident public servants) who were drawn to Alice Springs from 2007 onwards due to a federal government 'intervention' program aimed at managing Indigenous social issues in the region. The Yulara resort along with Voyages' assets at Watarrka and in Alice Springs were put up for sale in 2009, when the General Property Trust decided to get rid of its tourism properties in the wake of falling returns on investment. In addition, several airlines, bus tour operators and the Ghan tourist train reduced their services to Central Australia, with each announcement of service reduction causing a local industry outcry calling on the government to somehow intervene.

In reality, these shocks were the culmination of a longer trend rather than the instigation of a new crisis. Declining interest in standard passive sightseeing tours, paired with a persistent lack of new investment in infrastructure and experience development since the late 1990s, appear to have reduced tourist interest in Central Australia long before 2008. Nevertheless, the NT government, represented through Tourism NT (at times also called the NT Tourism Commission), has regularly denied the decline to be a result of structural weaknesses within the NT tourism system. The downturn in tourist numbers was almost exclusively blamed on external shocks and circumstances (such as the GFC, the high Australian dollar, various overseas terrorist attacks and epidemic diseases), and so the crisis was treated as an unfortunate temporary phenomenon. Instead of encouraging alternative destination-development pathways, the NT government poured more resources into maintaining the status quo and protecting previous developments: during that phase common government responses were new multi-million dollar marketing campaigns (essentially promoting the same old destination to new markets, such as the newly emerging markets in China), lobbying activities to attract airlines back to Central Australia, and various upgrades to existing infrastructure developments. In contrast, alternative development proposals from local stakeholders, for example, the development of off-road touring routes, a backpacker activity strategy, or an Indigenous cultural tourism centre in Alice Springs, only ever seemed to be pursued half-heartedly and never progressed much beyond the initial proposal stages.

It was not until the peak of the crisis in 2012 that Tourism NT, in the course of its new strategic plan development, started to call more on the local industry to come forward with new ideas to rejuvenate tourism in Central Australia (Chlanda 2012a). However, the local industry – primarily smaller local businesses in and around Alice Springs – has apparently struggled to come to grips with its new role of having to redefine tourism in the region. The long-term reliance on homogenous mass tourism and the lack of pre-existing industry diversity appear to have had a stifling effect on the emergence of alternative tourism pathways. For a system used to 'thinking big' in terms of infrastructure and tourist numbers, it seemed difficult to conceive of (and implement) small-scale development as an alternative way forward. Identified industry priorities have largely continued to centre around the return of the glorious past via increased government intervention (e.g. government assistance for crisis relief, more funding for marketing, more lobbying for new flights, more infrastructure investment in 'big' attractions, and more attention to attracting major events and conventions) (Chlanda 2012b; Finnane 2012). In addition, there seems to be an entrenched lack of creativity to think of product opportunities beyond the traditional 'tourism staple' (i.e. relatively unprocessed sightseeing activities around natural attractions). Initiatives to foster small niche market development, for example around various sports and adventure tourism opportunities, such as mountain biking, abseiling or skydiving, have been rare and have not gained much traction due to a lack of government endorsement and a lack of local industry leadership and coordination.

What has been recognized by the government as a niche worth pursuing is Indigenous cultural tourism development in local Indigenous communities. Indigenous cultural experiences have often been identified as desirable for international key markets, at least according to market research commissioned by Tourism NT and other marketing bodies in the country (Tremblay and Wegner 2009). As a result, there has been considerable public funding and in-kind support over the past decade to establish Indigenous tourism and art-related ventures in various remote communities, including Ntaria, Wallace Rockhole, Titjikala and Santa Teresa (see Figure 6.1). Some of them turned out to be not viable without continuous government support and quietly disappeared after funding programs and employment incentives were discontinued. Others, however, have managed to succeed on a longer-term basis by offering experiences to smaller niche markets, such as four-wheel-drive tourists or independent tourists looking for heritage and art experiences. Yet, these ventures have remained very small in terms of visitor volume and local employment opportunities. For example, Ntaria and Wallace Rockhole together had an estimated 20,000 visitor nights annually in the mid-2000s and around 20 local people working in tourism-related industries (hospitality, retail, arts and recreation services) – numbers that are clearly dwarfed by the size of the mainstream tourism industry in Alice Springs and Yulara (Carson and Carson 2014). As such, small Indigenous tourism ventures have remained disconnected from common mass tourism itineraries (in particular those offered by large tour operators) and the dominant mass tourism system. Not surprisingly, then, such small developments have not been considered in public debates as potential steps towards a new pathway that could rejuvenate tourism in the region.

A relatively weak culture of collaboration within the local tourism industry has also emerged as a constraining factor in the process of mobilizing local resources in innovative ways. Industry collaboration for product development and marketing had been relatively limited in the past when small operators were largely relying on big (and externally based) operators to get a piece of the tourism pie. Many small operators were therefore used to either competing against each other, or at best operating in isolation from each other. In addition, the local Central Australian Tourism Industry Association has traditionally been considered as a 'weak' representative body, having minimal influence on government policy and strategic directions in tourism due to the government's monopolistic 'big business' approach to tourism development (Pforr 2001). The association has repeatedly come under criticism for not being a strong lobbying force for local industry interests (Chlanda 2012b), and it has not been able to provide the industry with a useful platform to join forces in developing and implementing a shared vision.

Limited collective action at the local level could also be an outcome of continuous high turnover within the workforce and business environment, which may have stifled the formation of strong social bonds and long-term commitment to local development. Over half of all residents employed in tourism (including hospitality, tour and travel services) in 2006 and 2011 had lived in Central Australia for less than five years (ABS 2012b). Such high residential turnover has been a common feature of the NT's demography (Carson 2011), and it may be an indicator of a strongly embedded culture of 'temporariness' that has emerged around the staples trap (i.e. investors, labour and residents are expected to come and go with resource boom-and-bust cycles, thus limiting the gradual build-up of a more permanent stock of human capital with vested local interests) (Carson *et al.* 2010). What is critical is that the continuous influx of new people and investors in a remote staples environment like the NT does not seem to inject (and implement) new innovative ideas and practices – most likely because the entrenched way of doing business continues to attract similar types of people and organizations with similar knowledge, routines and attitudes. In turn, the NT government needs to keep chasing major projects and fast economic growth, because government cycles are themselves short term, and a large part of the NT electorate will simply not stay around to wait for the benefits of slow and long-term development strategies.

The ongoing reliance on short-term, external labour means that the integration of local Indigenous people in the NT staples workforce has continued to be marginal, and this has been the case in both mining and tourism. In 2011, only about 10 per cent of the Central Australian tourism workforce were Indigenous (160 jobs compared with 130 in 2006) (ABS 2012b). Particularly the Yulara resort has come under criticism for not employing local Indigenous people, despite massive unemployment rates in the surrounding Indigenous communities (Chlanda 2004). The resort was eventually sold in 2010 to the Indigenous Land Corporation – a step which was initially heralded as a major break-through in terms of getting Indigenous interests more involved in Central Australian tourism. However, the corporation is a federal government statutory authority based in Adelaide, and so one could argue that the new takeover has just meant more government-funded dependence on yet another externally based interest group. More importantly, this new government dependence is expected to continue as the resort has accrued an estimated AUD 200 million in debt that no private investor will be likely to take on in the near future (Aston 2014). Nevertheless, a new Indigenous training and employment program has been implemented in the meantime, resulting in a notable increase in Indigenous employees (from just a handful in 2005 to around 200 in 2014, according to official press releases). Still, many Indigenous employees appear to have actually come from outside Central Australia, and so the prevalence of external (and most likely also short-term) human capital is likely to continue.

Adding to the precarious situation of tourism in Central Australia is the fact that other staples industries in the NT – most notably offshore gas developments along the northern coast – have entered a substantial boom phase since the mid-2000s. Government attention has therefore increasingly shifted away from leisure tourism, at least for the time being, as the prospects for an imminent recovery to pre-crisis tourism demand and investment levels are slim in the current global economic climate. Central Australia in particular has fallen off the investment radar over the last decade, with no new major development proposals forthcoming and the only growing sector (in terms of employment) being the public service sector. Instead, the boom area has shifted north, where Darwin has managed to attract strong economic and population growth over the past decade as part of multi-billion dollar gas projects and a subsequent construction and real-estate boom in the city (Carson *et al.* 2010; Taylor and Carson 2014). This boom has indirectly boosted tourism in the city of Darwin (though not in the surrounding Top End region), as the general decline in leisure tourism during the GFC period was more than offset by a growing business-visitor market, which included large cohorts of short-term and non-resident (fly-in/fly-out) construction and gas workers. As a result, there is limited urgency for the government to step in and save tourism in the north, meaning that the crisis has largely remained a Central Australian experience.

Discussion and conclusion

Looking at Central Australia's tourism path in isolation, one could argue that its development trajectory has resembled one of Butler's (1980) classic S-shaped tourism-area life-cycle curves, traversing from a phase of low-volume exploration (1950s) and small-scale local involvement (1960s to 1970s), through to a phase of strong growth and maturation with increased development and large-scale industry involvement (1980s to 1990s), before entering a phase of stagnation and ultimately decline (since the early 2000s). However, tourism has not evolved as a self-contained, linear pathway but must be understood as embedded within the NT's overall development trajectory that has emerged around its historic political and economic role as a remote resource and defence frontier for Australia. The dominant political economy that has emerged out of this frontier role has become entrenched in a way that successive governments continue to prioritize the staples paradigm – through major projects, large-scale industrial interests and externally focused connection seeking – to stimulate fast yet temporary growth. Within this staples environment, 'cyclonic' boom-and-bust periods are accepted as inevitable, and so new boom industries need to be established to replace the busting ones. In this sense, the economic development path of the NT is not locked in to a particular industry, but it remains 'trapped' within a highly path-dependent political economy addicted to major projects, regardless of the nature of the staple (see Howlett and Brownsey 2008; Halseth *et al.* 2014).

The resulting institutional environment has become characterized by an entrenched culture of dependence (on government bodies and external investors) among local-industry players, a persistent lack of local entrepreneurial capabilities (including creativity and the willingness to invest and take leadership), and a weak local culture of collaboration to develop and implement alternative ideas on a collective level (also see Markey *et al.* 2006; Wellstead 2008). These micro-scale deficiencies within the tourism system appear to be the result of the prevalent institutional environment inherited from the NT's staples paradigm, particularly since the addition of new actors and organizations (as part of the high population and business turnover) has done little to change common practices, expectations or more formal institutions within the system.

The Central Australian tourism system currently appears to be locked in and heading towards path destruction, as developmental change (through, for example, 'layering', 'delayering', 'conversion' or 'recombination') has not gained much traction so far. On the one hand, tourism is unlikely to ever completely die and disappear as an industry in Central Australia, as the remote region continues to attract high levels of population mobility requiring service provision (e.g. from transit travellers, non-resident public servants, Indigenous travellers and people visiting friends and relatives) (Carson *et al.* 2012). On the other hand, however, traditional forms of leisure mass tourism (based on relatively superficial sightseeing) are unlikely to bounce back to previous levels, and so the system is facing the challenge to fundamentally redefine itself and its tourism focus in the absence of strong government and external leadership. Of course one could argue that this process is already underway, with small but noticeable changes such as the recognition to encourage more locally driven development (as a result of the government trying to shift development responsibilities to the local industry), or an increased attention to Indigenous involvement in tourism. The current bust and diminishing government interest may actually provide an opportunity for a local redesign of tourism based on the sorts of small-scale and activity-based experiences that have previously been overlooked or neglected. Potential for small-scale (including Indigenous) tourism development exists, and there is a demonstrated (if latent) market for such development. While it is clear that such small-scale and Indigenous tourism is unlikely to ever 'hold up' a regional economy on its own, it will probably be an important component of any future path, as it provides an opportunity to build a less transient economic base that will stick around during bust periods. However, new path creation after a disruptive shock may be a long and slow process, and whether a more resilient (and less volatile) local entrepreneurial class can emerge from the history of dependence on outsiders to make decisions and provide opportunities remains to be seen.

Conversely, the possibility always exists that tourism in Central Australia may re-emerge from its bust through the same mechanisms that created the previous boom – that is, large-scale external and government investment, and a concentration of resources on a few key attractions and pieces of infrastructure. Its historical development path predisposes the destination system to not only seek this (as described above) but to embrace it if it should occur. At some level, a continuing boom-and-bust tourism economy may not inherently be a bad thing (as one could argue that large but temporary development in a remote area is preferable to no development at all). However, chasing the boom is likely to become increasingly difficult and expensive because of the costs of replacing decaying infrastructure and seeking new markets, as well as the difficulties involved in 'out-bidding' the political and economic centre Darwin for government attention. Further entrenching 'boom-seeking' behaviour is also likely to continue to limit the prospects for local (particularly Indigenous) people to benefit directly from tourism employment and income.

This chapter has provided an example of how entrenched political economies and institutional legacies inherited from staples dependence may impact on the development trajectories of tourism in remote areas. Clearly, the case of Central Australia is an extreme case due to its remoteness, harsh desert environment, sparse population, and Indigenous context. As such, it may not be comparable with tourism destinations that have emerged in other types of rural areas – in particular destinations that are more accessible from major population centres, have scenic amenities that attract increasing counter-urbanization, and have more stable populations with strong levels of community attachment and vested local interests. Also important to consider is the fact that tourism in Central Australia did not replace a declining local resource industry (such as mining), but was more or less induced as a staples substitute by a government that was looking to establish a staples-like export industry in the region. Again, this makes Central Australia a bad example to compare with peripheral destinations that have experienced a decline in the resources sector before embarking on tourism as a means of economic diversification (George *et al.* 2009; Koster 2010; Carson and Carson 2011). However, the case emphasizes that integrating historic political and institutional perspectives from the macro- (or meso-) scale in the analysis of tourism development paths on the micro-scale is critical to enhance our understanding of how and why particular tourism pathways emerge in particular regions. Insights from the staples thesis add a useful explanatory layer to this analysis and provide a helpful tool to examine institutional environments emerging in the specific context of resource peripheries. Yet, more comparative research from other peripheries (especially within other jurisdictions) is needed to better conceptualize the impact of staples legacies on tourism pathways in remote areas.

References

ABS (Australian Bureau of Statistics). (2012a). Tourist accommodation, small area data, Northern Territory. [online] URL: www.abs.gov.au/AUSSTATS/abs@.nsf/Lookup/8635.7.55.001Main+Features1Jun%202011?OpenDocument (accessed on 17 July 2015).

ABS (Australian Bureau of Statistics). (2012b). Australian Census data, 2006 and 2011. [online] URL: www.abs.gov.au/websitedbs/censushome.nsf/home/tablebuilder?opendocument&navpos=240 (accessed on 17 July 2015).

Argent, N. (2013). 'Reinterpreting core and periphery in Australia's mineral and energy resources boom: An Innisian perspective on the Pilbara'. *Australian Geographer* 44(3), 323–40.

Aston, H. (2014, January 23). 'Row over Dawn Casey's "outrageous" Ayers Rock Resort comments'. *The Sydney Morning Herald.* [online] URL: www.smh.com.au/national/row-over-dawn-caseys-outrageous-ayers-rock-resort-comments-20140123-31acq.html (accessed on 15 July 2015).

Barnes, T. J. and Sheppard, E. (2010). '"Nothing includes everything": Towards engaged pluralism in anglophone economic geography'. *Progress in Human Geography* 34(2), 193–214.

Barnes, T. J., Hayter, R., and Hay, E. (2001). 'Stormy weather: Cyclones, Harold Innis and Port Alberni, BC'. *Environment and Planning A* 33(12), 2127–47.

Bathelt, H. and Glückler, J. (2011). *The Relational Economy: Geographies of Knowing and Learning.* Oxford: Oxford University Press.

Bathelt, H. and Glückler, J. (2014). 'Institutional change in economic geography'. *Progress in Human Geography* 38(3), 340–63.

Berzins, B. (2007). *Australia's Northern Secret: Tourism in the Northern Territory, 1920s to 1980s.* Sydney: self-published.

Boschma, R. and Frenken, K. (2006). 'Why is economic geography not an evolutionary science?' *Journal of Economic Geography* 6(3), 273–302.

Boschma, R. and Frenken, K. (2009). 'Some notes on institutions in evolutionary economic geography'. *Economic Geography* 85(2), 151–8.

Boschma, R. and Martin, R. (2007). 'Constructing an evolutionary economic geography'. *Journal of Economic Geography* 7(5), 537–48.

Bramwell, B. (2011). 'Governance, the state and sustainable tourism: A political economy approach'. *Journal of Sustainable Tourism* 19(4–5), 459–77.

Brouder, P. and Eriksson, R. (2013). 'Tourism evolution: On the synergies of tourism studies and evolutionary economic geography'. *Annals of Tourism Research* 43, 370–89.

Butler, R. W. (1980). 'The concept of a tourist area cycle of evolution: Implications for management of resources'. *Canadian Geographer* 24(1), 5–12.

Carson, D. A. and Carson, D. B. (2011). 'Why tourism may not be everybody's business: The challenge of tradition in resource peripheries'. *The Rangeland Journal* 33, 373–83.

Carson, D. B. (2011). 'Political economy, demography and development in Australia's Northern Territory'. *Canadian Geographer* 55(2), 226–42.

Carson, D. B. and Carson, D. A. (2014). 'Local economies of mobility in sparsely populated areas: Cases from Australia's spine'. *Journal of Rural Studies* 36, 340–9.

Carson, D. B., Schmallegger, D., and Harwood, S. (2010). 'A city for the temporary? Political economy and urban planning in Darwin, Australia'. *Urban Policy and Research* 28(3), 293–310.

Carson, D. B., Carson, D. A., Cartan, G., and Vilkinas, T. (2012). 'Saving Alice Springs tourism: Why it will never "bounce back" – but might leap forward'. *The Northern Institute Research Brief Series*, 2012/05. [online] URL: www.cdu.edu.au/northern-institute/ni-research-briefs (accessed on 10 August 2012).

Chlanda, E. (2004). 'Twenty years on: Looking back over resort's rocky road'. *Alice Springs News*, 1 December. [online] URL: www.alicespringsnews.com.au/1144.html (accessed on 17 July 2015).

Chlanda, E. (2012a). 'Wanted: Big fresh tourism ideas'. *Alice Springs News Online*, 8 March. [online] URL: www.alicespringsnews.com.au/2012/03/08/wanted-big-fresh-tourism-ideas/ (accessed on 16 July 2015).

Chlanda, E. (2012b). 'Tourism lobby has big wish list for new government'. *Alice Springs News Online*, 24 November. [online] URL: www.alicespringsnews.com.au/2012/11/24/tourism-lobby-has-big-wish-list-for-new-government/ (accessed on 15 July 2015).

Chlanda, E. (2014). 'Ayers Rock resort: What's in it for us?' *Alice Springs News Online*, 13 August. [online] URL: www.alicespringsnews.com.au/2014/03/28/ayers-rock-resort-whats-in-it-for-us/ (accessed on 16 July 2015).

Coe, N. M., Hess, M., Yeung, H. W., Dicken, P., and Henderson, J. (2004). '"Globalizing" regional development: A global production networks perspective'. *Transactions of the Institute of British Geographers* 29(4), 468–84.

Essletzbichler, J. (2009). 'Evolutionary economic geography, institutions, and political economy'. *Economic Geography* 85(2), 159–65.

Essletzbichler, J. and Rigby, D. L. (2007). 'Exploring evolutionary economic geographies'. *Journal of Economic Geography* 7(5), 549–72.

Finnane, K. (2012). 'PM will be asked to help Alice's flagging tourism industry'. *Alice Springs News Online*, 19 June. [online] URL: www.alicespringsnews.com.au/2011/07/17/pm-will-be-asked-to-help-alices-flagging-tourism-industry/ (accessed on 12 July 2015).

Fitzgerald, L. (2012). 'Struggle to keep the doors open'. *ABC Alice Springs*, 23 January. [online] URL: www.abc.net.au/local/stories/2012/01/23/3413899.htm (accessed on 18 July 2015).

Freudenburg, W. R. (1992). 'Addictive economies: Extractive industries and vulnerable localities in a changing world economy'. *Rural Sociology* 57(3), 305–32.

George, E. W., Mair, H., and Reid, D. G. (2009). *Rural Tourism Development: Localism and Cultural Change*. Bristol, UK: Channel View Publications.

Grabher, G. (1993). 'The weakness of strong ties: The lock-in of regional development in the Ruhr area'. In G. Grabher (ed.) *The Embedded Firm: On the Socio-Economics of Industrial Networks*. London: Routledge (pp. 255–77).

Gunton, T. (2003). 'Natural resources and regional development: An assessment of dependency and comparative advantage paradigms'. *Economic Geography* 79(1), 67–94.

Hall, C. M. (2007). 'North–south perspectives on tourism, regional development and peripheral areas'. In D. K. Müller and B. Jansson (eds) *Tourism in Peripheries: Perspectives from the Far North and South*. Wallingford, UK: CABI (pp. 19–37).

Halseth, G., Ryser, L., Markey, S., and Martin, A. (2014). 'Emergence, transition, and continuity: Resource commodity production pathways in northeastern British Columbia, Canada'. *Journal of Rural Studies* 36, 350–61.

Hassink, R., Klaerding, C., and Marques, P. (2014). 'Advancing evolutionary economic geography by engaged pluralism'. *Regional Studies* 48(7), 1295–307.

Hohl, A. E. and Tisdell, C. A. (1995). 'Peripheral tourism: Development and management'. *Annals of Tourism Research* 22(3), 517–34.

Horn, A. (2012). 'End of Indigenous Uluru guides blamed on funds'. *ABC Alice Springs*, 30 January. [online] URL: www.abc.net.au/news/2012-01-30/end-of-indigenous-uluru-tours-blamed-on-funds/3800246 (accessed on 15 July 2015).

Howlett, M. and Brownsey, K. (2008). 'Introduction: Toward a post-staples state?' In M. Howlett and K. Brownsey (eds) *Canada's Resource Economy in Transition: The Past, Present, and Future of Canadian Staples Industries*. Toronto: Emond Montgomery Publications (pp. 3–15).

Huskey, L. (2006). 'Limits to growth: Remote regions, remote institutions'. *The Annals of Regional Science* 40(1), 147–55.

Innis, H. A. (1933). *Problems of Staple Production in Canada*. Toronto: Ryerson Press.

Keller, C. P. (1987). 'Stages of peripheral tourism development: Canada's Northwest Territories'. *Tourism Management* 8(1), 20–32.

Koster, R. L. (2010). 'Local contexts for community economic development strategies: A comparison of rural Saskatchewan and Ontario communities'. In D. G. Winchell, D. Ramsey, R. L. Koster, and G. M. Robinson (eds) *Geographical Perspectives on Sustainable Rural Change*. Brandon, Manitoba: Rural Development Institute (pp. 461–83).

McKercher, B. and du Cros, H. (1998). 'I've climbed to the top of Ayers Rock but still couldn't see Uluru: The challenge of reinventing a tourist destination'. *Proceedings of the 8th Australian Tourism and Hospitality Research Conference*, 11–14 February, Gold Coast, Australia. Canberra: Bureau of Tourism Research (pp. 376–86).

MacKinnon, D., Cumbers, A., Pike, A., Birch, K., and McMaster, R. (2009). 'Evolution in economic geography: Institutions, political economy, and adaptation'. *Economic Geography* 85(2), 129–50.

Markey, S., Halseth, G., and Manson, D. (2006). 'The struggle to compete: From comparative to competitive advantage in Northern British Columbia'. *International Planning Studies* 11(1), 19–39.

Marshall, N. A., Fenton, D. M., Marshall, P. A., and Sutton, S. G. (2007). 'How resource dependency can influence social resilience within a primary resource industry'. *Rural Sociology* 72(3), 359–90.

Martin, R. (2010). 'Roepke lecture in economic geography – rethinking regional path dependence: beyond lock-in to evolution'. *Economic Geography* 86(1), 1–27.

Martin, R. (2012). '(Re)Placing path dependence: A response to the debate'. *International Journal of Urban and Regional Research* 36(1), 179–92.

Martin, R. and Sunley, P. (2006). 'Path dependence and regional economic evolution'. *Journal of Economic Geography* 6(4), 395–437.

Martin, R. and Sunley, P. (2015). 'Towards a developmental turn in evolutionary economic geography?' *Regional Studies* 49(5), 712–32.

Müller, D. K. and Jansson, B. (2007). 'The difficult business of making pleasure peripheries prosperous: Perspectives on space, place and environment'. In D. K. Müller and B. Jansson (eds) *Tourism in Peripheries: Perspectives from the Far North and South*. Wallingford, UK: CABI (pp. 3–18).

Nelson, R. R. and Winter, S. G. (1982). *An Evolutionary Theory of Economic Change*. Cambridge, MA: Harvard University Press.

Northern Territory Government. (2014). 'Major projects'. Department of the Chief Minister. [online] URL: www.dcm.nt.gov.au/territory_economy/major_projects (accessed on 16 July 2015).

Oosterlynck, S. (2012). 'Path dependence: A political economy perspective'. *International Journal of Urban and Regional Research* 36(1), 158–65.

Pforr, C. (2001). 'Tourism policy in Australia's Northern Territory: A policy process analysis of its tourism development masterplan'. *Current Issues in Tourism* 4(2–4), 275–307.

Sanz-Ibáñez, D. and Anton Clavé, S. (2014). 'The evolution of destinations: Towards an evolutionary and relational economic geography approach'. *Tourism Geographies* 16(4), 563–79.

Schmallegger, D. and Carson, D. B. (2010). 'Is tourism just another staple? A new perspective on tourism in remote regions'. *Current Issues in Tourism* 13(3), 201–21.

Taylor, A. and Carson, D. B. (2014). 'It's raining men in Darwin: Gendered effects from the construction of major oil and gas projects'. *Journal of Rural and Community Development* 9(1), 24–40.

TRA (Tourism Research Australia). (2013). National and International Visitor Survey data. Tourism Research Australia Student Online Database. www.tra.gov.au/tra-online.html (accessed on 26 July 2015).

Tremblay, P. and Wegner, A. (2009). *Indigenous/Aboriginal Tourism Research in Australia (2000–2008): Industry Lessons and Future Research Needs.* Gold Coast: Cooperative Research Centre for Sustainable Tourism. [online] URL: www.crctourism.com.au/wms/upload/Resources/110018%20Tremblay%20IndigenousAboriginalTRA%20WEB.pdf (accessed on 26 July 2015).

Watkins, M. H. (1963). 'A staple theory of economic growth'. *Canadian Journal of Economics and Political Science* 29(2), 141–58.

Wellstead, A. (2008). 'The (post) staples economy and the (post) staples state in historical perspective'. In M. Howlett and K. Brownsey (eds) *Canada's Resource Economy in Transition: The Past, Present, and Future of Canadian Staples Industries.* Toronto: Emond Montgomery Publications (pp. 19–37).

7 Knowledge transfer in the hotel industry and the 'de-locking' of Central and Eastern Europe

Piotr Niewiadomski

Introduction

Since Hjalager's (2002: 465) call for 'repairing innovation defectiveness in tourism', research on innovations in the tourism industry has gradually expanded in profile (Hall and Williams 2008; Williams and Shaw 2011). The same, although to a lesser extent, applies to knowledge transfer (KT) in tourism, which constitutes the key focus of this chapter and a critical component of what the topic of innovations encompasses. Important examples of the latter include the work of Cooper (2006) and Shaw and Williams (2009) who thereby give hope that the neglect of tourist firms in innovation studies deriving from the overall image of the industry as low-tech in nature (Hirsch-Kreinsen *et al.* 2006) is being steadily overcome.

However, despite acknowledging that KT processes in tourism are place dependent and that social relations as well as social systems and cultural contexts influence the effectiveness of KT (Pine 1992; Hjalager 2002; Brookes 2014), geographers have so far contributed little to this agenda. Given that the so-called spatial fixity of tourism supply (Urry 1990; Hall and Page 2006) and the simultaneity and co-presence of tourism production and consumption (Williams and Shaw 2011) are the most significant features of the tourism production system, this relative silence of geographers on the relations between various places and KT in tourism is surprising. While the influence of different characteristics of the host country on the recipient's absorptive capacity (i.e. ability to adopt and adapt new knowledge; Pine 1992; Cooper 2006; Jacob and Groizard 2007; Brookes 2014) has been well addressed in the management/business studies literature, the developmental implications of KT remain one of the most appealing gaps in research on tourism-related KT (see Jacob and Groizard 2007 for a noteworthy exception). Meanwhile, because this gap is spatial in nature, a geographical perspective might prove especially useful. As this chapter shows, particular potential could be attributed to the theoretical advancements popularized under the banner of evolutionary economic geography (EEG).

This chapter focuses on the expansion of international hotel groups into Central and Eastern Europe (CEE) following communism's collapse in 1989 and investigates the impact of the KT initiated by hotel corporations on the post-communist economic development. Given that, in contrast to the other sub-sectors of tourism, theories explaining KT in the hotel industry have been relatively well developed (Pine 1992; Orfila-Sintes *et al.* 2005; Jacob and Groizard 2007; Magnini 2008; Brookes 2014), the hotel industry constitutes an appropriate sectoral case through which the identified gap can be tackled. By the same token, because of the communist past and the current political, economic and institutional features, but also since the expansion of hotel groups into CEE is rather recent and its developmental impacts not yet fully accounted for, the various post-communist capitalisms of CEE (Swain and Hardy 1998) constitute interesting 'laboratories', where a combination of EEG and the theories developed within management and business studies can be tested.

The chapter's aim is twofold. Broadly, as is the purpose of the whole volume, the chapter argues that the assumptions of EEG are helpful in enhancing the general understanding of the tourism production system and its developmental impacts. In this respect, the chapter constitutes a constructive response to the numerous calls for bridging the gap between mainstream economic geography and tourism studies (Britton 1991; Ioannides 1995, 2006; Ioannides and Debbage 1998) and for applications of economic geography theories to research on tourism (Agarwal *et al.* 2000). Specifically, the chapter addresses the impact of international hotel groups on economic development in host countries, which is one of the most under-researched aspects of the globalization of the hotel industry (Niewiadomski 2014, 2015).

The chapter contends that the KT initiated by international hotel groups is one of the most critical categories of long-term impact that the international hotel industry has on economic upgrading in CEE. It demonstrates that, crucially for the CEE countries whose development is often constrained by communist legacies, the KT fostered by hotel groups functions as an important mechanism of 'de-locking', thus helping the CEE economies overcome post-communist path-dependence and develop in a more path-shaping manner. The chapter argues that the extent of such impact depends on the business model adopted by the group for a given hotel on the one hand and the specific features of the host economy on the other.

The data derive from extensive research carried out in Poland, Estonia and Bulgaria in 2009. The research process focused on all 23 international hotel groups from the world's top 50 (Gale 2008) that were present in CEE when the research commenced. The fieldwork generated 90 interviews:

- Twenty-four corporate interviews with development executives from 21 out of the 23 hotel groups;
- Fifty-six interviews carried out in CEE with senior managers at internationally branded hotels, hotel developers and owners, local hoteliers, hotel industry consultants, local authorities and hotel industry trade unions, all conducted in ten main tourist and business destinations in the three focal countries where access to interviewees was the easiest;
- Ten interviews with hoteliers in other CEE countries and with hotel consultants based outside CEE.

The remainder of this chapter consists of four sections. The following section reviews the existing literature on KT in tourism and the hotel sector. It explains why the assumptions of EEG are useful in addressing the identified research gap. In order to better set the scene, the third section describes the broader context in which the processes analysed in the empirical section take place. The status of the CEE hotel sector following the fall of communism is discussed and the applicability of the key concepts of EEG to the CEE context is justified. The penultimate section offers an empirical example. It is shown how the KT initiated by hotel groups manifests itself in different post-communist contexts and what developmental impacts it has on CEE destinations. The final section provides a brief summary and conclusions.

Technology and KT in tourism and the hotel industry

The literature on KT in services in general and in tourism and the hotel sector in particular is gradually growing (Jacob and Groizard 2007; Shaw and Williams 2009). The ideas related to KT, which originally developed with regard to other industries and have gradually found their way into research on the tourism industry revolve around three main, closely interrelated, topics (although this list is by no means exclusive and other categorizations are also possible):

– Types of knowledge and innovations,
– Types and vehicles of KT,
– Factors determining the effectiveness of KT.

This section briefly reviews these theoretical advancements in order to set the scene and to better explain where and how the assumptions of EEG can prove helpful in adding to the general understanding of KT in tourism.

First, knowledge is usually conceptualized as the company's most meaningful resource and important source of innovation and competitive advantage (Drucker 1991; Spender and Grant 1996; Hjalager 2002; Cooper 2006; Jacob and Groizard 2007; Shaw and Williams 2009). Indeed, generation and acquisition of new knowledge are critical tasks for firms looking for novel solutions to improve their market position. An innovation may pertain to products, production processes, management procedures but also various logistical solutions (Hjalager 2002; Orfila-Sintes *et al.* 2005). In this respect, firms are repositories of knowledge and sites of innovation (Amin and Cohendet 2004; Williams and Shaw 2011). The knowledge a firm possesses is residing in the firm's employees, technology, structure, routines and coordination processes (Argote and Darr 2000; Brookes 2014).

At the most general level, two kinds of knowledge can be distinguished: explicit and tacit (Nonaka 1991). Whilst explicit knowledge (i.e. know-that) is easily codified and articulated (for instance in such forms as databases, manuals or other documents) and is, therefore, relatively simple to imitate and transfer, tacit knowledge (i.e. know-how) pertains to habits and experiences and is harder to formalize and articulate, and hence harder to transfer between individuals and firms (Nonaka 1991; Cooper 2006; Magnini 2008; Shaw and Williams 2009). Thus, tacit knowledge is often considered a much more important source of competitive advantage than explicit knowledge (Jacob and Groizard 2007; Shaw and Williams 2009). Although this distinction is fully applicable to research on KT in tourism and the hotel industry (e.g. Cooper 2006; Jacob and Groizard 2007; Magnini 2008; Shaw and Williams 2009), this chapter relies on the typology offered by Enz *et al.* (2006) that is specifically tailored to the hotel sector and distinguishes three kinds of knowledge and intellectual capital that hotel firms possess:

- Systems capital (i.e. operational knowledge, including processes, policies and procedures);
- Human capital (i.e. knowledge, skills and experience possessed by employees);
- Customer capital (i.e. the value of a brand).

The first two categories are adopted in the penultimate section of this chapter as a framework for analysing the KT initiated by international hotel groups in CEE.

The second main topic pertains to KT itself. Knowledge transfer can be defined as a transmission of knowledge and technology from the transferor to the transferee such as from a franchisor to its franchisees or from a foreign firm to its local partners (Pine 1992). Rather than using the terms 'knowledge' and 'technology' together or interchangeably (e.g. Pine 1992; Jacob and Groizard 2007), this chapter adopts solely the term 'knowledge' to account both for equipment and technological solutions and methods, processes, procedures and policies. Not without relevance in KT research are also different types of KT. A useful categorization in relation to tourism has been provided by Williams and Shaw (2011), who distinguish between intra-sectoral, inter-sectoral and extra-workplaces types of KT. Although this typology has been elaborated with regard to the knowledge, which tourist firms seek to accumulate in the host market, it can also be applied to the knowledge, which expanding firms import to the host area.

Due attention should also be paid to different vehicles of KT. Inspired by the work of Kacker (1988) and Hjalager (2002), who distinguished between indirect conduits (e.g. observations, trade associations, conventions and human mobility) and direct conduits (e.g. those initiated through foreign direct investment, FDI; joint ventures; and contractual arrangements such as franchising and management contracts), Shaw and Williams (2009) focused on human mobility and different kinds of networks, including learning regions, communities of practice and FDI. Indeed, the role of FDI in diffusing professional knowledge in host areas, based on the assumption that internationalizing companies have superior knowledge over local firms (Shaw and Williams 2009; Williams and Shaw 2011), has long been recognized (Dunning and Norman 1983, 1987). 'Host firms . . . benefit from multinational companies (MNC) through imitation, competition effects, human capital mobility and vertical linkages' (Jacob and Groizard 2007: 976).

As Jacob and Groizard (2007) and Pine (1992) observed, the same important argument applies to the hotel sector. However, because the hotel industry relies mainly upon external sources of capital and since FDI is no longer a dominant mode of expansion in the sector (Go and Pine 1995; Contractor and Kundu 2000;

Endo 2006; Niewiadomski 2014), to better understand KT in the hotel sector it is necessary to acknowledge a variety of business models that hotel firms adopt (Table 7.1). Thus, various formal and less formal networking arrangements such as franchising, leasing or management agreements can be considered more significant vehicles of KT in the hotel industry than FDI. Indeed, it is mainly to gain access to external pools of knowledge, technology and expertise (and thus gain competitive advantage) that independently owned and operated hotels, which are usually classed as small and medium enterprises (SMEs), seek an affiliation in larger structures such as international hotel groups or consortia. As Hjalager (2002: 469) observed,

> constellations in collaborative structures can help SMEs overcome some of the innovation handicap, since the chain or franchise head office will be responsible for the screening and processing of vast amounts of information into something that member enterprises can use.

This argument is further supported by Brookes (2014), who analysed KT in master franchise agreements in the hotel industry, and by Magnini (2008), who enquired into the nature of knowledge sharing in hotel joint ventures. As shown by Pine (1992) and Cieslik (1983), the nature and effectiveness of KT differs widely between various business models. Indeed, as argued further in this chapter, the developmental implications of the KT initiated by hotel groups in CEE largely hinge upon the business model preferred by a given group.

Another important vehicle of KT is human mobility. Given that labour mobility and turnover are usually very high in the tourism industry and that tacit knowledge, which is highly personalized and embedded in the individual, is of particular importance in tourist services, this mechanism of KT often plays a key role in the tourism industry (Shaw and Williams 2009; Williams and Shaw 2011). At the same time, labour mobility may be also realized through migrations, both within firms (e.g. intra-firm transfers of managers such as those in hotel franchise and management contracts – see Magnini 2008; Brookes 2014) and between them (Shaw and Williams 2009). Despite that, it is essential to recognize that the key characteristics of the tourism industry such as high labour turnover (seasonality of work and a high proportion of casual and short-term jobs), low wages, non-standard working conditions, limited availability of professional training and scarce career opportunities, all of which result in relatively low levels of commitment to this career path and low levels of staff retention at the firm level, explain why the role of people as repositories of knowledge in tourism should not always be taken for granted (Hjalager 2002).

Finally, the third topic permeating the management/business studies literature concerns the factors determining the effectiveness of KT. Three groups of factors can be distinguished: sector-specific, firm-specific and place-specific. The pivotal sector-specific factors are those that reflect the overall nature of tourist services such as the co-terminality and co-presence of production and consumption, the intangible contents of products and processes, and the role of human resources

Table 7.1 Main business models of international hotel groups.

Business model	Features	Examples
Operator owning	– When the hotel is both owned and operated by a hotel group – The only form of hotel industry FDI – A high-commitment model with very high risk – The slowest mode of expansion	– Accor and some Spanish hotel groups such as Sol Meliã still own some real estate – mainly in their home markets
Managing	– When the hotel owner employs a hotel group to operate the business on the owner's behalf for a fee – A medium-commitment model with moderate risk – Currently one of the most popular business models in the hotel sector	– Many groups such as Four Seasons or Hyatt exclusively focus on management – For groups such as Starwood or Hilton, it is a dominant model
Joint-venture	– When the hotel operator co-owns the real estate with the hotel owner – A mixture of the two models described above – Just like operator owned, it is less and less popular	– Such a model is usually adopted on an individual basis depending on a given hotel project (usually by those groups that own some real estate)
Leasing	– When a hotel group rents the property from the owner to operate the business independently and pays the owner a rent – A high-commitment model with relatively high risk – A relatively quick mode of expansion	– Despite the risk, it is one of the main models of expansion for, e.g. Accor, NH Hoteles and Rezidor
Franchising	– When the hotel owner and/or operator employs a hotel group to flag the hotel for a fee – A low-commitment model with low risk – Currently the quickest and most popular mode of expansion in the hotel sector	– Some groups such as Choice and Wyndham are purely franchise firms – For groups such as Marriott, Hilton and, especially, InterContinental, it is a dominant mode of expansion
Hotel consortia	– When the hotel joins an affiliation of independent hotels to jointly conduct marketing activities – The range of services offered by consortia is similar to that of franchisors	– Best Western is the most prominent example here, although hotel consortia are normally not included in the ranking of hotel groups

Source: Author's elaboration on the basis of Athiyaman and Go (2003), Cunill (2006), Go and Pine (1995), León-Darder *et al.* (2011), Littlejohn (2003) and Niewiadomski (2013, 2014).

Note: FDI, foreign direct investment.

(Sirilli and Evangelista 1998; Jacob and Groizard 2007). Moreover, the tourism industry is still dominated by SMEs (e.g. single hotels) whose capacity to develop innovations is considerably smaller than that of transnational corporations (TNCs) (Hjalager 2002). This, in turn, explains why many hotels seek membership in larger structures and why – especially in emerging markets such as CEE – there is scope for expansion for international hotel groups. Also, because of the relatively transparent nature of tourist services, novel ideas in tourism (such as sophisticated holiday packages offered by travel agents or innovative and modern facilities at hotels) cannot be protected to the same extent as, for example, high-tech solutions in manufacturing, which are often patented and used behind closed doors (Hjalager 2002). According to Cooper (2006), one of the barriers to an effective implementation of knowledge-management systems in tourism (especially in SMEs) is also high cost. However, given that the tourism industry has a composite nature (Smith 1998) and that knowledge-management activities in each sub-sector may be organized in a different way (Williams and Shaw 2011), it is also essential to consider the hotel sector separately. As Orfila-Sintes *et al.* (2005) point out, the most important factors in the hotel industry include the differentiation of hotels in terms of standard, the organization of hotel firms as chains and the variety of business models evident in the industry (as discussed previously).

Orfila-Sintes *et al.* (2005) list various firm-specific characteristics that shape innovativeness in the hotel industry. Amongst them are the existence of technologies, departments and managers employed to support innovation-generating activities, the size and class of the hotel and the intensity of forward linkages developed by the hotel in the market. In addition, Jacob and Groizard (2007) point to the amount of training offered by the firm to its staff, the cultural distance between partners and the level of dissimilarity between their business practices (see also Simonin 1999). Finally, it is essential to acknowledge that where these factors are at work the most is in determining the company's absorptive capacity (Cohen and Levinthal 1990; Brookes 2014).

In contrast to the previous two, the most important group of factors from geography's perspective, those that are place-specific, has received limited attention in the literature. Meanwhile, place-specific factors both determine the firm's access to external pools of knowledge and mould its absorptive capacity. The most critical place-specific factors are the economic status of the region in which the firm is embedded (Pine 1992) and its so-called global connectivity, both of which translate into the firm's ability to attract and domesticate global flows (Williams and Shaw 2011). The absorptive capacity of the tourist firm depends also on the cultural, social and institutional context from which the firm derives (Hjalager 2002). Pine (1992) has analysed the influence of place-specific factors on the absorptive capacity of local hotels, focusing on the provision of vocational education in hospitality, the ability of local people to benefit from this education and the existence of an appropriate attitude and mental set that helps locals to accept change (see Stewart and Nihei 1987). As Pine (1992: 4) noted, attitudes and values of the host community may inhibit effective KT and therefore 'the . . . transfer process must . . . allow for accommodation of such attitudes and values or provide the means through which they can be developed or modified'. However, as he also noted, attitudinal change is usually difficult to achieve.

Unfortunately, research on relations between the host territory and the KT processes initiated by expanding tourist firms very rarely goes beyond the influence of place-specific factors on the absorptive capacity of local firms. Despite the fact that, 'multinational hotel chains' innovative activities in low and middle income countries have a high potential for promoting domestic development' (Jacob and Groizard 2007: 986, see also Pine 1992), the impact of KT on host territories remains a lacuna in research on KT in tourism. Meanwhile, KT has long been recognized in economic geography as a key category of impact that expanding TNCs may have on the host territory (Dicken 2011). Therefore, an economic–geographical perspective could prove helpful in addressing this gap, thus adding to the general understanding of KT in tourism and solidifying the contribution of economic geographers to tourism research. In this respect, this chapter makes the case for EEG as an effective platform from which the identified gap can be tackled.

As Brouder (2014: 2) contends, 'EEG has emerged in the last decade as a powerful explanatory paradigm and has led to an improved understanding of long-term economic change and why it differs between regions' (see also Boschma and Frenken 2006; Boschma and Martin 2007, 2010). In essence, EEG draws from evolutionary economics (Witt 2003, 2006) in order to address one of the most under-theorized topics in economic geography – how the economic landscape (i.e. the spatial organization of production, distribution and consumption) evolves and is transformed over time and what the role of history is in this set of processes. In other words, EEG is concerned with four main sub-topics (Boschma and Martin 2007, 2010):

- The spatialities of economic novelty;
- The emergence of the spatial structures of the economy;
- The processes of self-organization of the economic landscape;
- The role of the processes of path dependence and path creation in shaping geographies of economic development and transformation.

EEG considers the economy as dynamic and subject to continuous change and the processes of economic evolution as historically influenced, place-dependent and irreversible (Martin and Sunley 2006; Boschma and Martin 2007, 2010).

Crucially for this chapter it is vital to recognize that EEG is concerned with novelty, its generation and its role in economic development and the creative capacity of economic agents such as firms, institutions and individuals (Boschma and Martin 2007, 2010). Indeed, the importance of knowledge and innovation in fostering economic growth and transforming the economic landscape lies at the heart of EEG. As Boschma and Martin (2007, 2010) argue, just like the economic landscape is the product of knowledge, the landscape's evolution is shaped by changes in knowledge, which never stands still but is continuously re-developed. Special attention is paid here to networks of agents, the knowledge such networks generate and the role this knowledge plays in driving the evolution of the economic landscape (Boschma and Martin 2010). It is for this reason that the assumptions of EEG can complement business and management theories in explaining the influence of KT on host economies.

The most important concepts of EEG are path dependence, lock-in and path creation. Thus, regarding the notion of path dependence, Martin and Sunley (2006) explain that the outcomes of a path-dependent process are always a consequence of its history. In this respect, future outcomes will always depend upon past events and the state of the economy at a given point in time will always be determined by the trajectory that the economy has been following to date (Martin and Sunley 2006).

The idea of path dependence is inevitably connected to the notion of lock-in, which denotes a state in which a system (e.g. a region) becomes committed to a particular technology, industry or an institutional context to the extent that it finds it difficult to alter its path of growth and stop reproducing itself over time (Setterfield 1997; Martin 2006; Martin and Sunley 2006; MacKinnon 2012). Thus, the term 'lock-in' relates to 'how regions can become "locked-in" to existing paths of development as the weight of inherited investments, practices and skills inhibits their capacity to adapt to wider processes of economic change' (MacKinnon 2012: 233, see also Grabher 1993).

The literature, however, lacks consent as to whether a state of lock-in can only be overcome by external forces or whether endogenous change is also possible (Martin and Sunley 2006). A discussion of different mechanisms of 'de-locking' is, therefore, especially important here. As Martin and Sunley (2006) indicate, amongst these mechanisms are the creation of a new endogenous development path, the upgrading and/or diversification of existing industries and, crucially for this chapter, the transplantation of new technologies from elsewhere, for instance by means of exposing regions to external networks and the extra-regional sources of innovation, expertise and investment, which such networks might provide access to (Bathelt *et al.* 2004; Coe *et al.* 2004; MacKinnon 2012). As Martin and Sunley (2006: 423) observe,

> new knowledge brought into a region by the inward transplantation of firms from elsewhere (through FDI or takeover or merger) may be critical in initiating a new technological or industrial path locally, though this will depend on the absorptive capabilities . . . of the existing industrial base.

A link between EEG and the role of networks in KT on the one hand and the absorptive capacity of local people on the other is, therefore, evident.

Finally, the idea of path creation suggests that actors may always reproduce, deviate from and transform existing socio-economic structures, practices and trajectories of growth or, to put it more simply, that new paths of development are also possible (Martin and Sunley 2006). As Coe (2010) and Martin and Sunley (2006) point out, the mechanisms that underpin path dependence, lead to lock-in and make path creation possible are locally contingent and, therefore, inevitably place dependent.

Most importantly for this chapter, an EEG perspective also proves useful in research on networks and KT in tourism. As Brouder (2014) and Brouder and Eriksson (2013) argue, the nature of KT in tourism networks and its ability to serve as an important mechanism of change is a significant gap in research on the tourism production system. The work of Larsson and Lindström (2014), who exposed the difficulties in knowledge transference from non-tourism sectors to tourism, and Halkier (2014), who stressed the importance of extra-regional and extra-sectoral sources of knowledge in overcoming path dependence, have paved the way for further research on KT in tourism and its role as a mechanism of de-locking.

By adopting an EEG approach to examine the influence of KT in the hotel sector on the post-communist restructuring in CEE, the rest of this chapter aims to contribute to this emerging agenda and thus to solidify the applicability of EEG to research on tourism and its economic impacts. In this respect, the chapter builds upon Brouder's (2014: 6) argument that 'evolutionary approaches to tourism research will not only enhance the theoretical development of tourism studies, but also strengthen the relevance of EEG by testing it in a very different context' – the context of low-tech services, which are still largely neglected in the EEG-related literature. The following section discusses the broader context in which the investigated processes take place and explains why the main assumptions of EEG are of relevance to the post-communist environments of CEE.

Post-communist transformations and the hotel industry in CEE

The post-Second World War reorientation of many CEE countries to socialism resulted in the profound institutional reorganization of their hotel industries and the transfer of existing hotels to the control of various state institutions (Johnson 1997; Błądek and Tulibacki 2003; Witkowski 2003; Johnson and Vanetti 2004). Due to the persisting lack of funds deriving from the communist governments' ideological preoccupation with the development of heavy industries (as opposed to services), the CEE hotel sector quickly found itself lagging behind its Western counterpart in terms of the number of hotels and their condition, the range of extra facilities, the quality of hotel services and the skills and knowledge of hotel cadres (Scott and Renaghan 1991; Hall 1992; Mitka-Karandziej 1993; Shcherbakova 2002; Williams and Balaž 2002; Błądek and Tulibacki 2003; Witkowski 2003; Johnson and Vanetti 2004). Most importantly, cut off from the global economy because of the political divide between CEE and the West, the CEE hotel sector was also cordoned off from the international flows of capital and people, not to mention the innovations that these flows might have brought (Buckley and Witt 1990; Johnson and Vanetti 2004).

The situation started changing in the late 1970s. As a result of the growing political openness of some countries (notably Hungary and Poland) and the increasing recognition of tourism as a hard-currency earner, the regulations pertaining to the hotel sector were gradually relaxed. The first franchise contracts with foreign hotel groups (mainly SIEH Novotel and InterContinental) were quickly followed by the first hotel joint ventures with foreign investors (Buckley and Witt 1990; Franck 1990; Medlik 1990; Jaakson 1996; Johnson 1997; Błądek and Tulibacki 2003; Witkowski 2003). Although foreign parties' participation was limited to 49 per cent and local (rather than foreign) management was enforced, it was argued that international partners would import much needed capital and Western expertise (Medlik 1990; Jaakson 1996; Johnson 1997; Błądek and Tulibacki 2003; Witkowski 2003). Unfortunately, due to the lack of proper management agreements with international hotel groups, the implemented changes, although significant, were still not in a position to satisfy the needs of the CEE hotel sector (Buckley and Witt 1990; Franck 1990).

In 1989 the CEE states defied communism and embarked on the ambitious endeavour of economic and political transition to capitalism and liberal democracy (Smith 1997; Sokol 2001). The road to capitalism was to be based on four pillars: stabilization, liberalization, internationalization and privatization (Smith and Pickles 1998; Sokol 2001; Bradshaw and Stenning 2004). The disintegration of the Council for Mutual Economic Assistance (CMEA) was meant to open the region to import competition, foster the development of competitive export industries and allow foreign companies to invest in CEE (Bradshaw and Swain 2004). Given that it quickly appeared to be 'beyond the capabilities of CEE simultaneously to implement far-reaching economic reforms and to finance the necessary investment' (Franck 1990: 335), great hopes were pinned on FDI and the expected influx of foreign firms (Pavlinek 2004). It was assumed that large inflows of capital from abroad would generate industrial restructuring, create jobs, foster productivity, facilitate access to international distribution networks and, most importantly for this discussion, implement modern production and management strategies, and provide access to the newest technology, knowledge and staff training (Pavlinek 2004). Similar arguments were put forward in relation to tourism and the hotel sector, albeit to a lesser extent (Franck 1990; Johnson and Vanetti 2004).

The openness to foreign firms, the prospects of strong economic growth, an increasing degree of macroeconomic stability, ambitious investment policies aimed at attracting foreign investors, and a cheap and educated labour force (Johnson and Iunius 1999; Healey 1994) seemed to offer unprecedented growth opportunities to international hotel groups. Unfortunately, because of various communist legacies, the reality proved to be different. Alongside the persisting low level of political and economic stability, the expansion of international hotel groups into CEE was hampered by bureaucracy and corruption, fiscal disorder, confusion over property rights, the poor condition of physical infrastructure, labour skill shortages and the lack of service culture (Scott and Renaghan 1991; Healey 1994; Williams and Balaž 2000; Błądek and Tulibacki 2003). The dearth of local capital and the lack of business culture of risk-taking and wealth ownership (Lockwood 1993; Healy 1994), which translated into the low number of local investments, determined the shortage of opportunities for international hotel operators and franchisors even further. Thus, communist legacies proved to be serious inhibitors to the development of the hotel sector and the adoption and assimilation of innovations, which, if properly imported, might have hastened this development. Although the expansion of international hotel groups into CEE gradually progressed and the number of international hotels increased over the years from a handful in the 1980s to over 500 in 2010 (Niewiadomski 2013), the CEE hotel sector found itself to a large extent locked into the post-communist path-dependence. Nowadays, many of the factors that relate back to communism continue to impact on the development of the CEE hotel sector (Niewiadomski 2013).

As the above discussion implies, the main assumptions of EEG can play a critical role in explaining the post-communist development of the tourism industry in CEE after 1989. Research by Williams and Balaž (2000, 2002) on the path-dependent/path-shaping growth of the tourism sector in the Czech Republic and Slovakia further attests to this assertion. By means of investigating the extent to which the KT initiated by hotel groups influences the post-communist development of the CEE hotel sector, this chapter solidifies the applicability of EEG to tourism studies, thus laying the foundations for further research on the role of networks and KT in tourism as important mechanisms of de-locking.

International hotel groups and KT in CEE

Alongside investing capital, upgrading infrastructure, creating employment and forging local linkages, KT has long been recognized as one of the most important categories of influence that expanding TNCs have on regional development in host countries (Dicken 2011). Its importance in fostering economic upgrading is clearly evident in CEE, where, since the beginning of post-communist transformations, bridging the technology gap between CEE and the West has been one of the highest priorities for the region's national governments. As the example of the hotel industry discussed below demonstrates, although not critical, the role of the tourism industry and its sub-sectors is highly significant in helping the CEE economies overcome the lingering impact of their communist heritage. Indeed, mainly because it is intertwined with other categories of impact, the KT initiated by international hotel groups in CEE plays an important role in de-locking the CEE hotel sector from the post-communist path-dependence. Based on the typology provided by Enz *et al.* (2006), this section discusses two categories of hotel-industry-specific knowledge – systems capital and human capital – and analyses how, depending on the hotel group's business model, they are transferred both at the property development stage and at the operational stage (i.e. once the hotel is open). Spillovers of both kinds of knowledge extending beyond the individual property are also discussed.

From the perspective of expanding hotel groups, the KT, which they foster in the new market, is determined by what is termed 'a confrontation element'; whenever an international hotel group expands into a new market, the standards it wants to implement to successfully launch its operations are confronted with what the host environment can provide. All potential gaps are normally identified through market research and feasibility studies carried out prior to the property development (in the case of hotel groups that invest themselves) or prior to signing a contract with the hotel owner (in the case of franchisors and operators) and then regularly verified by the management at the operational stage. In general, to ensure that the desired service standards can be offered, expanding hotel groups face the challenge of filling these gaps. While in some cases such gaps may discourage the group from expanding (not to mention that the knowledge gap between expanding firms and host firms may affect the absorptive capacity of host firms, thus seriously inhibiting the effectiveness of KT; Glass and Saggi 2002; Jacob and Groizard 2007), usually it is a part of the deal, which the hotel group expects to pay off in the longer term and which is therefore worth the extra effort. In the last two decades this has often been the case in CEE – a promising new market, which because of the communist heritage has had little to offer to expanding firms in terms of knowledge. As a hotel sector consultant from an international consulting firm put it:

> Hotel groups may be very sceptical when it comes to entering a new market in CEE because they know that the workload will be massive and that the expectations will be extremely high. It's not just about opening a new hotel, but compared to if they were to open their 10th or 20th or 30th hotel in Paris, London, Berlin or wherever, it means building up not only the first hotel belonging to their own family of brands, but it might mean opening up the first ever hotel of an international brand in the location. So yes, this means know-how transfer, this means building up structures. This is pioneer work and pioneer work means much more effort.
>
> (Interviewee, October 2009)

Systems capital

'Systems capital', defined by Enz *et al.* (2006) as the firm's operational knowledge, is used here to also include modern technologies, which international hotel groups rely on heavily (Mitka-Karandziej 1993). Indeed, even stylish hotels located in historic buildings are often a symbol of modernity in terms of their contents. The transfer of technical innovations, which expanding hotel groups initiate, begins as early as the property-development stage. Even if the group does not invest in the property directly, its input in the hotel project starts at the very moment it joins forces with the investor. Thus, based on their international experience, hotel franchisors and operators force investors and developers to maintain appropriate construction standards and advise on what facilities to include and in what way to organize them to develop a competitive product (Niewiadomski 2015). This may include modern spa facilities, fully equipped conference rooms and various services offered in guest rooms (e.g. wireless Internet and play stations) that are not always found in private households. This transfer of technological knowledge is inextricably linked to the hotel sector's influence on infrastructure upgrading; a category of impact, which, because of the obsolete condition of hotels inherited from the communist past, is of particular importance to the CEE states (Niewiadomski 2015).

Indeed, the role of hotels in these processes was recognized in the 1990s by the European Bank for Reconstruction and Development, which noted that 'the lack of modern hotels and commercial facilities [in CEE] is constraining the development of the private sector' (EBRD 1994: 27). In line with the influence observed at the stage of property development is the provision of specific software and other IT technologies that may give the hotel an important competitive advantage at the operational stage. The technology, which international hotel groups import to CEE (either directly or by means of passing it to developers) may include:

- Modern solutions pertaining to the construction process;
- Effective ways of designing, selecting, constructing and arranging facilities, depending on the construction budget, class of the hotel, targeted clientele, size of the plot, location of the hotel within the city and the overall nature of the destination;
- Hotel-specific software that can be used either at the property level or by the whole chain, where hotels of the same brand can store and exchange operating knowledge and through which they can communicate;
- Links to worldwide reservation systems such as GDS (global distribution systems) which are of significance in connecting the formerly closed CEE market to worldwide distribution networks, including travel agents, airlines, car-rental firms and other hotels.

However, while the role of international hotel groups in importing the aforementioned types of modern technology is often significant, it should be simultaneously acknowledged that such technology can be acquired independently of management or franchise packages. Also, as long as local hotels can afford it (which because of the shortage of local capital is still rarely the case in CEE), it can lead to similar development without international hotel groups' involvement. Conversely, operating knowledge, which to a large extent has a tacit nature, is far harder to acquire without appropriate guidance (Niewiadomski 2015). Although some elements of this knowledge can be made available to the staff in the form of handbooks and manuals, a significant proportion of it has a know-how nature (rather than know-that) and is impossible for local workers to adopt and adapt without liaising with experienced managers from more advanced service environments. It is mainly this category of hotel industry-specific knowledge that, owing to the lack of service culture under communism, the CEE market is largely short of and which is needed by the CEE tourism sector to break away from the post-communist path-dependence. Indeed, given that many hotel groups have extensive networks of hotels across the world and their knowledge has been tested in many economic, political and socio-cultural contexts, the knowledge they import to CEE can be expected to be far more efficient for the CEE tourism industry than that rooted in the communist heritage. It is mainly for this reason that the know-how imported to CEE by international operators and franchisors is for local hotel owners the most desired asset in developing competitive advantage in the market. As a hotel industry consultant from an international consulting company confirmed:

> If you have a hotel that was established in the communist regime and the management and structure and staff haven't changed significantly since then, then people will not be used to providing a service in a way that makes that hotel competitive against its peers, whereas as soon as you get an international operator they are more attuned to that. That's the way they're thinking now. They want to be better than the hotel down the road. So it is a cultural change and it will happen.
>
> (Interviewee, October 2009)

Although it is difficult to divide the operating knowledge of hotel groups into clear-cut sub-categories, the following list summarizes the categories mentioned by the interviewees during the research process:

- Management techniques, including:
    - General management and the organization of the hotel's daily routines (e.g. dividing the hotel into departments and distributing the responsibilities between them, building a management hierarchy and organizing the system of work);
    - Human resource management (e.g. effective ways of recruiting and training new staff, setting up clear and transparent procedures pertaining to, for example, submitting holiday requests or airing grievances, developing a system of incentivizing staff and providing other benefits such as pension schemes, life insurance or discounted health services);
    - Public relations issues (e.g. developing and maintaining appropriate relations with local authorities, important tourist bodies in the area and the press).
- Sales and marketing techniques (e.g. building and maintaining networks of sales partners, implementing effective pricing systems, elaborating and conducting effective promotional campaigns and maintaining suitable relations with regular clients – especially corporate customers);
- Rules underlying the organization of work that aim to create an optimal work environment and increase employees' efficiency (e.g. health and safety regulations, fire regulations);
- Customer service standards which are well developed in the West but which are one of the most serious downsides of the CEE hotel sector (see for instance Karhunen 2008 for an analysis of the hotel sector in St. Petersburg, Russia).

While hotel operators (regardless of whether they own the real estate or not) transfer all the above kinds of knowledge to CEE, hotel franchisors and consortia, which by the very nature of these business models stay away from operating issues, normally focus only on knowledge related to marketing, sales and brand standards (including customer service standards). Only very rarely (although more often in less advanced service environments such as CEE) do they also get involved in human resource management.

Human capital

According to the typology provided by Enz *et al.* (2006), 'human capital' consists of knowledge, skills and experience possessed by hotel staff and, therefore, it exclusively relates to the operational stage. Although distinguished here as a separate category of hotel-specific knowledge, human capital is closely intertwined with systems capital (especially operating knowledge) as the value of human capital is largely reflective of the extent to which the hotel staff adopt and utilize the operating knowledge passed to them by the hotel group. However, the knowledge which hotel groups require their employees to have may be of two different kinds. The first category encompasses general knowledge of services and the hotel sector (e.g. basic customer service rules), which, at least to some degree, should be available through formal education in a given country and which hotel staff should possess regardless of international hotel groups' input (Stewart and Nihei 1987; Pine 1992). The second category comprises firm-specific knowledge such as company philosophy and operating knowledge, which differ between hotel groups and which therefore have to be taught regardless of where the group expands into. As a development executive from an international hotel group active in CEE explained:

> Wherever you go, even in the most developed country, you will have to provide training – sometimes more, sometimes less. . . . It depends very much also on the situation, it depends where you open the hotel and when you open the hotel. But you will always have to explain to the staff your standards, your rules and regulations and that obviously includes training.
>
> (Interviewee, March 2009)

Thus, it is the gaps in the first category that determine the effort, which expanding hotel groups must invest in staff training to maintain the required levels of service. As Pine (1992) observed, such gaps are especially broad in less-developed markets where the system of education in hospitality is of relatively low quality. Owing to the lack of service culture in communism and the neglect of education in services in general and hospitality in particular, the same can be said about CEE (Buckley and Witt 1990; Scott and Renaghan 1991; Bell 1992; Błądek and Tulibacki 2003). For this reason the training provided by international hotel groups to local people in CEE is a critical category of KT, which the hotel sector initiates in CEE and which can be therefore expected to be a very important mechanism of de-locking the CEE tourism sector from the post-communist path-dependence. Its significance for the CEE region was captured well by a development executive from one of the biggest hotel groups in the world that is also present in CEE:

> If a local person works for an international company they have the opportunity to liaise with the organization . . . which gives them a very powerful

incentive. [Our hotel group] is a machine. We have [a few thousand] hotels around the world so we have certain standard operating procedures and ways of doing things and when you are trained and taught in those procedures and those ways you become a better business person and do things the way they're done by an international company. These are then transferable to whatever you may do in your life, whether you stay with the hotel business or you do something else on your own. You're learning proven ways of doing things. . . . And also you're being incentivized to look for better ways of doing things or to improve things.

(Interviewee, January 2009)

In practice, each hotel group, or each chain within the group, has a separate training system wherein the company philosophy and operating standards are taught. In order to secure a high level of consistency in terms of standards, every member of staff (regardless of the position) is exposed to professional training to the same degree (Niewiadomski 2015). Although the focus is always on the group's standards, in less-advanced service environments such as CEE this type of training also necessarily covers selected areas of general hotel sector-related knowledge. Thus, international hotel groups that expand into CEE also offer their staff different additional courses such as in management, sales and marketing or foreign languages. The idea of cross-training (i.e. when employees from one hotel department are trained in responsibilities of staff from other departments) also proves useful to the staff whose general hotel knowledge may not always be as extensive as desired. Crucially, given that training provided by hotel groups may have many forms (e.g. theoretical classes, manuals distributed amongst the employees, practical training), it enables the transfer of both explicit and tacit knowledge. Finally, many hotel groups also have special departments at the HQ level referred to as 'academies' or 'universities', which provide high-level courses for the most talented employees, whose personal development can benefit the company in the future (Niewiadomski 2015). Thus, Accor has the Académie Accor, Scandic has the Scandic Business School and Golden Tulip has the Golden Tulip Academy. Due to the shortage of quality hotel schools in CEE the opportunity to be trained at such academies is particularly precious for talented workers in CEE who are willing to pursue a career in hospitality. Given that professional training in tourism and hospitality is too expensive for local governments and tourism-related institutions in CEE (such as tourist chambers or convention bureaux) to organize or subsidize in order to foster development of hotel cadres in the location, this kind of input from international hotel groups is a valuable means of helping the tourism sector in the CEE region overcome its communist heritage.

Despite that, some representatives of the CEE hotel industry indicate that the KT initiated by international hotel groups in CEE also has certain negative aspects. For instance, since hotel groups tend to rely on strictly predefined procedures, there is a risk that local service habits are not paid enough attention by international hotel operators and franchisors who normally seek to maintain a uniform level of service across the chain. Assuming that even the best standards cannot be applied to the same degree all over the world, some CEE hoteliers who cooperate with international hotel corporations stress that too high a level of standardization may hamper individual initiatives and independent thinking (Niewiadomski 2015). As Pine (1992) contends, careless attempts to change the cultural norms and traditional behaviour patterns of local workers in order to tailor them to the expectations of foreign firms may often encounter resistance. Hence, careful consideration of the local context and sympathetic administration of professional training are required if KT is to prove effective (Pine 1992; Jacob and Groizard 2007). However, whether in the case of CEE such clashes originate from cultural differences or, for instance, from low levels of absorptive capacity requires further in-depth research.

As in the case of systems capital, the impact that the KT associated with professional training has on the CEE hotel sector is highest in the case of hotel operators (again, regardless of whether they own the real estate or not). However, although the training provided by hotel franchisors rarely encompasses general hotel knowledge and management skills, their role in transferring valuable knowledge to CEE, mainly in the field of customer service standards, marketing and sales, should not be downplayed. The same, however, does not apply to hotel consortia, which usually remain in the background and, apart from linking their member hotels to worldwide systems of sales and distribution, rarely offer any training to their affiliates.

Spillovers of knowledge beyond the individual property

Since the tourism industry is based on the cooperation of firms representing many different sub-sectors (Williams and Shaw 2011) and it is easy to observe what competitors are doing (Hjalager 2002), the KT initiated by international hotel groups is rarely confined to the hotels operated by hotel groups. Instead, such KT also often applies to local hotels, local institutions, various partner firms and other sectors of the economy. The CEE region is a very good example here.

First, because of the high labour turnover in the hotel sector, the knowledge imported to CEE by international hotel groups inevitably spills out to local hotels. Its role as a key mechanism of de-locking the CEE hotel sector from the post-communist path-dependence is thus significant. As a general manager from an international hotel in Lodz (Poland) observed:

> The advantage of international hotel groups is that they systematize work and implement good habits. Therefore, all people who have ever worked for international brands can transfer these habits to other, non-branded, hotels. If one takes a look at local hotels, they very often do not have appropriate procedures or standards elaborated and set up. They only constantly create them as they go along. . . . But when they employ someone who previously worked for an international hotel, they can be sure that these employees will draw examples from well-verified systems . . . and will look to introduce similar solutions to those local hotels.
>
> (Interviewee, August 2009)

This sort of impact was particularly evident in the early 1990s, shortly after the onset of post-communist transformations. As a hotel sector consultant from an international consulting company active in Poland commented on the first international hotel opened in the country after 1989:

> We must have somewhere to draw good examples from and fortunately there are already a few sources of those [in Poland]. It's just like the Marriott in Warsaw that opened in 1989. All the people who worked there and were trained there are now scattered across the country and work now as general managers at other hotels in Warsaw and elsewhere. It's because they got this know-how from an international operator.
>
> (Interviewee, May 2009)

Second, the knowledge of hotel groups also spills out to local suppliers of goods and services who 'are subjected to a level of quality control and management expertise which may trigger them to improve or expand their own business' (Pine 1992: 10). Indeed, apart from forging local linkages – one of the crucial categories of impact which foreign firms have on economic development in the host country (Hardy 1998; Pavlinek 2004; Dicken 2011) – international hotel groups are also instigators of qualitative changes. As important corporate clients, hotel groups constantly force supplier firms to improve the quality of their products and motivate them to extend the range of services (e.g. to include just-in-time deliveries), thus stimulating competition in the market and helping local firms to adopt the newest standards. This mainly pertains to upscale/luxury hotels whose requirements are normally stringent. As a result, what the market can guarantee becomes to some extent a function of what hotels need to buy. This may include things like local produce and meat on the one hand or building materials on the other. The CEE market where, since the fall of communism, local businesses have been mushrooming is undoubtedly a good example.

Third, amongst the most important beneficiaries of the knowledge imported to CEE by hotel groups are also local authorities. For instance, expatriate managers working for international hotels tend to be asked by local governments to act as international tourism and hotel industry experts. Indeed, their professional knowledge and international experience often prove useful in elaborating tourism strategies and city promotion and destination management activities (Niewiadomski 2015). Some Polish cities, but also Tallinn (Estonia), where hoteliers meet with local authorities on a more or less regular basis, can serve as good examples (interviews with representatives of the hotel sector in Warsaw and Tallinn, May to June 2009). Given that hotel groups (like all TNCs) also try to lobby local and national governments, for example, in the field of taxation and labour law, their expertise may be helpful in establishing new legislation. Finally, international customer service standards and corporate culture, which hotel groups import to CEE, are also acquired by the families and friends of hotel staff who transfer them further to other sectors (Fosfuri *et al.* 2001; Niewiadomski 2015) – something that in the CEE context is also an important de-locking mechanism.

Summary and conclusions

The KT fostered in CEE by expanding hotel groups is a vital mechanism of de-locking the CEE tourism industry from its post-communist path-dependence. Indeed, because of the fact that local hotels in CEE lack the resources to generate appropriate knowledge internally or to easily and cheaply obtain it from elsewhere without the international hotel industry's involvement, international hotel groups can be a valuable source of novelty for the CEE tourism sector and the CEE economies in general. Given that since the collapse of communism Western knowledge has been accorded an important role in stimulating economic development in CEE, the KT initiated by international hotel groups in CEE is one of the crucial categories of long-term impact which the international hotel sector has on the post-communist restructuring in CEE.

It has been also shown that the KT fostered by hotel groups in CEE starts as early as the stage of property development, when innovative technologies related to the construction process are recommended to hotel developers. However, where KT is most intensive and where its path-shaping and de-locking impact is particularly evident is at the operational stage. Thus, apart from bringing firm-specific operating knowledge, which includes modern management and sales and marketing techniques, and which has to be transferred regardless of where the group expands into, international hotel groups that are coming to CEE also import general hotel and business knowledge – something that, due to the lack of service culture under communism, the CEE market is still often short of. Indeed, the various forms of professional staff training which hotel groups provide play an important role in helping the CEE hotel industry break away from the communist heritage. Furthermore, because of the high labour turnover in the hotel sector, both the tacit and explicit knowledge brought to CEE easily spill out beyond the level of an individual property, for example to local hotels, partner firms, suppliers of goods and services, local administrations and even to other sectors.

Most importantly, the chapter has argued that the scale and extent of this impact depends on the business model adopted by the hotel group for a given hotel, thus reflecting how the hotel group's production network is structured in a given location. The impact is by far the highest in the case of hotel operators (regardless of whether they own the real estate or not). Not only do they train staff in their brand standards and company philosophy, but they also import their operating knowledge, implement it thoroughly in the new context and allow their staff and partners to benefit from it for the sake of their own development. Faced with the necessity to fill the gaps deriving from the neglect of the hotel sector under communism, hotel operators also provide general training, thus allowing the CEE tourism industry to adopt Western standards. In contrast, the role of franchisors is less significant. While the transfer of customer service standards and sales and marketing techniques is as intensive as in the case of operators, due to the fact that they do not get involved in management issues, the training that franchisors provide is rather limited. The same applies to hotel consortia, whose contribution is largely confined to the field of sales and marketing.

Apart from providing an empirical analysis of how the KT initiated by hotel groups can help the CEE tourism sector to grow, this chapter also has important theoretical implications. First, it has been shown that the key concepts of EEG such as path dependence, path creation and lock-in are of particular utility in explaining the role that the KT initiated by tourist firms plays in de-locking host destinations from path dependence. In this respect, the chapter has added to the literature on KT in tourism and its developmental impacts. Due to the fact that this gap is geographical in nature, an economic–geographical perspective such as EEG can serve as an effective theoretical platform from which this gap can be tackled, thus further enhancing the applicability of economic–geographical approaches to research on the tourism production system. Second, by means of paying attention to different business models of hotel groups (i.e. different types of hotel networks), the chapter has contributed to the general understanding of tourism networks and their role as external pools of knowledge, the transfer of which can help host territories to break away from path dependence (Brouder and Eriksson 2013; Brouder 2014).

However, the analysis also has some limitations. Although this chapter offers a foundation on which further research on the impact of KT in the hotel sector on economic development in host destinations could be based, because of space shortages the data have only been presented in generalized form at the level of CEE, that is, without any reference to the national or regional level. While, due to the communist past that the CEE countries share, it is possible to generalize about the whole region, it should not be assumed that KT processes in the hotel sector express themselves in every local context in the same way. Indeed, various other place- and firm-specific factors may also mould the developmental impacts of KT in the hotel sector. Thus, further research in this area should pay attention to various types of tourist destinations (e.g. summer resorts as opposed to big cities and business destinations), different market segments (e.g. luxury and upscale as opposed to budget/economy hotels), the number of establishments, which a given group operates and/or franchises in the market and the whole range of political, socio-cultural and institutional factors that are continuously at work at all scales and that differ widely between different contexts across CEE. Hence, while the KT initiated by international hotel groups in CEE is undoubtedly an important mechanism of de-locking the CEE tourism industry from the post-communist path-dependence, more work is required if the role these processes play in fostering post-communist transformations is to be fully accounted for.

Acknowledgements

This chapter draws from the author's PhD thesis, completed at The University of Manchester, UK in 2011. The author is grateful to his supervisors Dr Martin Hess (The University of Manchester) and Professor Neil Coe (currently the National University of Singapore) for supervising the PhD project. Two interview quotes used in the text have been re-printed courtesy of Taylor & Francis Ltd. (www. tandfonline.com) and the *Tourism Geographies* journal where they appeared for the first time. The quotes derive from the article entitled 'International hotel groups and regional development in Central and Eastern Europe', written by Piotr Niewiadomski and published in *Tourism Geographies* in 2015.

References

Agarwal, S., Ball, R., Shaw, G., and Williams, A. (2000). 'The geography of tourism production: Uneven disciplinary development'. *Tourism Geographies* 2(3), 241–63.

Amin, A. and Cohendet, P. (2004). *Architectures of Knowledge: Firms, Capacities and Communities*. Oxford: Oxford University Press.

Argote, L. and Darr, E. (2000). 'Repositories of knowledge in franchise organizations: Individual, structural, and technological'. In G. Dosi, R. Nelson, and S. Winter (eds) *Nature and Dynamics of Organizational Capabilities*. Oxford: Oxford University Press (pp. 1–69).

Athiyaman, A. and Go, F. (1993). 'Strategic choices in the international hospitality industry'. In B. Brotherton (ed.) *The International Hospitality Industry: Structure Characteristics and Issues*. Oxford: Butterworth-Heinemann (pp. 124–59).

Bathelt, H., Malmberg, A., and Maskell, P. (2004). 'Clusters and knowledge: Local buzz, global pipelines and the process of knowledge formation'. *Progress in Human Geography* 28, 31–57.

Bell, C. (1992). 'Opening up Eastern Europe: New opportunities and new challenges'. *The Cornell Hotel and Restaurant Administration Quarterly* 33, 53–63.

Błądek, Z. and Tulibacki, T. (2003). *Dzieje krajowego hotelarstwa – od zajazdu do współcze-sności: Fakty, obiekty, ludzie*. Poznań: Palladium Architekci – Błądek, Mańkowski.

Boschma, R. and Frenken, K. (2006). 'Why is economic geography not an evolutionary science? Towards an evolutionary economic geography'. *Journal of Economic Geography* 6, 273–302.

Boschma, R. and Martin, R. (2007). 'Editorial: Constructing an evolutionary economic geography'. *Journal of Economic Geography* 7, 537–48.

Boschma, R. and Martin, M. (2010). 'The aims and scope of evolutionary economic geography'. In R. Boschma and R. Martin (eds) *The Handbook of Evolutionary Economic Geography*. Cheltenham, UK: Edward Elgar (pp. 3–39).

Bradshaw, M. and Stenning, A. (2004). 'Introduction: Transformation and development'. In M. Bradshaw and A. Stenning (eds) *East Central Europe and the Former Soviet Union*. Harlow, UK: Pearson (pp. 1–32).

Bradshaw, M. and Swain, A. (2004). 'Foreign investment and regional development'. In M. Bradshaw and A. Stenning (eds) *East Central Europe and the Former Soviet Union*. Harlow, UK: Pearson (pp. 59–86).

Britton, S. (1991). 'Tourism, capital and place: Towards a critical geography of tourism'. *Environment and Planning D: Society and Space* 9, 451–78.

Brookes, M. (2014). 'The dynamics and evolution of knowledge transfer in international master franchise agreements'. *International Journal of Hospitality Management* 36, 52–62.

Brouder, P. (2014). 'Evolutionary economic geography: A new path for tourism research?'. *Tourism Geographies* 16(1), 2–7.

Brouder, P. and Eriksson, R. (2013). 'Tourism evolution: On the synergies of tourism studies and evolutionary economic geography'. *Annals of Tourism Research* 43, 370–89.

Buckley, P. and Witt, S. (1990). 'Tourism in the centrally-planned economies of Europe'. *Annals of Tourism Research* 17, 7–18.

Cieslik, J. (1983). *Contractual Arrangements for the Transfer of Technology in the Hotel Industry*. Vienna: UNIDO.

Coe, N. (2010). 'Geographies of production I: An evolutionary revolution?' *Progress in Human Geography* 35(1), 81–91.

Coe, N., Hess, M., Yeung, H., Dicken, P., and Henderson, J. (2004). '"Globalizing" regional development: A global production networks perspective'. *Transactions of the Institute of British Geographers* 29, 468–84.

Cohen, W. and Levinthal, D. (1990). 'Absorptive capacity: A new perspective on learning and innovation'. *Administrative Science Quarterly* 35(1), 128–52.

Contractor, F. and Kundu, S. (2000). 'Globalization of hotel services: An examination of ownership and alliance patterns in a maturing service sector'. In Y. Aharoni and L. Nachum (eds) *Globalization of Services*. London: Routledge (pp. 296–319).

Cooper, C. (2006). 'Knowledge management and tourism'. *Annals of Tourism Research* 33(1), 47–64.

Cunill, O. (2006). *The Growth Strategies of Hotel Chains: Best Business Practices by Leading Companies*. New York, NY: Haworth Hospitality Press.

Dicken, P. (2011). *Global Shift: Mapping the Changing Contours of the World Economy*, 6th edition. London: Sage.

Drucker, P. (1991). 'The new productivity challenge'. *Harvard Business Review* 69(6), 69–79.

Dunning, J. and Norman, G. (1983). 'The theory of the multinational enterprise: An application of an international office location'. *Environment and Planning A* 15, 675–92.

Dunning, J. and Norman, G. (1987). 'The location choice of offices of international companies'. *Environment and Planning A* 19, 613–31.

EBRD (1994). *Annual Report 1994*. European Bank for Reconstruction and Development.

Endo, K. (2006). 'Foreign direct investment in tourism – flows and volumes'. *Tourism Management* 27, 600–14.

Enz, C., Canina, L., and Walsh, K. (2006*). Intellectual capital: A key driver of hotel performance*. Report by the Centre for Hospitality Research, Cornell University. Ithaca, NY: Cornell University.

Fosfuri, A., Motta, M., and Ronde, T. (2001). 'Foreign direct investment and spillovers through workers' mobility'. *Journal of International Economics* 53, 205–22.

Franck, C. (1990). 'Tourism investment in Central and Eastern Europe'. *Tourism Management* 11, 333–8.

Gale, D. (2008). 'Hotels' 325'. *Hotels* 7, 38–52.

Glass, A. and Saggi, K. (2002). 'Multinational firms and technology transfer'. *Scandinavian Journal of Economics* 104, 495–513.

Go, F. and Pine, R. (1995). *Globalization Strategy in the Hotel Industry*. London: Routledge.

Grabher, G. (1993). 'The weakness of strong ties: The lock-in of regional development in the Ruhr area'. In G. Grabher (ed.) *The Embedded Firm: On the Socio-economics of Industrial Networks*. London: Routledge (pp. 255–77).

Halkier, H. (2014). 'Innovation and destination governance in Denmark: Tourism, policy networks and spatial development'. *European Planning Studies* 22(8), 1659–70.

Hall, C. and Page, S. (2006). *The Geography of Tourism & Recreation: Environment, Place and Space*, 3rd edition. London: Routledge.

Hall, C. and Williams, A. (2008). *Tourism Innovation*. London: Routledge.

Hall, D. (1992). 'The challenges of international tourism in Eastern Europe'. *Tourism Management* 13, 41–4.

Hardy, J. (1998). 'Cathedrals in the desert? Transnationals, corporate strategy and locality in Wrocław'. *Regional Studies* 32, 639–52.

Healey, N. (1994). 'The transition economies of Central and Eastern Europe: A political, economic, social and technological analysis'. *The Columbia Journal of World Business* 29, 61–70.

Hirsch-Kreinsen, H., Jacobson, D., and Robertson, P. (2006). '"Low-tech" industries: Innovativeness and development perspectives – a summary of a European research project'. *Prometheus* 24(1), 3–21.

Hjalager, A. (2002). 'Repairing innovation defectiveness in tourism'. *Tourism Management* 23, 465–74.

Ioannides, D. (1995). 'Strengthening the ties between tourism and economic geography: A theoretical agenda'. *Professional Geographer* 47, 49–60.

Ioannides, D. (2006). 'The economic geography of the tourist industry: Ten years of progress in research and an agenda for the future'. *Tourism Geographies* 8(1), 76–86.

Ioannides, D. and Debbage, K. (1998). 'Introduction: Exploring the economic geography and tourism nexus'. In D. Ioannides and K. Debbage (eds) *The Economic Geography of the Tourist Industry: A Supply-Side Analysis*. New York: Routledge (pp. 1–14).

Jaakson, R. (1996). 'Tourism in transition in post-Soviet Estonia'. *Annals of Tourism Research* 23, 617–34.

Jacob, M. and Groizard, J. (2007). 'Technology transfer and multinationals: The case of Balearic hotel chains' investments in two developing economies'. *Tourism Management* 28, 976–92.

Johnson, C. and Iunius, R. (1999). 'Competing in Central Eastern Europe: Perspectives and developments'. *International Journal of Hospitality Management* 18, 245–60.

Johnson, C. and Vanetti, M. (2004). 'Market developments in the hotel sector in Eastern Central Europe'. *Advances in Hospitality and Leisure* 1, 153–75.

Johnson, M. (1997). 'Hungary's hotel industry in transition 1960–1996'. *Tourism Management* 18, 441–52.

Kacker, M. (1998). 'International flow of retailing know-how: Bridging the technology gap in distribution'. *Journal of Retailing* 64(1), 41–67.

Karhunen, P. (2008). 'Managing international business operations in a changing institutional context: The case of the St. Petersburg hotel industry'. *Journal of International Management* 14, 28–45.

Larsson, A. and Lindström, K. (2014). 'Bridging the knowledge-gap between the old and the new: Regional marine experience production in Orust, Västra Götaland, Sweden'. *European Planning Studies* 22(8), 1551–68.

León-Darder, F., Villar-Garcia, C., and Pla-Barber, J. (2011). 'Entry mode choice in the internationalization of the hotel industry: A holistic approach'. *The Service Industries Journal* 31, 107–22.

Littlejohn, D. (2003). 'Hotels'. In B. Brotherton (ed.) *The International Hospitality Industry: Structure Characteristics and Issues*. Oxford: Butterworth-Heinemann (pp. 5–29).

Lockwood, A. (1993). 'Eastern Europe and the former Soviet States'. In P. Jones and A. Pizam (eds) *The International Hospitality Industry: Organizational and Operational Issues*. New York: Pitman Publishing/John Wiley & Sons (pp. 25–37).

MacKinnon, D. (2012). 'Beyond strategic coupling: Reassessing the firm-region nexus in global production networks'. *Journal of Economic Geography* 12, 227–45.

Magnini, V. (2008). 'Practicing effective knowledge sharing in international hotel joint-ventures'. *International Journal of Hospitality Management* 27, 249–58.

Martin, R. (2006). 'Economic geography and the new discourse of regional competitiveness'. In S. Bagchi-Sen and H. Lawton Smith (eds) *Economic Geography: Past, Present and Future*. London: Routledge (pp. 159–72).

Martin, R. and Sunley, P. (2006). 'Path dependence and regional economic evolution'. *Journal of Economic Geography* 6, 395–437.

Medlik, S. (1990). 'Focus on Eastern Europe'. *Tourism Management* 11, 95–8.

Mitka-Karandziej, U. (1993). *Hotelarstwo*. Zespół Prywatnych Szkół Zawodowych nr 1, Warszawa, Working Paper.

Niewiadomski, P. (2013). 'The globalisation of the hotel industry and the variety of emerging capitalisms in Central and Eastern Europe'. *European Urban and Regional Studies*, DOI: 10.1177/0969776413502658.

Niewiadomski, P. (2014). 'Towards an economic–geographical approach to the globalisation of the hotel industry'. *Tourism Geographies* 16(1), 48–67.

Niewiadomski, P. (2015). 'International hotel groups and regional development in Central and Eastern Europe'. *Tourism Geographies* 17(2), 173–91.

Nonaka, I. (1991). 'The knowledge creating company'. *Harvard Business Review* 69(6), 96–104.

Orfila-Sintes, F., Crespi-Cladera, R., and Martinez-Ros, E. (2005). 'Innovation activity in the hotel industry: Evidence from Balearic islands'. *Tourism Management* 26, 851–65.

Pavlinek, P. (2004). 'Regional development implications of foreign direct investment in Central Europe'. *European Urban and Regional Studies* 11, 47–70.

Pine, R. (1992). 'Technology transfer in the hotel industry'. *International Journal of Hospitality Management* 11, 3–22.

Scott, J. and Renaghan, L. (1991). 'Hotel development in Eastern Germany: Opportunities and obstacles'. *The Cornell Hotel and Restaurant Administration Quarterly* 32, 44–51.

Setterfield, M. (1997). *Rapid Growth and Relative Decline: Modelling Macroeconomic Dynamics with Hysteresis*. London: Macmillan.

Shaw, G. and Williams, A. (2009). 'Knowledge transfer and management in tourism organisations: An emerging research agenda'. *Tourism Management* 30, 325–35.

Shcherbakova, S. (2002). Stan współczesny i kierunki rozwoju przemysłu hotelarskiego Rosji. *Turystyka i Hotelarstwo* 2, 133–7.

Simonin, B. (1999). 'Ambiguity and the process of KT in strategic alliances'. *Strategic Management Journal* 20(7), 595–623.

Sirilli, G. and Evangelista, R. (1998). 'Technological innovation in services and manufacturing: Results from Italian surveys'. *Research Policy* 27(9), 881–99.

Smith, A. (1997). 'Breaking the old and constructing the new? Geographies of uneven development in Central and Eastern Europe'. In R. Lee and J. Wills (eds) *Geographies of Economies*. London: Edward Arnold (pp. 331–44).

Smith, A. and Pickles, J. (1998). 'Theorising transition and the political economy of transformation'. In J. Pickles and A. Smith (eds) *Theorising Transition: The Political Economy of Post-communist Transformations*. London: Routledge (pp. 1–24).

Smith, S. (1998). 'Tourism as an industry: Debates and concepts'. In D. Ioannides and K. Debbage (eds) *The Economic Geography of the Tourist Industry: A Supply-Side Analysis*. New York: Routledge (pp. 31–52).

Sokol, M. (2001). 'Central and Eastern Europe a decade after the fall of state-socialism: Regional dimensions of transition processes'. *Regional Studies* 35, 645–55.

Spender, J. and Grant, R. (1996). 'Knowledge and the firm: Overview'. *Strategic Management Journal* 17, 5–9.

Stewart, T. and Nihei, Y. (1987). *Technology Transfer and Human Factors*. Lexington, MA: Lexington Books.

Swain, A. and Hardy, J. (1998). 'Globalization, institutions, foreign investment and the reintegration of East and Central Europe and the former Soviet Union with the world economy'. *Regional Studies* 32, 587–90.

Urry, J. (1990). *The Tourist Gaze: Leisure and Travel in Contemporary Societies.* London: Sage.

Williams, A. and Balaž, V. (2000). *Tourism in Transition: Economic Change in Central Europe.* London: I.B. Tauris.

Williams, A. and Balaž, V. (2002). 'The Czech and Slovak republics: Conceptual issues in the economic analysis of tourism in transition'. *Tourism Management* 23(1), 37–45.

Williams, A. and Shaw, G. (2011). 'Internationalization and innovation in tourism'. *Annals of Tourism Research* 38(1), 27–51.

Witkowski, C. (2003). *Hotelarstwo – cz. II: Międzynarodowe systemy hotelowe w Polsce.* Warszawa: Wyższa Szkoła Ekonomiczna w Warszawie.

Witt, U. (2003). *The Evolving Economy: Essays on the Evolutionary Approach to Economics.* Cheltenham, UK: Edward Elgar.

Witt, U. (2006). 'Evolutionary economics'. *Papers on Economics and Evolution.* No. 0605. Jena: Max Planck Institute of Economics, Evolutionary Economics Group.

8 Co-evolution and sustainable tourism development

From old institutional inertia to new institutional imperatives in Niagara

Patrick Brouder and Christopher Fullerton

Introduction

Regional tourism growth often occurs around a central theme or central place which has the most appeal to the broadest audience, usually leading to an identifiable regional brand. This pattern is seen all over the world in mass tourism destinations. Throughout the development of mass tourism in recent decades this approach was not generally seen as a problem by local stakeholders. However, as concerns over the sustainability of mass tourism have been raised (Saarinen 2006), a clear need to take a closer look at tourism development has emerged. This chapter identifies two challenges to sustainable tourism development. First, mass tourism development often tends towards homogenization by both espousing a limited view of what a particular destination has to offer and obfuscating the heterogeneous nature of tourism supply in regions with an established brand. As a result, diversity is not necessarily embraced or understood in many destinations. Second, as more and more mass tourism destinations face persistent stagnation, or even decline, there is a need to reassess the internal path development of tourism. Thus, while success breeds success, the self-reinforcing nature of tourism development is not without its limits. These two challenges are of particular importance as the sustainable development agenda has gained traction in recent times and as questions of governance have been assessed (Bramwell 2011).

Consistently ranking among the world's top tourist destinations, Niagara Falls attracts millions of visitors each year and is instantly recognizable with one of the most established names in global tourism and one of the world's most enduring mass tourism destinations. However, the Niagara region, in which the Falls are situated, is so much more than just the mass tourism of the Falls and the entertainment district which most people think of when they think of Niagara. For example, Niagara is a well-established wine region and is developing related activities such as culinary tourism (Gayler 2010; Telfer and Hashimoto 2013).

In this chapter we investigate the intra-regional co-evolution of the various tourism paths in the Niagara region of Canada, building on our recent exploratory research in Niagara (Brouder and Fullerton 2015). Through semi-structured interviews with regional tourism stakeholders, as well as regular participation in local tourism development meetings, a new perspective on tourism in the Niagara region is revealed and informs further development of evolutionary theory on the ongoing processes of co-evolution in the Niagara region. Path dependence has led to a dominant unilineal view of tourism as an economic development strategy radiating out from the Falls area. However, multiple tourism development paths are co-evolving and contesting the status quo. The findings illustrate how this co-evolution is not only beneficial but necessary for sustainable regional development, since some of the less noticed tourism development paths may prove robust over the long term and the laggards of today may be the leaders of tomorrow. We also build on the concept of co-evolution by supplementing our recent claim of co-evolution as co-evolving intra-regional paths – we ask whether (and how) the regional institutional evolution enables (or constrains) new path development.

Aim and research questions

This chapter contributes to tourism studies by developing the concept of co-evolution and showing why it is important for long-term, sustainable tourism development. By focussing on Niagara Falls, an iconic mass-tourism destination, it is possible to empirically interrogate unilineal conceptualizations of tourism development. Thus, the chapter aims to link research on complexity in tourism to the concept of co-evolution taken from evolutionary economic geography (EEG) (Brouder and Eriksson 2013a; Ma and Hassink 2013).

We see co-evolution occurring in a number of ways: between distinct groups of tourism businesses (grouped possibly by sub-region or sub-sector), between tourism development paths and other economic development paths (across the Niagara region), and between tourism businesses and regional institutions (standard co-evolutionary approach). Each of these is explored in the empirical material. This requires a focus on the institutional geographies of the region, since successful long-term regional development through tourism may require a reconfiguration of regional institutions. The level of institutional coherence and cohesion across the region reveals the level of dynamism in the regional tourism evolution.

The following research questions guide the empirical analysis:

1. What are the relative development stages of tourism paths in Niagara?
2. What are the interrelationships and interdependencies of the existing paths?
3. How do tourism institutions shape the evolution of the regional tourism economy?
4. How do tourism stakeholders influence the regional institutional environment?

These questions help to assess the heterogeneity within the Niagara region's tourism economy and institutions, and raise questions over how tourism development is governed. Ultimately, we discuss why co-evolution matters for sustainable tourism development.

Theory

Economic geography attempts to understand the development of regional economies from a spatial perspective and examines why some regions prosper while others do not. The tourism economy is not always studied from an economic geography perspective even though such studies have opened new avenues for exploration in the past (e.g. Ioannides and Debbage 1998). Tourism development has often been simplistically perceived as being the result of inherent locational advantages or unilineal development (Cohen 1979), but this only partially explains the long-term evolution of destinations. In tourism, slow and incremental developments have been shown to occur in regions not traditionally associated with tourism entrepreneurship (Marchant and Mottiar 2011; Brouder 2012; Conway and Cawley 2012; Brouder 2013), and this implies that there are subtle change processes at play. Thus, it is necessary to analyse these processes of change at the grassroots level.

Debbage and Ioannides (2004) have called for a more active, closer connection between tourism studies and economic geography, with a view to finding new perspectives on change in tourism. In this regard, one recent development in economic geography which has received attention from tourism scholars is EEG (Brouder 2014a). With its focus on the historical factors which condition the future courses of regional development (Boschma and Martin 2010), EEG draws attention to long-term and ongoing processes of change. EEG also highlights the heterodox nature of regional economies – with not one, but many possible development paths present in any given region at any given time. EEG can thus help 'academic understanding of small-scale tourism in regions where it is not the dominant sector, or where it is made up of multiple (perhaps even contesting) paths' (Brouder 2014b: 542; see also Papatheodorou 2004).

Ruhanen (2013) highlighted how local government can impact the possibilities for sustainable tourism development, acting as either facilitators or inhibitors of positive change. We build on her argument by conceptualizing the regional tourism economy as a heterodox grouping (i.e. consisting of multiple tourism paths); this heightens the role of local government, since regional authorities (as well as private investors) will prefer some paths over others and support them accordingly. This is ultimately reflected in the regional institutional geography: 'New institutions emerge, old institutions are challenged and individuals with particular skill sets become marginalised while others become central and still others manage to adapt their skills to the new institutional reality' (Brouder and Ioannides 2014: 422).

Thus, the existing (and changing) power relations among regional stakeholders become important research subjects (Reed 1997; Dredge 2006; Viken and Aarsaether 2013) and analysing them improves our understanding of the long-term potential of all regional tourism paths, as well as any inhibitors which may be limiting the community of stakeholders. Of course, these networks may be entangled with other (non-tourism) regional stakeholders, and their priorities and loyalties may not necessarily lie with tourism but rather with other sectors or with community development in general (George *et al.* 2009; Haugland 2011).

Co-evolution is a useful concept drawn from EEG, as it highlights the hetero-dox nature of the tourism economy within the regional economy (Ma and Hassink 2014; Brouder and Fullerton 2015), a fact often overlooked in empirical studies, which still tend to use unilineal explanatory models. That the tourism economy is a complex system is axiomatic in tourism studies today (Milne and Ateljevic 2001), but co-evolution, in particular, has been scarcely explored empirically (Ma and Hassink 2013; García-Cabrera and Durán-Herrera 2014; Larsson and Lindström 2014). While Larsson and Lindström (2014) focus on cross-sectoral co-evolution, it is also necessary to explore co-evolution within the tourism sector (Ma and Hassink 2013; García-Cabrera and Durán-Herrera 2014). Brouder and Eriksson (2013b) found that related experience and local experience helped new tourism firms stay in business and contribute to tourism development in a region not traditionally associated with tourism entrepreneurship, thus showing that regional branching into tourism is possible and this further implies that tourism develop-ment of any kind is not necessarily dependent on the dominant regional path.

Co-evolution also has implications for questions of sustainable development, including sustainable tourism development. A growing number of lifestyle entrepreneurs in the tourism sector are not primarily interested in the achieve-ment of economic goals, such as profit-making or job creation, but are most concerned about making a living and enjoying a good quality of life as their business evolves over time (Ateljevic and Doorne 2000; Andersson Cederholm and Hultman 2010; Marchant and Mottiar 2011). This further suggests that the range of stakeholders which are involved, as well as the institutional impera-tives of different groups, may be broader than most evolutionary studies usually consider; this implies not just tourism firms but also non-business stakeholders in the community. Therefore, the study of co-evolution must include a broader conceptualization of regional (community) development.

Background to the study area

The Niagara region of Canada consists of twelve urban and rural municipalities. With just over 431,000 residents, Niagara's population increased by only 6.9 per cent between 1996 and 2011, one of the lowest growth rates in Southern Ontario. This is largely due to the weak economic climate in recent decades. Historically, manufacturing (including steel products, automotive components, food and bever-ages, and paper goods, among others) has been one of the region's three economic pillars, along with agriculture and tourism. The region has lost thousands of fac-tory jobs since the 1970s, however, with dozens of firms relocating to the United States and various overseas locations where production costs are far lower (Fuller-ton 2013). Manufacturing employment in Niagara fell from 47,000 jobs to just over 25,000 between 1987 and 2007 (Hickey 2008). Economic shocks have also been felt in the historically strong agricultural sector. Niagara is one of Canada's most important grape and tender fruit crop regions. Many of these products had long been processed locally, but these value-added activities have largely ceased. For exam-ple, the Welch's grape juice plant closed in 2007 and the CanGro cannery closed in

2008. These shut-downs eliminated hundreds of manufacturing jobs and also left hundreds of Niagara farmers without a buyer for their produce (Fullerton 2013).

Tourism has been the most resilient of the region's three traditional economic pillars, but it has also been stagnating over the past few decades. Niagara's tourism industry has always centred on the iconic waterfalls on the Niagara River and the surrounding city of Niagara Falls (Figure 8.1). The flow of tourists to 'the Falls' (as they are known colloquially) grew throughout the twentieth century, particularly after the rise of the automobile in the 1950s (Dubinsky 1999). By the 1980s and 1990s, however, visitor numbers began to stagnate as some of the area's tourist districts suffered from neglect on the part of property owners and attraction operators (Gayler 1994). In his study of Niagara Falls' relevance to the Tourism Area Life Cycle Model, Getz (1992: 758) noted: 'The Clifton Hill area is basically a strip development dominated by small attractions and services and is to many visitors "tacky" in appearance and atmosphere'.

Jayawardena *et al.* (2008) also point out that, in the late 1990s, Niagara Falls suffered from further product and marketing challenges, including: stagnating traveller expenditures and lengths of stay; a lack of expanded or diversified investment in tourism infrastructure, products and services (despite the changing demands of domestic and international tourists); and a lack of response to rising quality standards, as well as a lack of package offerings that integrated tourism offerings for different market segments (e.g. wine tourists, affluent visitors or families). As an outcome of these challenges, Jayawardena *et al.* (2008: 271) noted: 'the

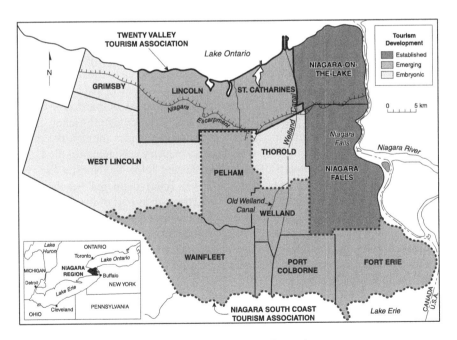

Figure 8.1 Tourism evolution in the Niagara region of Canada.

powerful Niagara brand, one of the world's great tourist icons, was being eroded by outdated, poor quality attractions, accommodations and food establishments'.

Tourism in the area suffered further setbacks shortly after the turn of the twenty-first century due to events such as the 9/11 terrorist attacks in the United States, which prompted much tighter security measures at the Canada–United States border, and the 2003 Severe Acute Respiratory Syndrome (SARS) epidemic in Toronto, which scared away many potential visitors to Southern Ontario, as there were dozens of SARS deaths in the nearby metropolis.

The stagnation and decline of Niagara Falls' tourism economy in the 1990s and through the early 2000s prompted an intensive search for potential remedies (Jayawardena *et al.* 2008; Ontario Tourism Competitiveness Study 2009). Efforts to bolster the local tourism economy led to an increase in the number of visitor attractions after the mid-1990s, most notably through the provincial government's opening of two casinos (in 1996 and 2004) (MacLaurin and Wolstenholme 2008). These initiatives have prompted the mass entry of transnational hotel, restaurant and other chains (such as Hilton, Radisson and Sheraton) into the Niagara Falls tourism market (Jayawardena *et al.* 2008) through both the upgrading of existing properties and the construction of new ones (including some of Canada's tallest buildings). Today there are about 15,000 hotel rooms in Niagara Falls, and the Niagara region now has the third-highest concentration of hotel rooms in Canada (Jayawardena *et al.* 2008). Despite these developments, visitation levels continue to stagnate (Brooker and Burgess 2008). It is estimated that Niagara currently attracts about 12 million tourists per year, down significantly from the 16 million who routinely visited in the pre-9/11 years (Deloitte and Touche 2008).

A recurring conclusion of Niagara-focused tourism studies has been that municipalities throughout Niagara possess assets that might be used to diversify the region's tourism offering beyond only those in Niagara Falls and, with this, that there is great potential for tourism development to contribute to the region's economic revitalization. Certainly, some diversification was already underway by the late 1990s in a few parts of Niagara, most notably in Niagara-on-the-Lake, which has worked vigorously to promote its cultural and built heritage (Mitchell *et al.* 2001). Furthermore, the growing reputation of Niagara wines through the early 2000s helped to cultivate a thriving wine-tourism industry in Niagara-on-the-Lake and, successively, in other parts of the region situated below the Niagara Escarpment (Fullerton 2013; Telfer and Hashimoto 2013). Today, municipalities throughout Niagara have, to various degrees, embraced tourism as part of their economic development strategies. Niagara Falls has placed a strong emphasis on reversing the decline in tourist visits and on growing the amount of tourism spending within the city. At the same time, many of the region's more rural communities are only recently looking to tourism development as a means of compensating for agricultural and industrial decline.

With all Niagara municipalities standing to benefit from an enhanced tourism sector, it would appear that opportunities exist for a region-wide tourism development strategy to be implemented. Up to now, however, there has been a lack of coordination in tourism marketing across the region's towns and cities, with

Niagara having been identified in a provincial government report as being a place in Ontario where the existence of multiple-destination marketing organizations has resulted in a duplication of tourism promotion efforts (Jayawardena *et al.* 2008; Ontario Tourism Competitiveness Study 2009).

In turn, both academic and consultant studies have asserted that there is a lack of a clear 'Niagara' brand beyond the Falls, leading to an inconsistent international brand image for Niagara (Deloitte and Touche 2008; Jayawardena *et al.* 2008). The Government of Ontario addressed this concern in 2010 through the creation of the Tourism Partnership of Niagara (TPN), whose mandate is 'to provide leadership and coordination to attract more visitors, generate more economic activity and create more jobs across the Niagara region' (Tourism Partnership of Niagara 2012). The TPN is responsible for representing all twelve Niagara-region municipalities in tourism marketing and is expected to work closely with the municipalities, tourism agencies and businesses. Whether this constellation leads to a more focussed brand or to a more contested tourism economy is a central question for the regional stakeholders and is also of particular interest for research on the evolution of Niagara's tourism economy.

Method

The chapter uses semi-structured, in-depth interviews with regional tourism stakeholders and regular participation in local tourism-development meetings to investigate new path-development in tourism in the Niagara region. Qualitative fieldwork was conducted in 2013 and 2014. Respondents were purposively chosen (Valentine 2005) to include a range of tourism stakeholders in the region. Eight formal interviews were conducted across Niagara, including representatives of local and provincial government agencies and NGOs, in an effort to ensure that insights from across the region would be gathered. These were complemented by four shorter informal interviews further interrogating issues raised in earlier interviews. Interviews were conducted with both authors present, with Chris leading and Patrick interjecting at times. This led to dynamic and open exchanges with our interviewees. The interview study was augmented by regular participation in the Niagara Tourism Network, a grassroots-based organization that meets once a month to share information and consists mostly of the more peripheral and smaller-scale tourism stakeholders of the Niagara region.

Thematic analysis was employed in the post-interview stage (Quinn Patton 2002). The interviews were analysed several times, with broad themes being identified at first. An iterative process between the researchers, through discussion of and reflection on the materials and the extant literature, facilitated a robust and critical analysis, with each author analysing the material independently first and then comparing emerging themes later. Only the results which were strongly evidenced in the material are included. The study is part of an ongoing research project building on the work of Brouder and Fullerton (2015) and includes approximately one additional year of local participation since our previous publication.

Results and discussion

Tourism path development in Niagara – existing paths across the region

Not all places in Niagara have pursued tourism development for as long, nor to the same extent, as others. Given the iconicity of the Falls, and with almost two centuries of tourism development within the vicinity, the Niagara region's tourism economy has traditionally centred on the Niagara Falls area. As noted earlier, tourism in Niagara Falls has expanded well beyond the edge of the Niagara River and now includes two large casinos, a number of family waterpark resorts and a variety of other amenities and services. The building boom that followed the opening of the Niagara Fallsview Casino in 2004 brought about notable changes to the city's skyline, with several major hotel chains having built high-rise hotels adjacent to the casino. Explored later in this chapter are the potential long-term impacts of Niagara Falls having followed this tourism-development path, particularly as it relates to the development of a broader tourism economy across the Niagara region.

Beyond 'the Falls', several of Niagara's other urban and rural municipalities (see Figure 8.1) have also become more active players in the regional tourism economy in recent decades. The specific type of tourism offering has varied considerably, depending somewhat on the nature of each municipality's place-based assets, which are largely based on the region's agricultural and industrial legacies. The municipalities that have the right soil and climate conditions – namely Niagara-on-the-Lake, St. Catharines, Lincoln and Grimsby – have been able to centre their efforts upon Niagara's emerging wine industry. Those communities straddling the Lake Erie shoreline (Wainfleet, Port Colborne and Fort Erie) have focused their efforts on growing their water-based tourism and recreation industries, such as sport fishing and second-home tourism. Port Colborne, Welland and Thorold have also used the presence of the Welland Canal to their advantage. Built to enable ships to by-pass the Niagara River while en route between Lakes Erie and Ontario, this waterway has been rerouted numerous times. One of the now closed-off sections, located in Welland, serves as a flat-water sport venue and hosts numerous national and international events and competitions. The Welland Canal also provides the backdrop to Port Colborne's Canal Days Marine Heritage Festival. At the same time, however, one interviewee noted that the 'tourism industry has under-valued the Welland Canal' (Interviewee #6) and that there were many more ways in which the Canal could be harnessed for tourism development. Several municipalities have also witnessed the development of a burgeoning agri-tourism industry, with businesses such as pumpkin farms and horse-riding stables.

Niagara-on-the-Lake has been most able to tap into the Niagara Falls tourism market due to its close proximity and its easy accessibility via the Niagara River Parkway. Furthermore, the public transportation services provided by the Niagara Parks Commission (via its WEGO buses) enable tourists without an automobile to access Niagara-on-the-Lake, but not any other municipalities. Over time, however, Niagara-on-the-Lake has come to rely less on the cascade of tourists from the Falls and instead has become more independent as a tourism destination, as it has built a niche for itself as a centre for wine, cultural and heritage tourism. Many people now come to Niagara-on-the-Lake without also visiting Niagara Falls.

Perhaps the next most developed cluster of municipalities is the group promoted through the Twenty Valley Tourism Association (TVTA). The TVTA serves as the official tourism agency for the Town of Lincoln and also includes the City of St. Catharines as a member, although the latter also does its own independent tourism marketing through its economic development and tourism services office. Twenty Valley began as a grassroots-based organization made up of merchants in the village of Jordan, but over time has grown to become a prominent regional tourism organization that routinely brings together businesses such as wineries and restaurants for wine and culinary weekends, as well as other events.

Tourism-development paths are less advanced in other parts of Niagara. The most significant development in recent years has been the creation of the Niagara's South Coast Tourism Association (NSCTA) in 2013. The five municipalities that have partnered to create this organization (Port Colborne, Fort Erie, Wainfleet, Pelham and Welland), none of which had any extensive history of commercial tourism development before the NSCTA's creation, felt that they would have to work collaboratively if they were to make any real progress in promoting tourism. As Interviewee #3 put it, 'tourists don't pick destinations based on municipal boundaries'. Since no single municipality had enough attractions on its own to attract visitors in any great numbers, the most effective approach was deemed to be a collaborative marketing effort in which the communities are promoted as a package.

The remainder of the Niagara municipalities have far less advanced tourism development paths. The City of Thorold contracts its tourism marketing to an organization called Thorold Tourism that has focused thus far on the community's Welland Canal related assets and bicycle tourism. Notably, however, this organization is not part of any of the larger formal regional networks and is, for the most part, marketing itself independently. Similarly, in the research interviews it was found that Grimsby has been exploring the potential to engage more actively in tourism development (beyond its currently very limited level), but that little local appetite for this has been found among residents and business owners. Finally, the Township of West Lincoln, which is largely an agricultural rural community, is virtually invisible within regional tourism circles.

Tourism path-development in Niagara – path dependence and new path creation

Breaking from path dependence is notoriously difficult, and this has been no different in the Niagara region, where there has sometimes been a lack of capacity to act on the new opportunities which tourism presents. Niagara has historically based its economy on a mix of agriculture, manufacturing and tourism. However, as described above, for a long period the balance was heavily skewed towards manufacturing in many municipalities. This created high wages but also high dependency on those manufacturing jobs and, once they were gone, the region was 'ruined' (Mah 2012). Regional 'lock-in' became the order of the day with institutional practices unable to adjust to the changes. Many Niagara municipalities paid only scant attention to the tourism industry as a potential growth sector and instead resorted to interminably longing for the good old days by maintaining a 'smokestack chasing' approach to economic development that focused on what many perceive to be 'real' industries, such as light manufacturing and renewable energy technology. This highlights how path dependence in other sectors can potentially inhibit new tourism development through institutional inertia.

In Niagara, path dependence is not only inter-sectoral in nature – there are several examples of tourism path-dependence. At the regional level, the emphasis on the Falls as the central place and focus of tourism promotion has meant that the rest of the region has not received the attention it deserves in regional tourism development (Brouder and Fullerton 2015). The recent desire of Niagara municipalities to diversify their economies by stimulating tourism development would, perhaps intuitively, seem to be more easily achieved by acting upon the proximity of a world-famous attraction such as Niagara Falls. To be sure, all interviewees acknowledged the value of having an iconic attraction in the region. For example, one participant commented that having 'major attractions in the region is a huge advantage' (Interviewee #3). Another illustrated what he saw as the potential for the region to benefit from Niagara Falls' heavy tourism visitation numbers by comparing Niagara with another New World wine region (California's Napa Valley) noting that 'maybe the Falls is our Napa City' (Interviewee #2). These statements imply that the region can benefit from the cascade effect of visitors spreading out from the central attraction in the region. However, a contrasting observation also emerging strongly during the interviews was that the presence of the Falls has been somewhat of a 'double-edged sword', since many people think the Niagara region is the Falls and nothing else (Interviewee #1). Thus, despite the availability of many marketable tourism assets across the region, a major challenge for peripheral parts of Niagara has been to convince that ever-present and consistent group of Niagara Falls visitors to extend their stay in the Niagara region and spread out from the Falls to the rest of the region.

Recent developments within Niagara Falls have also complicated the picture. The last decade (since the opening of the Niagara Fallsview Casino in 2004) has seen a classic case of path dependence in Niagara Falls. There has been (and continues to be) huge capital investment in accommodation facilities in the Falls, even though visitor numbers are stagnating (having peaked at the turn of the century around 16 million but now ranging around 11–12 million visitors per annum). This is reinforcing the notion that Niagara Falls is central, as the individual accommodation-providers compete with each other, with the rest of the region, with the rest of the province and also with destinations on the opposite side of the Canada–United States border, for the limited tourist overnight stays available. The increasing level of internal competition is particularly interesting when compared with the sustainable development limits set in Whistler, Canada (Gill and Williams 2011), and it raises two interesting empirical questions: First, can Niagara Falls sustain its current stock of accommodation providers, and, if not, who will be the winners and losers? Second, how does the lock-in present in Niagara Falls affect the regional institutional relations, including the dissonant voices within the Falls (of which, surely, there are some)?

Beyond Niagara Falls and across the region, the research participants regularly mentioned the power of the Niagara Falls-centred tourism stakeholders. Most notably, some consternation was expressed about the ways in which the TPN has operated since its creation by the provincial government in 2010. The TPN, whose headquarters is located a stone's throw from the Falls, is mandated to serve the entire Niagara region, but was widely viewed in the interviews as focusing largely on Niagara Falls in its marketing efforts, with only a few exceptions. Stakeholders in the more peripheral parts of Niagara were often critical of what they saw as a short-term view on the part of the TPN, with several interviewees repeating that the TPN knows how to market mass tourism in Niagara Falls but has no idea what tourism is in rural Niagara (Interviewee #5). One interviewee went so far as to state that the TPN was not serving the partners at all, since it did not actively engage all of them in its marketing activities (Interviewee #6). This path-dependent legacy is reflected in the make-up of the TPN, which is dominated by board members from Niagara Falls and its geographically proximate municipalities. This constellation made sense in the past, but, as tourism is growing across the region, it has become a barrier to cooperation and mutual understanding among regional stakeholders.

While a lack of support from the TPN was cited as one reason that tourism development has not evolved considerably in some places, several peripheral stakeholders admitted in the interviews that the municipalities themselves were also partly responsible for this problem. As one noted, some communities and businesses have established little presence in the regional tourism promotional material 'because we haven't got our act together' (Interviewee #1) and that, up until recently, the peripheral parts of the Niagara region have not had a clear identity or purpose (Interviewee #4). Interviewee #5 also noted that it was up to the rural municipalities to become more proactive in building recognition of their tourism offerings. This type of change takes time and shows the incremental nature of tourism development over the long term, which is typical of rural areas (Brouder 2012).

Interviewee #6 noted that 'We all have assets', but that more time needs to be spent mapping the assets and matching them to specific tourism niches. Adding to the challenge of further developing the local tourism economy was the fact that residents and business owners in some places did not see their communities as potential tourism destinations. For example, Wainfleet is mainly an agricultural community and Grimsby is primarily a commuter town. This makes it more difficult to garner support for local tourism development for the few tourism entrepreneurs who exist, but also shows that not every municipality or community can or should be focussed on tourism. Diversity across the region is not limited to tourism supply but also to the various industries which persist in Niagara and this must also be understood when planning for tourism development and supporting all communities within the region.

Co-evolution in Niagara tourism – existing relations across the region

This preliminary research across Niagara found different tourism groups at different stages of evolution, with groups of businesses in the various municipalities also co-evolving at the sub-regional level. The recent establishment of the NSCTA illustrates the challenges of tourism development. Made up of five municipalities, the NSCTA was formed following a recognition that the communities have to work together to bundle their offerings. As Interviewee #3 noted, potential visitors haven't been aware of what the communities have had to offer because it has never been marketed as a distinct package or destination. The NSCTA is made up primarily of business members, but is operated as a public–private partnership. In order to build the necessary operating budget, the member municipalities were asked to contribute 50 cents per capita each year, while individual businesses pay a membership fee based on their category (e.g. bed-and-breakfast, hotel) and the size of their operation. The pent-up demand for this tourism development initiative was evident in the large turnout of people to the early NSCTA development meetings – what was expected to be a small turnout at one meeting actually became a standing-room-only crowd.

The NSCTA's first director was central in order 'to get it going . . . get the ball rolling', while acknowledging that the association itself should be industry led (Interviewee #3). The NSCTA board of directors aims to build the capacity of the association in its embryonic stage and, once the members are ready to engage more fully, then the board could take a back seat in the development. However, the director of the NSCTA left his post to pursue other opportunities during the nascent stages of development and the organization did not seem to move forward in the year which followed. This shows the importance of maintaining key personnel in the early stages of new path development and the early risk of new path atrophy.

The importance of maintaining continuity in the nascent stage of development cannot be emphasized enough and the benefits of this are seen in the contrasting cases of the more established tourism associations in the region. For example, the creation and development of the TVTA 'has driven a lot of us together' (Interviewee #2). In fact, the self-reinforcing nature of success is clear, since 'exhibitors as well as tourists want to be part [of the association] due to the buzz' (Interviewee #2). Thus, a successful local network facilitates the emergence of positive processes over time and, once embedded locally, such ongoing processes become self-reinforcing.

The TVTA has grown rapidly and now reaches out beyond its original limit of Lincoln to include members from St. Catharines, and the Association is also interested in recruiting members from the neighbouring town of Grimsby. Given the experience and success of the Association, their growth means rapid knowledge transfer to neighbouring stakeholders and a faster pace of capacity building among its new members.

The cooperation among tourism stakeholders across the Niagara region has potential to aid the long-term development of the region. However, the question of how this cooperation will extend to the dominant regional tourism player – Niagara Falls – is yet to be seen. Even though cooperation between Niagara Falls and the more peripheral parts of the region is desirable, the varying goals of the stakeholders make cooperative alignment difficult in the short-term. The regional institutional relations will need to adapt for positive change to occur.

Co-evolution in Niagara tourism – old institutional inertia and new institutional imperatives

Much of the tourism development that Niagara communities hope to achieve is contingent on the ability of the Tourism Partnership of Niagara to build awareness of the region's tourism offerings beyond its already well-established and well-known attractions. Many interviewees expressed a general sense of dissatisfaction with how this has played out so far. As noted earlier, the TPN was seen as being far too locked in to a Niagara Falls centred tourism marketing strategy. However, it is important to note that this feeling was not universal. For example, the TVTA, which aims to promote tourism in Lincoln and St. Catharines (both of which are some distance away from Niagara Falls), has leveraged its representation on the TPN board of directors into a notable presence within the TPN's marketing materials. For example, the TVTA figures prominently in a recent edition of the *Niagara Travel* magazine, which is produced by the TPN and has a circulation of 775,000 (Tourism Partnership of Niagara 2013). This connection between the horizontal and vertical actors is centred on the former director of the TVTA, an industrious and charismatic man who also sits on the TPN's marketing committee, but his position is not the only point of note.

The success of the TVTA in leveraging marketing dollars in its favour is also the result of long-term processes of change which have seen significant product development in the Twenty Valley area. Twenty Valley has had to work hard to get to this point: first, by building its membership, developing a critical mass of quality local-tourism products and establishing a reputation as a well-managed and successful destination marketing organization; and second, by initiating and nurturing its relationship with the TPN. All of this has been focussed through a change in formal network relations which is allowing meaningful dialogue to occur – dialogue which is leading to knowledge transfer and closer cooperation. This has also taken a long time, but is clearly now paying off and is probably why the other marginal stakeholders are getting together slowly but surely to develop tourism in their own locales (such as in the case of the NSCTA). New tourism development is occurring but at a much more modest pace in the more peripheral parts of the region and, over time, these highly localized developments should lead to noticeable regional institutional change.

Conclusion

In this chapter we have examined the relative development stages of Niagara's tourism paths and discussed the new path development and institutional changes occurring in the Niagara region. These themes show how tourism development in the region is in many ways a product of the region's industrial and agricultural legacies, but also how innovative action over an extended period of time is bringing about institutional change in the tourism economy. We also built on the concept of co-evolution by exploring how the institutional inertia associated with the more central actors of the region (in both tourism and non-tourism development) is being organically changed by the force of the institutional imperatives embodied by the more peripheral stakeholders (see Papatheodorou 2004; García-Cabrera and Durán-Herrera 2014).

In conclusion, let us turn to the question we raised at the beginning: why is co-evolution important for sustainable tourism development? There are several co-evolving tourism paths in the Niagara region. Even though the web of tourism stakeholders is quite tangled, with some individuals serving multiple roles, there are a number of distinct paths in this relatively small region. While it is obvious that not all paths are the same (there are some large, capital-intensive paths and some small, community-driven paths), they are all an important part of the local tourism development mix. Only by actively supporting all viable paths can the region avoid the danger of lock-in to one or two larger but unsustainable paths. Destinations need to be understood as complex development environments (see Milne and Ateljevic 2001; Brouder and Eriksson 2013a). The inertia of the dominant tourism (and non-tourism) institutions is beginning to be changed by the new developments, ultimately leading to a more sustainable regional economic portfolio for Niagara. Regional stakeholders need to understand that positive change takes time and that the laggards of today may be the leaders of a more resilient regional economy tomorrow.

Acknowledgements

We would like to thank the Banting Postdoctoral Fellowships for supporting Patrick's research and the Council for Research in Social Sciences at Brock University for supporting our early collaboration. We would also like to acknowledge Loris Gasparotto for his map-making expertise.

References

Andersson Cederholm, E. and Hultman, J. (2010). 'The value of intimacy – Negotiating commercial relationships in lifestyle entrepreneurship'. *Scandinavian Journal of Hospitality and Tourism* 10(1), 16–32.

Ateljevic, I. and Doorne, S. (2000). 'Staying within the fence: Lifestyle entrepreneurship in tourism'. *Journal of Sustainable Tourism* 8(5), 378–92.

Boschma, R. and Martin, R. (eds) (2010). *The Handbook of Evolutionary Economic Geography*. Cheltenham, UK: Edward Elgar.

Bramwell, B. (2011). 'Governance, the state and sustainable tourism: A political economy approach'. *Journal of Sustainable Tourism* 19(4–5), 459–77.

Brooker, E. and Burgess, J. (2008). 'Marketing destination Niagara effectively through the tourism life cycle'. *International Journal of Contemporary Hospitality Management* 20(3), 278–92.

Brouder, P. (2012). 'Creative outposts: Tourism's place in rural innovation'. *Tourism Planning and Development* 9(4), 383–96.

Brouder, P. (2013). 'Embedding Arctic tourism innovation in "creative outposts"'. In R. H. Lemelin, P. Maher, and D. Liggett (eds) *From Talk to Action: How Tourism is Changing the Polar Regions* .Thunder Bay: Centre for Northern Studies Press (pp. 183–98).

Brouder, P. (2014a). 'Evolutionary economic geography: A new path for tourism studies?' *Tourism Geographies* 16(1), 2–7.

Brouder, P. (2014b). 'Evolutionary economic geography and tourism studies: Extant studies and future research directions'. *Tourism Geographies* 16(4), 540–5.

Brouder, P. and Eriksson, R. H. (2013a). 'Tourism evolution: On the synergies of tourism studies and evolutionary economic geography'. *Annals of Tourism Research* 43, 370–89.

Brouder, P. and Eriksson, R. H. (2013b). 'Staying power: What influences micro-firm survival in tourism?' *Tourism Geographies* 15(1), 124–43.

Brouder, P. and Fullerton, C. (2015). 'Exploring heterogeneous tourism development paths: Cascade effect or co-evolution in Niagara?' *Scandinavian Journal of Hospitality and Tourism* 15(1), 152–66.

Brouder, P. and Ioannides, D. (2014). 'Urban tourism and evolutionary economic geography: Complexity and co-evolution in contested spaces'. *Urban Forum* 25(4), 419–30.

Cohen, E. (1979). 'Rethinking the sociology of tourism'. *Annals of Tourism Research* 6(1), 18–35.

Conway, T. and Cawley, M. (2012). 'Organizational networking in an emerging ecotourism destination'. *Tourism Planning and Development* 9(4), 397–409.

Debbage, K. G. and Ioannides, D. (2004). 'The cultural turn? Toward a more critical economic geography of tourism'. In A. A. Lew, C. M. Hall, and A. M. Williams (eds) *A Companion to Tourism*. Oxford: Blackwell (pp. 99–109).

Deloitte and Touche (2008). *Making it Happen: Shaping Niagara and Other Canadian Regional Tourism for Tomorrow*. Toronto: Deloitte and Touche LLP.

Dredge, D. (2006). 'Networks, conflict and collaborative communities'. *Journal of Sustainable Tourism* 14, 562–81.

Dubinsky, K. (1999). *The Second Greatest Disappointment: Honeymooning and Tourism at Niagara Falls*. Toronto: Between the Lines.

Fullerton, C. (2013). 'The growing place of wine in the economic development of the Niagara region'. In M. Ripmeester, P. G. Mackintosh, and C. Fullerton (eds) *The World of Niagara Wine*. Waterloo: Wilfrid Laurier University Press (pp. 47–63).

García-Cabrera, A. M. and Durán-Herrera, J. J. (2014). 'Does the tourism industry co-evolve?' *Annals of Tourism Research* 47, 81–3.

Gayler, H. (1994). 'Urban development and planning in Niagara'. In H. Gayler (ed.) *Niagara's Changing Landscapes*. Ottawa: Carleton University Press (pp. 241–78).

Gayler, H. (2010). 'Niagara's emerging wine culture: From a countryside of production to consumption'. In J. Nicks and N. Baxter-Moore (eds) *Covering Niagara: Studies in Local Popular Culture*. Waterloo: Wilfrid Laurier University Press (pp. 195–212).

George, E. W., Mair, H., and Reid, D. G. (2009). *Rural Tourism Development: Localism and Cultural Change*. North York: Channel View.

Getz, D. (1992). 'Tourism planning and destination life cycle'. *Annals of Tourism Research* 19(4), 752–70.

Gill, A. M. and Williams, P. W. (2011). 'Rethinking resort growth: Understanding evolving governance strategies in Whistler, British Columbia'. *Journal of Sustainable Tourism* 19(4–5), 629–48.

Haugland, S. (2011). Development of tourism destinations: An integrated multilevel perspective. *Annals of Tourism Research* 38(1), 268–90.

Hickey, R. (2008). *Challenges and Opportunities for Improving Employment Conditions in Niagara's Hotel Sector*. Report prepared for UNITE HERE Canada.

Ioannides, D. and Debbage, K. G. (1998). *The Economic Geography of the Tourist Industry: A Supply-Side Analysis*. London: Routledge.

Jayawardena, C., Patterson, D. J., Choi, C., and Brain, R. (2008). 'Sustainable tourism development in Niagara: Discussions, theories, projects and insights'. *International Journal of Contemporary Hospitality Management* 20(3), 258–77.

Larsson, A. and Lindström, K. (2014). 'Bridging the knowledge-gap between the old and the new: Regional marine experience production in Orust, Västra Götaland, Sweden'. *European Planning Studies* 22(8), 1551–68.

Ma, M. and Hassink, R. (2013). 'An evolutionary perspective on tourism area development'. *Annals of Tourism Research* 41, 89–109.

Ma, M. and Hassink, R. (2014). 'Path dependence and tourism area development: The case of Guilin, China'. *Tourism Geographies* 16(4), 580–97.

MacLaurin, D. J. and Wolstenholme, S. (2008). 'An analysis of the gaming industry in the Niagara region'. *International Journal of Contemporary Hospitality Management* 20(3), 320–31.

Mah, A. (2012). *Industrial Ruination, Community, and Place: Landscapes and Legacies of Urban Decline*. Toronto: University of Toronto Press.

Marchant, B. and Mottiar, Z. (2011). 'Understanding lifestyle entrepreneurs and digging beneath the issue of profits: Profiling surf tourism lifestyle entrepreneurs in Ireland'. *Tourism Planning and Development* 8(2), 171–83.

Milne, S. and Ateljevic, I. (2001). 'Tourism, economic development and the global–local nexus: Theory embracing complexity'. *Tourism Geographies* 3(4), 369–93.

Mitchell, C., Atkinson, G., and Clark, A. (2001). 'The creative destruction of Niagara-on-the-Lake'. *The Canadian Geographer* 45(2), 285–99.

Ontario Tourism Competitiveness Study (2009). *Discovering Ontario: A Report on the Future of Ontario Tourism*. Toronto: Queen's Printer for Ontario.

Papatheodorou, A. (2004). 'Exploring the evolution of tourism resorts'. *Annals of Tourism Research* 31(1), 219–37.

Quinn Patton, M. (2002). *Qualitative Research and Evaluation Methods*. London: Sage.

Reed, M. (1997). 'Power relations and community-based tourism planning'. *Annals of Tourism Research* 24(3), 566–91.

Ruhanen, L. (2013). 'Local government: Facilitator or inhibitor of sustainable tourism development?' *Journal of Sustainable Tourism* 21(1), 80–98.

Saarinen, J. (2006). 'Traditions of sustainability in tourism research'. *Annals of Tourism Research* 33(4), 1121–40.

Telfer, D. and Hashimoto, A. (2013). 'Wine and culinary tourism in Niagara'. In M. Ripmeester, P. G. Mackintosh, and C. Fullerton (eds) *The World of Niagara Wine*. Waterloo: Wilfrid Laurier University Press (pp. 281–99).

Tourism Partnership of Niagara (2012). [online] URL: www.niagarasrto.com/about (accessed on 28 September 2013).

Tourism Partnership of Niagara (2013). *Niagara Travel*. Niagara Falls: Tourism Partnership of Niagara.

Valentine, G. (2005). 'Tell me about . . . . Using interviews as a research methodology'. In R. Flowerdew and D. Martin (eds) *Methods in Human Geography: A Guide for Students Doing a Research Project*. Harlow: Pearson (pp. 110–27).

Viken, A. and Aarsaether, N. (2013). 'Transforming an iconic attraction into a diversified destination: The case of North Cape tourism'. *Scandinavian Journal of Hospitality and Tourism* 13(1), 38–54.

9 Regional development and leisure in Fryslân

A complex adaptive systems perspective through evolutionary economic geography

Jasper F. Meekes, Constanza Parra and Gert De Roo

Introduction

In September 2013 a European jury chose Leeuwarden, the capital of the Dutch province of Fryslân, as European Capital of Culture for 2018 (Joustra 2013). This title might have come as a surprise to some, given the competition of larger and better-known Dutch cities such as The Hague, Utrecht and Eindhoven; nevertheless, the designation of Leeuwarden matches the development in the north of the Netherlands, where regional development is increasingly focused on creating an environment in which people enjoy being. The route towards 2018 consists of a programme that specifically aims at making the area 'optimally attractive' (Stichting Kulturele Haadstêd 2015, 2018). This is part of the development that Hermans and De Roo (2006) call a 'leisure economy'. The rationale is that rural or peripheral areas such as Fryslân cannot compete with the core economic areas in Europe. However, the peripheral location and lower population density do result in qualities that are important for leisure, such as green spaces, waterscapes and tranquillity. Leisure, in this context, is seen not just as an economic activity, but also as relating to well-being, identity and status, and even a state of mind or attitude, for instance a feeling of freedom (cf. Gospodini 2001; Walmsley 2003; Greenwood Parr and Lashua 2004). Particularly for areas in the face of population decline, as is the case for many rural regions in the EU (see Haartsen and Venhorst 2010; Provincie Fryslân 2013: 8), focusing on leisure development can generate social, cultural and political advantages, which go far beyond economic benefits (e.g. Stebbins 1982; Parra 2010a).

The current transformations in Fryslân are related to a broader debate within academia and regional development policy on the role of leisure in rural and peripheral areas (e.g. Ravenscroft and Reeves 1999; Parra 2010b). Regions that lack a strong industrial or service sector turn to leisure, tourism and recreation as a way of improving employment and production in the area. However, planning for leisure is not a simple challenge to address. Leisure is fragmented, both as a spatial phenomenon and as a policy issue. It is comprised of several subsectors, making it dependent on various policy departments, regulations and funding streams. Leisure often exists on the fringes of urban and rural areas. Where it occurs in rural areas, it falls outside the spatial categories of nature and agriculture traditionally used in rural land-use policy. Additionally, although leisure is often used as a means of economic development, there are prominent cultural, social and ecological issues to be considered, for instance the quality and aesthetics of landscape. A traditional economic approach fails to capture many of these factors' importance for analysing the role of leisure in regional development.

This chapter provides an alternative and more inclusive perspective on regional development and the role of leisure, by calling for an evolutionary economic geography (EEG) approach based on complex adaptive systems (CAS). In our view, this perspective can produce a more complete understanding of the unpredictable and non-linear development of a region. We aim to explore the insights into regional development that can be gained by applying this perspective, which do not surface through traditional approaches. We argue that this can be especially valuable for elucidating the inherently complex role of leisure in regional development. This chapter builds on the case of Appelscha, a village in the north of the Netherlands well known regionally for its leisure cluster, to illustrate and discuss the complexities involved in regional development through leisure. In 2001 the amusement park Duinen Zathe, which formed the heart of the local leisure cluster in the Frisian village of Appelscha, was moved to a location 500 m to the west, just outside the village. This relocation, implemented to allow the amusement park to grow without nuisance to the village inhabitants, led to harsh and unexpected results. In short, several leisure-related companies located in the village went bankrupt, investments by the municipality to upgrade the village centre did not lead to a revival and in general moving the amusement park was seen as a 'blunder'. Based on traditional analytical frameworks, these developments are difficult to explain. On the basis of a discussion of the perspective offered by CAS and its specific application within EEG, we highlight tools for grasping the non-linear nature of regional development through leisure. Applying this framework to the case of Appelscha, we then illustrate how this perspective can reveal underlying processes influencing a regional system's ability to adapt to changes in its environment. We conclude with a discussion of how this CAS perspective to examine leisure and its role in regional development can help to better comprehend the effects of planning measures and institutional settings on long-term processes in the region.

A complex evolutionary perspective on leisure and regional development

The complexity of leisure and the interactions between many factors of regional development make predicting the effects of specific changes in an area difficult, if not impossible. The case of Appelscha, briefly described in the introduction, provides a good example of such unpredictable developments. To provide a theoretical framing for the case study, a review of the key constructs of EEG and CAS is presented.

Evolutionary economic geography

Evolutionary economic geography aims to explain (uneven) economic development through a combination of a region's past and present, taking different aspects of the region into account and not concentrating only on price and demand. The idea that 'history matters' is given a spatial dimension through this approach (Gill and Williams 2014). As Boschma and Martin (2007: 540, emphasis in original) state, EEG is:

> quintessentially concerned with *the spatialities of economic novelty* (innovations, new firms, new industries), with how the *spatial structures of the economy emerge* from the micro-behaviours of economic agents (individuals, firms, institutions); with how, in the absence of central coordination or direction, the *economic landscape exhibits self-organization*; and with how the processes of *path creation* and *path dependence* interact to shape geographies of economic development and transformation, and why and how such processes are themselves place dependent.

Based on these concepts EEG can be useful in providing tools to analyse the role of leisure and tourism in regional development (Brouder 2014). However, it is important to stress that a variety of approaches exist within EEG. Boschma and Martin (2010) state that complexity sciences, path dependency and neo-Darwinism, are the three major theoretical frameworks for EEG. Martin and Sunley (2007) elaborate on the concept of complexity within EEG, and state that the complexity of an economy stems from its spatial distribution. Change is difficult to predict and the effects of certain measures perhaps even more so. The non-linear development of spatial arrangements, as well as the interactions between social, economic, ecological and political factors in space, can cause plans that are made with all the right intentions to lead to unwanted results and sometimes deterioration of the existing situation. We hold that this specific form of EEG, focusing on CAS, can provide a new perspective on unpredictable non-linear developments. In the following sections we discuss the concept of CAS, its meaning for EEG and the way it can be applied to understanding leisure planning in the case of Appelscha.

Complex adaptive systems

The call for the use of complexity sciences when dealing with regional development comes from the observation that, due to the large number of actors involved, as well as interactions between social, economic and ecological issues, spatial transformations are often characterized by a high degree of complexity. The term 'complexity' in this context is used to denote two main ideas: through complex interactions the whole is greater than the sum of the parts and evolution over time progresses non-linearly. Complex-systems sciences focus on the links or connective properties that exist between elements of a system. Examining these connective properties, we can discover processes that create order in complexity (Foster 2006). According to Martin and Sunley (2007), complex systems are distinguished by the way they show emergent, self-organizing behaviour, driven by co-evolutionary interactions, and by an adaptive capacity that allows them to spontaneously rearrange their internal structure. This interpretation of complexity centres on the adaptivity of a system: How does a system react to internal and external changes? Levin (2003) defines adaptivity as stemming from the diversity of components, interactions among these components and a process of selection of components for replication or enhancement based on the interactions. Local small-scale interactions cause the emergence of large macroscopic patterns (Rammel *et al.* 2007). The nested hierarchy that takes place in such systems causes a complex and non-linear development that defies accurate prediction. However, as Levin (2003) explains, broad features of a system are knowable, implying the ability to understand the functioning of the system to the extent that it is clear what properties of the system are unknown but knowable, and what is truly unknowable.

The complexity of space and the unpredictability of change is not a new observation in planning and spatial sciences. As Healey (2003: 117) states, her work on collaborative planning is 'a plea for understanding complexity and diversity, in a way that does not collapse into atomistic analyses of specific episodes and individual achievements, or avoid recognizing the way power consolidates into driving forces that shape situational specificities'. However, the further advancement of complexity theories has led to a number of concepts that can be of benefit to the understanding of how complex systems work. Most prominently, the work on CAS – using the concepts of self-organization, emergence and co-evolution to discuss complex interactions – shows potential for providing a useful dynamic perspective on spatial development (Rammel *et al.* 2007; McDonald 2009; Rauws *et al.* 2014). CAS are open systems, connected to an environment that contains other systems (Foster 2005). A CAS absorbs the information from this environment, which leads to adaptation and learning through self-organization, co-evolution, and emergence. These processes can reveal consistent patterns in an ever-changing world. Although this does not mean that planners will be able to accurately predict the future (nor is that the aim), understanding these patterns can help form a more adaptive planning approach.

The term self-organization refers to 'a property of [complex systems] which enables them to develop or change internal structure spontaneously and adaptively in order to cope with, or manipulate, their environment' (Cilliers 1998, in McDonald 2009: 460). Self-organization in complex systems is thus the driving force behind the adaptivity of a system. It can cause spontaneous order to arise from chaos, not as a result of the properties of the individual components of the system, but based on the interactions between these components. Each component adapts only to local information, but the combined process of many components can lead to structure on a high level (McDonald 2009). Rauws (2015) gives the example of a shopping street to explain self-organization in a spatial manner. The uncoordinated and relatively independent actions of multiple individuals or sub-groups (for instance shop owners) can create changes on a higher scale, for instance when stores are transformed into a bar or café. Over time, these actions can result in the shopping street being transformed into a public 'living room', without the predetermined intent of any of the individual shop owners to create this new spatial pattern. This transformation can be triggered by external circumstances, for instance the rise of online shopping, but the final spatial pattern that arises, i.e. the way the system adapts, is highly unpredictable. According to Rotmans and Loorbach (2009), such self-organization is not a sufficient criterion for complex adaptive systems: only systems that exhibit self-organization as well as emergence are truly complex and adaptive.

The concept of emergence is an important aspect of the irreducibility of complex systems, as the properties on a higher level cannot be explained solely as a summation of those on lower levels. Rotmans and Loorbach (2009: 186) describe emergence as 'the arising of novel and coherent structures, patterns and properties during the process of self-organization in complex systems'. Properties can be called 'emergent' when the combined changes on lower levels lead to new and often unexpected properties on a higher level, such as the transformation of a shopping street into a public 'living room' in the example given above. Emergence is crucial in CAS not only due to the fact that it links different levels, but also because this creates memory, as the structure on a higher level will through feedback loops affect the self-organization of the low-level components (McDonald 2009). This is what Martin and Sunley (2012) call 'third-order emergence', where first-order emergence only involves amplified forms of changes on lower levels, second-order emergence includes downward causal effects, but third-order emergence adds an evolutionary character to the system. In their words, 'specific past higher-order states repeatedly shape the lower-order dynamics of a systems' micro-components that in turn lead to future emergent states' (Martin and Sunley 2012: 342). They compare this form of emergence to selective path-dependence, where the subsequent path of the system is shaped by particular significant events, in which some events matter more than others. Therefore, emergence not only refers to bottom-up processes exhibiting influence on higher levels, but also includes the feedback loops and path-dependency of the system.

In the analysis of regional development through leisure as a CAS, the concept of co-evolution is perhaps the most relevant of the three concepts discussed in this section, as it depicts the way in which different subsystems influence each other's evolution. In economics, the term 'co-evolution' is commonly used for the relation between technology and industrial structures (Rammel *et al.* 2007). However, the concept of co-evolution can be used more broadly as the way in which two evolving populations, or sub-systems, significantly impact each other's evolution and ability to persist (Murmann 2003). In the case of tourism, Ma and Hassink (2013) see the interaction between tourism sectors, tourism products and their institutional environment occurring at multiple levels as a co-evolutionary process. In an even broader sense, co-evolution can also describe the way in which the evolution of an economic sector is mutually dependent with other sectors or with the same economic sector in a different region. As such, the role of leisure in regional development can be seen as co-evolutionary with other sectors of the economy, with formal and informal institutions, with changes in society and with the evolution of leisure in other regions.

Complexity and leisure

The use of the concepts of self-organization, emergence and co-evolution lies in their ability to reveal the links and interactions between different parts of the system. They can clarify the way in which subsystems influence each other. The interactions between different subsystems are crucial in analysing a complex adaptive system, as is stressed by, among others, Anderies *et al.* (2004) and Liu *et al.* (2007), or by Ramstad (1986) when discussing holism. This systemic approach can show for instance how (formal and informal) institutions shape and are shaped by changes in the leisure sector or how the agricultural sector and leisure co-evolve. By attempting to distinguish the processes of self-organization, emergence and co-evolution, the evolutionary process can be broken down for a subsystem into internal and external influences. These processes, and most specifically emergence and co-evolution, can also express the multi-level nature of regional development processes. Regional development does not only take place at the regional level. It is influenced by changes at a lower level that materialize on the regional level. Additionally, the national and supranational levels influence the regional level. However, these vertical interactions are not the only multi-level aspects of regional development. The co-evolution of different (sub) systems gives rise to horizontal interactions. Economy, culture, society, politics, institutions and ecology all dynamically interact, co-evolve and influence each other. These interactions are an important part of what keeps a CAS adaptive.

As such, CAS can be useful for the analysis of regional development in a holistic manner. Within regional development the topic of leisure offers a specific opportunity to see how different aspects of the system of regional development interact. This is based, first of all, on the various meanings assigned to the concept of leisure. Leisure can be seen simply as free time, time that is left over after work and essential personal care (Walmsley 2003), but also as the activities that fill this time. It can be defined as a state of mind or attitude (Greenwood Parr and Lashua 2004), such as a feeling of freedom (Gospodini 2001; cf. Rojek 2001). Leisure relates to the concepts of tourism and recreation, where recreation is often defined as the activities that fill leisure time and tourism involves overnight stay and travel; but, as Walmsley (2003: 64) states, attempts to distinguish leisure, tourism and recreation 'are ultimately doomed and . . . the three forms of behaviour are best viewed as parts of the same whole'. The importance of leisure has been linked to: well-being (e.g. Stebbins 1982; Gilbert and Abdullah 2004); identity and status (Veblen 1994; Stebbins 2001; Kaltenborn 2009); economy, for instance as part of the 'experience economy' (e.g. Andersson 2007; Smidt-Jensen *et al.* 2009); and regional development (e.g. Ravenscroft and Reeves 1999; Parra 2010a, 2010b).

Related to the many definitions and conceptions of leisure is the fact that many different values are attached to leisure. There are different rationales for developing the leisure sector, which range from purely economic reasons to broader quality-of-life issues in the region (e.g. Hermans and De Roo 2006). These values attached to leisure are based on the way in which the interactions between different subsystems – for instance social, economic and ecological – are judged. The importance of these interactions coincides with the focus on the relations between system parts within the framework presented here. Another characteristic of leisure that makes it a suitable topic for a complexity viewpoint lies in its spatial manifestation. Leisure, from a regional development perspective, is a fragmented issue. It takes place on the fringes of urban and rural areas. In rural areas, leisure does not fit in the traditional divide between nature and agriculture, as it has links to both (Hadjimichalis 2003; Buijs *et al.* 2006; Hartman and De Roo 2013). These characteristics make planning for leisure more challenging, especially when combined with the intersectoral nature of leisure and leisure policies.

Given the fragmented spatial manifestation of leisure, as well as the different and changing meanings that can be attached to the concept, we call for a non-reductionist approach that considers these complexities and allows for the analysis of the whole of definitions and manifestations of leisure. This entails a holistic ontology, in which reality and, therefore, also leisure, is seen as an integrated whole, and not as a set of logically separable structures and processes (Ramstad 1986). Complexity serves this requirement well. As Martin and Sunley (2007: 575) state, 'by its very nature as a holistic concept the notion of complexity resists easy reduction to a set of law-like statements or universal theoretical principles' (cf. O'Sullivan 2004). Leisure is therefore not reduced to a purely economic concept or a specific land use type, but a complex and evolving mix of meanings and manifestations. This holistic approach also matches our view of regional development, which goes beyond its economic dimension to include ecological, cultural, social and political processes. Additionally, the regional development of one region, in this case Fryslân, cannot be seen in isolation of the development of other (nearby) regions.

However, even though we take a holistic stance, not all things related to leisure are of equal value for this research. Those leisure activities that are neither spatially nor economically relevant (for instance watching TV at home) are not likely to have an impact on the development of the region or, to the extent that they do, fall outside of the scope of this research. We choose to take leisure activities that are both spatially and economically relevant as a starting point. For these activities, we discuss how they relate to the broader aspects of both leisure and regional development. This means that we include in our approach the impacts such activities might have on people's well-being or on the cultural or ecological development of the region. Given this starting point, we follow Walmsley (2003) in his statement, discussed above, that it is not possible and not useful to distinguish leisure, tourism and recreation. Leisure activities undertaken by people in the region as well as by tourists visiting from other areas are of interest for regional development. Therefore, when using the term 'leisure', we include both recreation and tourism, without the need to distinguish precisely between the various manifestations of this phenomenon.

Adaptivity in the evolution of leisure

Based on the CAS approach presented here, the development of a complex system depends on the capacity to adapt to changes within the system as well as in the external environment. This adaptation takes place through processes of self-organization, co-evolution and emergence. However, a system's capacity to adapt – its adaptivity – is not always the same. The interactions between different parts of the system play an important role in adapting to changing circumstances. CAS evolve over time, not only in the composition of subsystems, but also in the way in which these subsystems are linked and interact with each other. The intensity of linkages can grow or decline, and the influence these linkages can exert on different subsystems changes as well. These changes are, however, not completely random. They influence a system's adaptivity through influencing the conditions a system must possess in order to adapt to change. We, therefore, propose a framework that discusses the changes in functioning of the system based on aspects of robustness, dynamics, unity and diversity.

Based on CAS theory it is possible to deduce a set of criteria that a CAS must fulfil to stay 'alive' and adaptive. CAS are often said to be on the edge of order and chaos (Waldrop 1992; Martin and Sunley 2007). This spectrum between order and chaos can be seen as depending on various aspects. Potts (2000) views the spectrum as a matter of connectivity: an ordered system has low connectivity, whereas a chaotic system has a very high level of connectedness. Duit and Galaz (2008), by contrast, centre on the balance between robustness and adaptive capacity as vital for a CAS. De Roo (2012) combines these two positions and rephrases them as 'unity versus diversity' (connectivity) and 'robustness versus dynamics'. A CAS must retain a balance between these extremes, or, somewhat paradoxically, must possess all four traits at the same time. This is possible because robustness and dynamics, as well as unity and diversity, are diametrically opposed but not mutually exclusive. A complex system can be both robust and dynamic, having a strong capacity to withstand external shocks, but still possess the dynamics to adapt to changes in the environment. A diverse system, which combines many different functions, can still have an internal unity through a small number of strong connections.

When we understand a system's capacity to adapt as a combination of the conditions of unity, diversity, robustness and dynamics, this allows for the relative comparison of the adaptivity of a system over time. These conditions determine the extent to which a system can self-organize, co-evolve and show emergent behaviour. However, these conditions are not stable. They change due to developments within the system, as well as external influences. Because the amount of adaptivity that is required changes, there is no ideal state for the system in terms of robustness, dynamics, unity and diversity. However, if these conditions are seen as a spectrum (for example, from complete robustness to a complete lack thereof), the extremes will result in a very low adaptivity, as this implies a lack of balance. Although no absolute values can be attached to a system's score on such conditions, relative comparisons are possible. By evaluating a system over time, conclusions can be drawn as to the robustness, flexibility, unity and diversity in comparison to an earlier state of the system. This is especially valuable when the situation before and after drastic changes in the system's structure or function is compared.

Exploring a system's adaptivity through conditions of robustness, dynamics, unity and diversity creates a promising perspective when applied to leisure and regional development. The fragile reciprocity in many tourism- and leisure-oriented regions between nature protection and economic development comes down to a balance between these conditions. Liu *et al.* (2007) discuss this issue, stating that economic development in tourism can degrade the qualities that attract tourists. In order to be maintained, a dynamic development must, therefore, be accompanied by robustness within a system. Simultaneously, a region's attractiveness is based both on its unity, being recognized as one destination, and its diversity, offering a variety of activities. Russell and Faulkner (1999) conceive the evolution of tourism in a region as a balance between entrepreneurs as agents of change and planners as moderators or controllers, which in our framework can be interpreted as a balance between dynamics and robustness. Using this perspective of a system's adaptivity for the topic of leisure can provide new insights in the complex processes that shape its development, which is further illustrated through the example of Appelscha in the following section.

Appelscha: an example of non-linear development

The province of Fryslân has a number of areas with an economic orientation towards leisure and tourism. The islands off the Wadden Sea coast are popular tourism destinations, and the lakes and canals in the south-west and central parts of the province attract visitors interested in water-related recreation, such as boating, sailing and windsurfing. The eleven historical cities in the province, famous for the epic 200-km eleven cities ice-skating tour, provide a cultural attraction. These three areas – the Wadden islands, the Frisian lakes and the eleven Frisian cities – are marketed by the province as the 'unique selling points' the province has to offer when it comes to leisure, recreation and tourism (Provincie Fryslân 2011: 6). The village of Appelscha, in the south-east of the province, does not fit into any of these unique selling points, but does have a long-standing reputation as a leisure cluster in the north of the Netherlands. This reputation, as well as the long history as a tourism and leisure destination, makes this village an interesting illustration for the complexity perspective presented here.

Appelscha, in the municipality of Ooststellingwerf, is a village of just over 4,500 inhabitants (Centraal Bureau voor de Statistiek 2011) that lies on the edge of the National Park Drents-Friese Wold. The local tourist office was established in 1911, and since then tourism, recreation and leisure in Appelscha have gone through various transitions. Originally, leisure facilities in Appelscha were to a large extent based on the natural surroundings, which combine the second-largest stretch of forest in the Netherlands, with sand dunes, heathlands, and fens and peat bogs. Since the 1970s some of the canals historically used for peat transport have been reopened and renovated, creating possibilities for recreational boating. Additionally, the village houses a number of attractions not directly related to the surrounding landscape, most notably the amusement park Duinen Zathe. This facility started out as a children's playground, but has evolved into an amusement park with a roller coaster and other thrill rides. The owner of this amusement park in 1989 also opened the Miniature Park Appelscha. This park, with scale models of buildings from all over the north of the Netherlands, was intended to be complementary to the amusement park and was located immediately besides Duinen Zathe so it could easily be visited by the same crowd. Based on the different camp sites surrounding Appelscha, the amusement park and the miniature park, Appelscha has a tradition of being a destination for school field trips, making it well known in the north of the Netherlands. Although tourism, recreation and leisure remain on a relatively small scale when considered from an (inter)national viewpoint, a large part of the population is directly or indirectly employed within the sector (Gemeente Ooststellingwerf 2009) and the village's reputation in the north of the Netherlands is quite strong.

The development of the leisure sector in Appelscha has, however experienced ups and downs. The most drastic event in this regard was related to the amusement park Duinen Zathe. In the early 1990s the park's growth had reached the limits of what was possible at the location at the time, both in terms of space available and nuisance levels for the surrounding neighbourhood (Nicolai 1991). After a discussion over several years between the municipality, the amusement park and other actors involved, the decision was made to move the park to a new location where it would have the required space to expand and grow (Arendz 1997). The move was realized in 2001, and although this new location was only about 500 m west of the old one, the results of the relocation were quite harsh and unexpected. The increased distance between the amusement park and the recreational centre of the village caused a reduction in the number of visitors to the local cafés and restaurants. The Miniature Park also suffered from no longer being adjacent to the amusement park. No new user was found for the terrain that was previously occupied by Duinen Zathe. Attempts by the municipality and other actors to move the visitor centre for Staatsbosbeheer (the forestry and nature management organization) to this location failed. According to popular opinion, Appelscha was left with a hole in the heart of its leisure centre (Vogelzang 2006). In 2007, six years after Duinen Zathe moved, the Miniature Park went bankrupt due mainly to a declining visitor rate. By this time, many of the cafés and restaurants had gone bankrupt as well and changed owners or disappeared. New investments by the municipality to upgrade the central leisure area have not led to a revival, although some positive developments can be seen in which a local outdoor sports and events company plays an important role. In general, however, the moving of the amusement park is seen as a 'blunder' (according to several interviewees) with extremely detrimental effects for the entire leisure sector in Appelscha.

Applying a CAS perspective

The theoretical framework presented in this chapter offers a different perspective on regional development through leisure and a framework for understanding the non-linear processes that shape such development. The case of Appelscha offers the opportunity to illustrate this perspective. Based on an analysis of policy documents and newspaper articles, as well as a number of semi-structured interviews with actors in the region, conducted in the summer of 2014, we illustrate the contribution of an EEG approach through CAS to the understanding of the way in which leisure developments shape and are shaped by processes in the wider CAS. Although this illustration is based on an actual case, the goal is not to give an exhaustive description of the developments in Appelscha.

To apply this framework to the case of Appelscha, we start by defining the CAS in this case. Based on the EEG approach, we take the physical space of Appelscha as the basis for this CAS. Building on this physical space, the leisure companies within this area, the national park, the inhabitants of, as well as the visitors to, the village of Appelscha and the institutions set up by the municipality or by other local actors all interact within the complex system. Because CAS are by definition open (Foster 2005), it is difficult to define a concrete boundary. Although Appelscha has a defined space, processes outside of this region influence the village as well, such as policy on a regional level, but also macroeconomic conditions. As this local system is nested within systems on a higher scale, effects from the regional level – such as the provincial policy on tourism and leisure – as well as the (supra)national level will have their impact on Appelscha and are influenced by emergent properties from the local level. In the end, systems are not defined by predetermined boundaries, but by the mechanisms that govern them.

The complex system of leisure in Appelscha has shown adaptivity throughout its history. No specific plan was made to create a leisure cluster, yet this did not prevent the different leisure companies from self-organizing into a pattern of interacting leisure facilities offering complementary touristic and recreational services. A representative of the local association of tourism and leisure-related companies describes this development as something that grew in an independent process:

> You can't build it. It all coincides, yes, that's the right word. You don't organize this. You can change it, [. . .], but the entire situation just grew around it.
>
> (Appelscha, 15 July 2014)

The development of the leisure sector in this area has had an impact on the surrounding natural areas. At times, Staatsbosbeheer, the Dutch governmental organization responsible for forestry and managing nature reserves, has expressed its concerns about the amount of people frequenting the woods, heathlands and sand dunes near Appelscha. However, the growth of the leisure sector in Appelscha has co-evolved with a changing perspective in the policy of Staatsbosbeheer, where, instead of closing off the natural areas for people wanting to visit, the organization has put up paths and signage to lead visitors through the area in a way that minimizes damage to its natural qualities. Through the years this has led to more recreational services offered by Staatsbosbeheer, for instance in the visitor centre. Also, according to a local forester, the presence of a significant leisure function in the reserve played an important role in assigning the area as National Park in 2000, which in his view is first and foremost a marketing tool to promote recreation, tourism and leisure in the area:

> You really have to see the National Parks as a sort of advertising and marketing tool, not as a protective measure.
>
> (Assen, 21 August 2014)

The development of the cluster of leisure companies in the village has also influenced the population of the village. A large percentage of the inhabitants have a job that is directly or indirectly linked to the leisure sector. According to a representative of the local association of tourism and leisure-related firms, this has resulted in a high tolerance towards the nuisance that leisure-related activities might produce:

> We are a real tourist village in that sense, that knows where their living comes from, and that therefore you have to be tolerant towards the tourists.
>
> (Appelscha, 15 July 2014)

This illustrates what could be called a co-evolution between the leisure sector and the population of Appelscha. On the one hand, the growth of the leisure sector has increased the population's tolerance of developments related to this sector, while on the other hand this tolerance has been an important factor in allowing this development to take place. Additionally, the composition of the village and the larger municipality in terms of political support has influenced the leisure cluster in a rather profound way. According to a former civil servant who worked for the municipality for forty years, the local labour party, which had until 2010 always been the largest party in the municipal council, specifically chose to stimulate forms of leisure that were accessible for the low-income groups:

> It was historically a low budget story, that's been the case for a long time. And it was also an objective for the municipality to offer opportunities for recreation to people on a tight budget.
>
> (Groningen, 26 August 2014)

This has led to leisure facilities mainly directed at the lower market segment, with, for instance, lower price-scale restaurants.

The description of the leisure cluster in Appelscha prior to the relocation of the amusement park can form the basis for the assessment of the conditions shaping its adaptivity. First of all, the reputation the area had – and perhaps to a lesser extent still has – has contributed to a robust system. This robustness was also achieved through the co-evolution and self-organization of different leisure firms and (the management of) the National Park. However, for the village as a whole, this has had an influence on its diversity. As an employee of the municipality puts it:

> It has a huge reputation, so people have been coming there for a long time and because of that a large part of the economy is based on recreation and tourism.
>
> (Ooststellingwerf, 13 August 2014)

Within the leisure sector of Appelscha, diversity is also limited, as is testified by the focus on low-income groups and fewer upscale facilities. However, although this suggests a lack of diversity, several actors in the village see this focus as an important factor in the success and branding of Appelscha. Diversity is seen as important, but mainly as a balance of facilities aimed at both day visitors and people staying in the area for longer periods. In terms of unity, the fact that many of the leisure services were aimed at the lower market segment created a cluster with a clear signature for Appelscha. In terms of dynamics, developments such as the miniature park and a live-music café testify to the exploration of new options within the existing structures.

The main question at hand is what happened to this system after the amusement park was moved to the new location. Although it is difficult to determine the adaptivity of the system before the move retrospectively, in general the unity and robustness of the system seemed to be quite high, the diversity was limited and the system was moderately dynamic. The decision to move the park was based on a discourse of dynamics, growth and expansion. The amusement park needed room to expand, in order to not lag behind the competition of other parks in the country. An employee of the municipality said about this:

> The times were different back then, I think they expected there would be something new there right away, it was still in the hosanna days.
>
> (Ooststellingwerf, 13 August 2014)

However, moving the amusement park had important effects on the leisure cluster. The main attraction of the cluster was no longer located near the other facilities in the manner in which it had evolved over the years. According to another civil servant working at the municipality of Ooststellingwerf, the response of the local leisure entrepreneurs lacked coordination:

> It's every man for himself, it's not as if they're saying: come on, let's make something nice out of this together! […] They still, so to speak, don't understand that if they strengthen each other, you strengthen the entire area and therefore also attract more people.
>
> (Ooststellingwerf, 13 August 2014)

The combination of the physical replacement of the amusement park and the response of the local leisure entrepreneurs led to a decline of the unity of the system. Additionally, the structures that had evolved over the years and had proven to be quite robust were broken down, leading to decreased robustness. The diversity of the system, which had not been extremely high before, was not improved, as no new facilities replaced the amusement park. As such, the balance between the robustness, dynamics, unity and diversity of the system was lost. In terms of the perspective offered by the CAS approach presented above, this caused a significant deterioration of the adaptivity of the system.

The lower adaptivity that we argue was the result of the moving of the amusement park is of course not the whole story. External influences, such as the economic crisis starting in 2008, were of great importance in the decline of the cluster. The representative of the local association of tourism and leisure-related firms stated:

> The plans to move the amusement park were based on a glorious future and growth. Due to the economic crisis we were faced with a hole in the middle of the village where no one dared to invest. This hole is still there and has really damaged us.
>
> (Appelscha, 15 July 2014)

In this perspective, the timing of the moving of the amusement park was extremely unfortunate. Because this move decreased the systems adaptivity, the economic crisis probably hit the village harder than it would have done without the move. In hindsight, it might seem that the decision to move the amusement park was a bad one. However, as the same tourism representative said:

> Moving the amusement park was of course a first class blunder, but to some point you can't really blame the municipality, because they also can't see five, six, seven years into the future. They're also, well, well-intentioned amateurs is perhaps a bit harsh, but it's not as if they can look into a crystal ball and say . . . . But by the same token they could have been right and we would have had a bright future.
>
> (Appelscha, 15 July 2014)

Predicting the effects of specific measures is extremely difficult, if not impossible, in a complex system such as the leisure cluster in Appelscha. Minor changes can have large consequences and external influences can also have profound effects on the local system. We do not argue that the perspective we present allows an accurate prediction of the future. However, the holistic and integrated approach, focusing on the connections between different parts of the system, can reveal the conditions that lie at the heart of a systems adaptivity. A local entrepreneur also stresses the necessity of an integrated approach when he states:

I think the government should recognize, well, that everything is interwoven. We had a discussion the other day about nature, is nature a cost item or an investment? The government sees roads as, you know, that's infrastructure, but nature is also infrastructure. You know, every euro you invest in nature, it comes back.

(Appelscha, 15 August 2014)

The approach we have presented here provides a first attempt at explaining complex regional and local processes through EEG and CAS. However, further research is needed to fully grasp the processes underlying the development of Appelscha and especially the influence of the regional level. Also, comparison with other cases can help clarify to what extent transformations can be attributed to the properties of the local system, or are a result of effects that find their source on the regional, national or even supranational scale.

Conclusion

This chapter shows how a perspective based on evolutionary economic geography through CAS can provide new insights in the non-linear processes that shape the development of leisure. This perspective is an attempt to deal with the unpredictability of future development, whilst still acknowledging the interactions between the various parts of a regional system. This approach can be specifically valuable for leisure, due to its complex and interrelated nature. By examining the robustness, dynamics, unity and diversity of leisure as an aspect of regional development, the changes of both content, and structure and function of the system of regional development can be explored.

The case of Appelscha illustrates some of the processes that play a role in the evolution of leisure. The interdependencies of various leisure companies, but also the relations between the nature areas, the local population and the leisure sector, must retain or continuously seek a certain balance to stay adaptive. If this balance is lost, for instance because of too strong an emphasis on the dynamics of the sector, changes in the environment can lead to detrimental effects for the leisure sector and the region's development. The case of Appelscha illustrates how moving the amusement park, which changed structures that had evolved over the years, caused a loss of balance. As such, the system's ability to adapt to external shocks, for instance the economic crisis, was diminished as the unity and robustness of the system decreased. Although a more thorough examination of the case is required to draw strong conclusions, this example shows the contribution of an approach that combines an EEG perspective with CAS. The illustration given here focuses on the local level. This is a first step towards a more extensive analysis that explores the evolution on a regional or provincial level. By looking at more cases and further integrating a multi-level perspective, the effects of provincial policies to stimulate leisure development can be explored and the potential for a more adaptive approach in planning can be considered.

We posit that the discussion of regional development through leisure in the framework presented in this chapter provides the opportunity to gain better insights in the role leisure might play in the future. An improved comprehension of the way in which different subsystems interact can also be used to estimate the consequences of specific advancements or policy measures in a specific field. In Fryslân, specifically, this perspective could contribute to ensuring that the effects of the 2018 European Capital of Cultural title have a lasting positive effect on the province as a whole. Exploring the CAS of leisure in Fryslân can facilitate learning from past developments such as those in Appelscha. It can reveal the mechanisms that allow the region to adapt to internal and external circumstances. Such lessons could of course also contribute to the wider debate on regional development in rural and peripheral areas. This research can elucidate the links between leisure and regional development, further exploring the potential for an economy in which leisure plays a central role. Although this does not mean that accurate predictions of future changes are possible, it can strengthen the ability to respond to changes that are already perceived.

Acknowledgements

This work is part of a research programme which is financed by the Province of Fryslân. The authors wish to thank the respondents for their willingness to cooperate in this research, as well as the reviewers and editors for their comments on previous versions of this chapter.

References

Anderies, J. M., Janssen, M. A., and Ostrom, E. (2004). 'A framework to analyze the robustness of social–ecological systems from an institutional perspective'. *Ecology and Society* 9(1), 18.
Andersson, T. D. (2007). 'The tourist in the experience economy'. *Scandinavian Journal of Hospitality and Tourism* 7(1), 46–58.
Arendz, J. (1997). 'Pretparkbaas krijgt veel gedaan'. *Leeuwarder Courant*, 28 March, p. 7.
Boschma, R. and Martin, R. (2007). 'Editorial: Constructing an evolutionary economic geography'. *Journal of Economic Geography* 7(5), 537–48.
Boschma, R. and Martin, R. (2010). 'The aims and scope of evolutionary economic geography'. In R. Boschma and R. Martin (eds) *The Handbook of Evolutionary Economic Geography*. Cheltenham, UK: Edward Elgar (pp. 3–39).
Brouder, P. (2014). 'Evolutionary economic geography and tourism studies: Extant studies and future research directions'. *Tourism Geographies* 16(4), 540–5.
Buijs, A. E., Pedroli, B., and Luginbühl, Y. (2006). 'From hiking through farmland to farming in a leisure landscape: Changing social perceptions of the European landscape'. *Landscape Ecology* 21(3), 375–89.
Centraal Bureau voor de Statistiek. (2011). 'Gemeente Op Maat Ooststellingwerf. The Hague'. [online] URL: www.cbs.nl/NR/rdonlyres/3454F215-ACB2-411C-A702-CBB6331E3119/0/Ooststellingwerf.pdf (accessed on 10 November 2015).
De Roo, G. (2012). 'Spatial planning, complexity and a world "out of equilibrium": Outline of a non-linear approach to planning'. In G. De Roo, J. Hillier, and J. Van Wezemael

(eds) *Complexity and Planning: Systems Assemblages and Simulations*. Farnham, UK: Ashgate (pp. 129–65).

Duit, A. and Galaz, V. (2008). 'Governance and complexity – emerging issues for governance theory'. *Governance: An International Journal of Policy, Administration, and Institutions* 21(3), 311–35.

Foster, J. (2005). 'From simplistic to complex systems in economics'. *Cambridge Journal of Economics* 29(6), 873–92.

Foster, J. (2006). 'Why is economics not a complex systems science?' *Journal of Economic Issues* 40(4), 1069–91.

Gemeente Ooststellingwerf. (2009). 'Ooststellingwerf: De Grenzeloze Toekomst; Structuurvisie 2010-2020-2030 Identiteit en Ontwikkeling'. [online] URL: www.ooststellingwerf.nl/document.php?m=29&fileid=3521&f=d02e9cc30cdf521aecf9c0cd989a79e6&attachment=0 (accessed on 22 October 2015).

Gilbert, D. and Abdullah, J. (2004). 'Holidaytaking and the sense of well-being'. *Annals of Tourism Research* 31(1), 103–21.

Gill, A. M. and Williams, P. W. (2014). 'Mindful deviation in creating a governance path towards sustainability in resort destinations'. *Tourism Geographies* 16(4), 546–62.

Gospodini, A. (2001). 'Urban design, urban space morphology, urban tourism: An emerging new paradigm concerning their relationship'. *European Planning Studies* 9(7), 925–34.

Greenwood Parr, M. and Lashua, B. D. (2004). 'What is leisure? The perceptions of recreation practitioners and others'. *Leisure Sciences* 26(1), 1–17.

Haartsen, T. and Venhorst, V. (2010). 'Planning for decline: Anticipating on population decline in the Netherlands'. *Tijdschrift Voor Economische En Sociale Geografie* 101(2), 218–27.

Hadjimichalis, C. (2003). 'Imagining rurality in the New Europe and dilemmas for spatial policy'. *European Planning Studies* 11(2), 103–13.

Hartman, S. and De Roo, G. (2013). 'Towards managing nonlinear regional development trajectories'. *Environment and Planning C: Government and Policy* 31(3), 556–70.

Healey, P. (2003). 'Collaborative planning in perspective'. *Planning Theory* 2(2), 101–23.

Hermans, E. and De Roo, G. (2006). *Lila en de planologie van de contramal*. Assen: In Boekvorm.

Joustra, W. (2013). '"Feest van heel Europa" Leeuwarden unaniem uitgekozen tot Culturele Hoofdstad'. *Leeuwarder Courant*, 7 September, p. 1.

Kaltenborn, B. P. (2009). 'Nature of place attachment: A study among recreation home-owners in Southern Norway'. *Leisure Sciences* 19(3), 175–89.

Levin, S. (2003). 'Complex adaptive systems: Exploring the known, the unknown and the unknowable'. *Bulletin of the American Mathematical Society* 40(1), 3–19.

Liu, J., Dietz, T., Carpenter, S. R., Alberti, M., Folke, C., Moran, E., Pell, A. C., Deadman, P., Kratz, T., Lubchenco, J., Ostrom, E., Ouyang, Z., Provencher, W., Redman, C. L., Schneider, S. H., and Taylor, W. W. (2007). 'Complexity of coupled human and natural systems'. *Science* 317(5844), 1513–16.

Ma, M. and Hassink, R. (2013). 'An evolutionary perspective on tourism area development'. *Annals of Tourism Research* 41, 89–109.

Martin, R. and Sunley, P. (2007). 'Complexity thinking and evolutionary economic geography'. *Journal of Economic Geography* 7(5), 573–601.

Martin, R. and Sunley, P. (2012). 'Forms of emergence and the evolution of economic landscapes'. *Journal of Economic Behavior & Organization* 82(2–3), 338–51.

McDonald, J. R. (2009). 'Complexity science: an alternative world view for understanding sustainable tourism development'. *Journal of Sustainable Tourism* 17(4), 455–71.

Murmann, J. P. (2003). *Knowledge and Competitive Advantage: The Coevolution of Firms, Technology, and National Institutions*. Cambridge: Cambridge University Press.

Nicolai, F. (1991). 'Pieter Jasper slachtoffer van eigen succes: Uitbreiding recreatie bij Boerestreek stuit op verzet'. *Leeuwarder Courant*, 28 August, p. 21.

O'Sullivan, D. (2004). 'Complexity science and human geography'. *Transactions of the Institute of British Geographers NS* 29, 282–95.

Parra, C. (2010a). *The governance of ecotourism as a socially innovative force for paving the way for more sustainable development paths: The Morvan regional park*. Doctoral thesis. Lille: Université de Lille 1, Science et Technologies.

Parra, C. (2010b). 'Tourisme et développement durable'. In B. Zuindeau (ed.) *Développement Durable et Territoires*. Villeneuve d'Ascq: Presses Universitaires du Septentrion (pp. 363–72).

Potts, J. D. (2000). *The New Evolutionary Microeconomics: Complexity, Competence and Adaptive Behaviour*. Cheltenham, UK: Edward Elgar.

Provincie Fryslân. (2011). Fryslân Toeristische Topattractie Uitvoeringsagenda 2011– 2013. Leeuwarden: Provincie Fryslân.

Provincie Fryslân. (2013). De Steat fan Fryslân 2013. Leeuwarden: Provincie Fryslân.

Rammel, C., Stagl, S., and Wilfing, H. (2007). 'Managing complex adaptive systems – A co-evolutionary perspective on natural resource management'. *Ecological Economics* 63(1), 9–21.

Ramstad, Y. (1986). 'A pragmatist's quest for holistic knowledge: The scientific methodology of John R. Commons'. *Journal of Economic Issues* 20(4), 1067–105.

Rauws, W. S. (2015). 'Civic initiatives in urban development: Self-governance versus self-organization in planning practice'. In W. S. Rauws (ed.) *Why Planning Needs Complexity*. Groningen, the Netherlands: InPlanning PhD Series (pp. 75–98).

Rauws, W. S., Cook, M., and van Dijk, T. (2014). 'How to make development plans suitable for volatile contexts'. *Planning Practice and Research* 29(2), 133–51.

Ravenscroft, N. and Reeves, J. (1999). 'Planning for recreation in rural England'. *Journal of Planning Education and Research* 18(4), 345–52.

Rojek, C. (2001). 'Leisure and life politics'. *Leisure Sciences* 23(2), 115–25.

Rotmans, J. and Loorbach, D. (2009). 'Complexity and transition management'. *Journal of Industrial Ecology* 13(2), 184–96.

Russell, R. and Faulkner, B. (1999). 'Movers and shakers: Chaos makers in tourism development'. *Tourism Management* 20(4), 411–23.

Smidt-Jensen, S., Skytt, C. B., and Winther, L. (2009). 'The geography of the experience economy in Denmark: Employment change and location dynamics in attendance-based experience industries'. *European Planning Studies* 17(6), 847–62.

Stebbins, R. A. (1982). 'Serious leisure: A conceptual statement'. *The Pacific Sociological Review* 25(2), 251–72.

Stebbins, R. A. (2001). 'Serious leisure'. *Society* (May/June), 53–7.

Stichting Kulturele Haadstêd 2018. (2015). Waarom Leeuwarden-Fryslân 2018. [online] URL: www.2018.nl/nl/waarom-leeuwarden-fryslan-2018 (accessed 22 October 2015)

Veblen, T. (1994). *The Theory of the Leisure Class*. New York: Dover Publications.

Vogelzang, E. (2006). 'Vergane glorie'. *Leeuwarder Courant*, 15 April, p. 1.

Waldrop, M. M. (1992). *Complexity The Emerging Science at the Edge of Order and Chaos*. New York: Simon & Schuster.

Walmsley, D. J. (2003). 'Rural tourism: A case of lifestyle-led opportunities'. *Australian Geographer* 34(1), 61–72.

10 Tourism and economic geography redux

Evolutionary economic geography's role in scholarship bridge construction

Dimitri Ioannides and Patrick Brouder

Tourism's marginal status

Almost two decades ago, Ioannides and Debbage (1998) passionately made the argument for bridging the considerable theoretical gap which at the time they perceived to exist between tourism research and one of the geographic discipline's key branches, namely economic geography. Their edited volume was inspired by their own backgrounds in economic geography, regional development and planning studies but also, to a major extent, by the work in tourism of several influential geographers such as Pearce (1989), Britton (1991), Shaw and Williams (1994) and Smith (1998), to name but a few. Happily, over the years since *The Economic Geography of the Tourist Industry* (Ioannides and Debbage 1998) made its appearance, a growing number of authors have offered their own valuable contributions relating to the interlinkages of tourism to economic geography (e.g. Milne and Ateljevic 2001; Papatheodorou 2004; Shaw and Williams 2004; d'Hauteserre 2006; Mosedale 2006; Bianchi 2009; Hjalager 2010; Brouder and Eriksson 2013). These insights, in turn, have led Ioannides and Debbage (2014) to reflect that we must no longer talk about a singular economic geography of tourism. Rather, just as we now must perceive the pluralistic nature of research relating to tourism's overall spatial characteristics (Hall and Page 2009), we must also recognize the existence of the '*economic* geograph*ies* of tourism' (Ioannides and Debbage 2014: 115).

Hall and Page (2009: 3) argue that overall 'the geography of tourism appears at first glance to be reasonably healthy'. They back up their statement by arguing that, in general terms, geographers have made several important contributions to the study of tourism, pointing out that more than a third of the 25 most cited researchers on this topic have graduate degrees in geography. At the educational level, many geography departments across the globe have developed courses and programs directly relating to tourism, while specialty groups relating to this theme have also been developed by various academic organizations, such as the Association of American Geographers and the International Geographical Union. Meanwhile, a number of compilation texts relating to the geography of tourism have made their appearance in recent years (e.g. Wilson 2012; Lew *et al.* 2014), including one on the non-Anglophone contributions to tourism geographies

(Wilson and Anton Clavé 2013). Moreover, since the late 1990s there has been a geography journal specifically related to tourism (*Tourism Geographies*).

Yet, unfortunately, despite this considerable strengthening of the ties between tourism and geography, not to mention between tourism and economic geography (Debbage and Ioannides 2012; Ioannides and Debbage 2014) a fundamental critique that continues to be valid to this day is that almost all of this scholarship has been developed for consumption by tourism scholars. In other words, practically all researchers involved in tourism research as it relates to economic geography or indeed any branch of human geography tend to 'preach to the choir', by writing for audiences that are specifically interested in tourism itself rather than seeking to also distribute this knowledge within the mainstream of (economic) geography. Thus, we are guilty of embracing ideas and theoretical constructs developed in economic geography, adapting them for use in our own research on tourism and then publishing our work in primarily tourism-related journals, and we rarely seek to disseminate our findings to journals aimed at broader audiences in the field (e.g. *Economic Geography, Progress in Human Geography* and *Geoforum*). To illustrate this point, Hall and Page (2009) show that during the period 1997–2007 only a very small number of tourism-specific articles appeared in journals such as these. In turn, this implies that mainstream geographers have rarely been exposed to what it is that much of tourism research is all about, which means that at the end of the day the topic reinforces its marginality within the overall subject of human geography, including economic geography.

In our view, the appearance of what arguably is one of the major 'turns' in the overall study of economic geography over the last decade or so, namely evolutionary economic geography (EEG) (Boschma and Martin 2010), constitutes a fundamental step forward in allowing not only tourism scholars but also so-called mainstream economic geographers and/or regional development specialists to gain a superior understanding of tourism's relationship to the overall development of localities and entire regions. While plenty of other contributors such as the ones we have already referred to have each in their own right been instrumental in terms of knowledge accumulation in the economic geography of tourism, we firmly believe that EEG constitutes the ideal pathway forward towards embedding tourism research within mainstream economic geography. Arguably it can help convince some of the more sceptical representatives of this academic branch of the need to take tourism seriously in the manner advocated by Britton (1991) and Ioannides and Debbage (1998). In part, this is because EEG provides the ability *inter alia* to view tourism in the context of a region's development not in isolation but in terms of how this sector co-evolves with the – often competing – development paths of several other sectors; if tourism is viewed as one component of a destination's entire, complex economic structure, then it becomes clearer to comprehend its evolutionary track over time and pinpoint the forces that determine its pathway.

In the rest of this concluding chapter we briefly remind the reader why the synergies of EEG and the study of tourism are an endeavour worth pursuing, while identifying an agenda for further research. We also provide a cautionary note by reminding the reader that we should go beyond a mechanistic interpretation of a destination's evolution and recognize the implications of this approach in the context of matters of uneven development, social inequities and capital accumulation (MacKinnon *et al.* 2009; Bianchi 2012).

Tourism's evolution through time and space

As several contributors to this volume have persuasively argued, examining the manner in which tourism evolves over time and also spatially within destinations of varying sizes has long been a subject of preoccupation of tourism geographers, regional scientists and other scholars (Wolfe 1952; Christaller 1964; Plog 1973; Miossec 1977; Stansfield 1978; Butler 1980, 2006 Gormsen 1981). Undoubtedly the most famous of these contributions is Butler's extremely well cited, though oft-criticized, Tourism Area Life Cycle (TALC), which despite (or because of) its apparent simplicity has been utilized in several guises by numerous researchers over the last 35 years to explain the manner in which destinations shift through time and the key forces behind their evolution. Hall and Page (2009: 5) contend that the TALC 'remains a clear indicator of the importance of theory in tourism research' and they go on to say that the model is ideal in terms of highlighting the need for theory in tourism studies.

A key strength of Butler's model has been, according to Pearce (1989), its portrayal of the key local as well as exogenous actors who determine the manner in which a destination evolves through time; though several other observers have argued that the model suffers from shortcomings, such as its inability to easily account for seasonality, its lack of prescriptive powers and the fact that within one major destination there might be a number of sub-destinations, each of which might be at a varying stages of its own respective resort cycle (Ioannides, 1994; Hall and Page 2009). Added to these criticisms is the not-so-insignificant point that, in almost all examinations that apply the TALC lens, the emphasis has been on tourism's pattern of growth and decline largely in isolation from the evolutionary behaviour of other key sectors within the destination and, indeed, the evolution of the place itself as part of a socioecological as well as a socioeconomic system.

The embrace of an EEG lens within the study of tourism enables us to begin to understand the manner in which tourism behaves in a complex economic system where it is not necessarily the only or indeed the major sector (Brouder 2014). A prime approach that has been reinforced in several of this volume's contributions (e.g. Chapters 2, 3, 6, 8) has to do with examinations of path dependence and associated issues such as regional lock-in, as well as path creation and path plasticity (Brouder 2014). It quickly becomes obvious, as Niewiadomski (Chapter 7) argues, that for a region to escape its historical legacy is far from easy, as it oftentimes may be shaped by a particular rigid political system and/or a region's inherited sociocultural traits. Consider, for instance, the near impossibility that several destinations worldwide face when seeking to effectively react to calls to make their tourism product evolve in a more sustainable manner than in the past. Ioannides and Holcomb (2003) have noted, in the context of various rapidly evolving coastal mass-tourism destinations (e.g. Cyprus, Malta), that despite strong recognition that rapid and uncontrolled development undoubtedly leads to long-term adverse negative environmental and sociocultural impacts, the common suggested solution is one reinforcing a 'tourism-first' mind-set. This 'failure to learn from failure' is not uncommon in tourism and is so entrenched it consistently proves difficult to overcome (Hall, 2011).

Elsewhere, natural disasters from South-East Asia to Mexico tend to result in updated forms of capital-intensive investment (e.g. from time-shares to all-inclusive resorts) rather than leading to a more sustainable form of local tourism development (e.g. small-scale community-based tourism). Thus, natural disasters are seen as a clean slate to modernize the stock rather than to rethink the nature of tourism development. This is despite the fact that the sector might have actually outlived its value for the destination and might indeed have to be replaced by another economic strategy. Thus, we regularly see calls for luxury-based tourism under the pretext that such an approach should serve to attract smaller numbers of high spenders, supposedly enabling the destination to improve its environmental health without compromising economic gains. This narrow view of sustainable development that emphasizes economic gains through the constant growth of tourism receipts whilst relegating environmental goals to the utility they have in serving the aforementioned economic priorities reflects the strong path-dependence of tourism's evolution in these destinations that is constantly shaped by a powerful pro-business lobby. Meanwhile, in other regions tourism struggles to gain recognition as a real economic sector as institutional legacies are tied to 'real' industries such as manufacturing (Brouder and Fullerton 2015).

Escaping such path dependency is far from easy, but when it does occur, this happens following what Sanz Ibáñez *et al.* (see Chapter 5) describe as 'moments' or key points of inflection when certain circumstances combine, forcing a shift in the destination's evolutionary trajectory. Gill and Williams (see Chapter 3) point out that a new path occurs to a major extent as a result of human agency, embodied in actions such as entrepreneurship and innovation (see also Chapters 4 and 7), which might also coincide with certain key events (e.g. the announcement that a destination has been selected for a major sporting event). Halkier and James (see Chapter 2) indicate that such moments occur following a crisis that necessitates a new course of action. They use the concept of resilience and specifically a complex adaptive systems (CAS) approach to examine how two Danish destinations adapted to the impacts of both long-term economic downturn and the more sudden financial crisis. CAS has also been used by Meekes *et al.* (see Chapter 9) in combination with EEG to examine what they see as non-linear forms of regional development associated with leisure. They conclude that their approach is valuable, since it aims to account for the unpredictability of the future while also appreciating that the evolution of leisure within a destination is strongly interrelated to many other parts of the regional system, including private companies, natural areas and the local population.

Though several chapters in this book (see, for instance, Chapters 3 and 8) implicitly account for the role of institutions and indeed some contributors adopt a relational economic geography approach in their examination of EEG (see Chapter 5), Carson and Carson (see Chapter 6) are the only authors who *explicitly* call for an approach in EEG that clearly demonstrates the link between 'evolutionary concepts to political economy approaches, arguing that the evolution of the economic landscape must be related to processes of capital accumulation and uneven development' (MacKinnon *et al.* 2009: 129). In this way, they seek a move away from an EEG approach that borrows concepts from evolutionary economics (Nelson and Winter 1982), since this tends to focus heavily on micro-level firm dynamics as key in explaining regional path-dependence, while it sees the role of institutions as secondary and deriving from industrial dynamics.

Carson and Carson's (Chapter 6) argument is that political systems and institutional structures, among others, can have a significant bearing on the manner in which companies behave at the micro-level and that this in turn influences the development trajectory of a particular sector. Their case study of tourism development in Central Australia demonstrates that in this situation, despite the existence of a crisis reflected in a decade-long downturn in arrivals, inertia on the part of major stakeholders meant that this situation has been hard to reverse. In other words, the key argument of Carson and Carson is that, although a sudden event or crisis may act as an instigator for a new path creation, that new pathway will always be mediated by the destination's past (political system, historical contingency, cultural traits, etc.; see also Chapter 7).

In the final analysis, Carson and Carson's principal argument is that the development of tourism at a destination cannot be understood simply by focusing narrowly on the sector itself and the stakeholders directly associated with this. Their emphasis on the institutional environment and by extension the overall political economy coincides with earlier calls to develop a 'theorisation that explicitly recognises, and unveils, tourism as a predominantly capitalistically organised activity driven by the inherent and defining social dynamics of that system, with its attendant production, social, and ideological relations' (Britton 1991). This call matches earlier calls specific to EEG (Essletzbichler 2012) and EEG in the context of tourism (Brouder and Ioannides 2014), with Essletzbichler, in particular, arguing for a strong role for political-economy approaches within EEG research.

Setting an agenda for future directions in research

We began this chapter by reminding the reader that, despite the fact that many positive steps have been made over the last two decades or so in terms of bridging the gap between tourism and economic geography, to a large extent much of this scholarship has gone unnoticed by academics who are not directly interested in the study of this sector. This situation perpetuates misunderstandings that, in turn, lead a number of scholars to trivialize the importance of tourism and its interrelationship to the rest of the economy. This downgrading of tourism has serious implications – from research-grant applications to government planning – with tourism being poorly funded or isolated as a special interest rather than as an important part of a diverse economy. As tourism scholars, we are often told that if we are to be successful in gaining access to research funding we must carefully and creatively camouflage the topic and avoid using terms such as 'tourism' and 'travel industry' directly. That said, we believe that the embrace of EEG in tourism studies presents a new frame for tourism studies by shifting it from being a case on the margins of economic geography to an important part of an integrated economic framework.

For this to happen it is our contention to be mindful of the critique of MacKinnon *et al.* (2009), who maintain that it is important not to simply adopt a somewhat mechanistic approach to EEG without taking into account the broader institutional context and especially the political economy. As Bianchi (2009, 2012) has argued, we are sometimes guilty in tourism scholarship, which has gone through several so-called turns (e.g. critical turn, cultural turn, relational turn, evolutionary turn), of neglecting or at least underplaying the political economy context despite the calls of Britton (1991), Ioannides and Debbage (1998) and more recently Gibson (2008). At the end of the day we believe that 'the evolution of the economic landscape [within which tourism may be a part] needs to be related to processes of capital accumulation and uneven development' (MacKinnon *et al.* 2009: 131).

To a greater or a lesser extent, the contributions in this volume have implicitly already done this. The next step is to argue for future research that embraces an evolutionary approach to the study of tourism through a political economy lens and specifically ties to 'dynamics of capital accumulation, underpinned by the creation and realization of value through spatial circuits of production, circulation, consumption, and regulation' (MacKinnon *et al.* 2009: 137). Here, we provide a short list of possible research directions, which are not mutually exclusive, that could significantly strengthen the ties of economic geography to tourism by embracing an EEG approach.

Tourism work and workers: an EEG approach

The geography of tourism work and workers is a subject that hitherto has not received the attention it deserves despite the fact that employment in the sector is plagued by an image of long-standing inequities (Zampoukos and Ioannides 2011; see also Tufts 2004). Gibson (2009) has already argued that, as part of an agenda for tourism geographers to actively embrace a political economy approach in their studies, it is important to consider the dimensions of work and workers in this sector. His argument follows Herod's (1997) view that we must include workers in broad discussions relating to uneven development patterns, since these individuals have their own say in influencing geographic contingencies 'as authors of their own historical geographies under capitalism' (Herod 1997: 16). In other words, all workers within a region are actively agents who either directly or indirectly influence how their geography is shaped and evolves. Following the argument of MacKinnon *et al.* (2009) to take into account the role of work and workers in moulding innovation (e.g. through transfer of knowledge), within the context of EEG research we argue that the time is ripe to utilize a longitudinal lens in examinations of the manner in which workers in the various branches that constitute the tourism sector and the tasks they perform over time combine with other factors such as institutional practices in shaping the destination's evolutionary trajectory.

Policy entrepreneurship as agency in path formation

Some of the chapters in this volume (e.g. Chapters 2 and 3) have already shown how governance can emerge as an active ingredient in shaping new paths at destinations. What is not perhaps always very lucid is whether a particular individual can emerge as the key player at particular points who has an active role in allowing a place to escape its path dependency. Such an individual can be termed a 'policy' or even a 'political entrepreneur', a construct that has increasingly become a focal point of discussion in other social sciences such as political science and planning studies (Narbutaite Aflaki *et al.* 2015). Generally speaking, policy entrepreneurs are those 'entrepreneurs' who can either be elected officials or bureaucrats, as well as private citizen–activists who take certain risks in order to influence certain (sometimes important) shifts in policy. What drives these individuals as opposed to regular entrepreneurs in the private sector is not pure economic objectives, but rather ambitions such as to remain in or gain access to political office or even more altruistic motives such as to serve the public interest through lofty ambitions to eradicate homelessness, or reduce poverty and unemployment (Ioannides 2015).

Thus, the question emerges as to whether EEG can be used as a way to peel away the institutional layers and narrow down on the identity of the key movers and shakers within a destination that have a major say from time to time in causing path divergence. Such an approach dovetails with calls to more readily embrace the 'role of power and politics in structuring economic adaptation' (MacKinnon *et al.* 2009: 139), which in the final analysis is an important aspect of the political economy perspective. There is certainly ample empirical scope for such investigations. For example, Rogerson and Rogerson (2014) show how tourism path divergence is partly explained by institutional and entrepreneurial conditions both internal to and external of the tourism sector in eight South African metropolitan regions.

Tourism and contingent neoliberalism through an EEG lens

Mosedale (2014: 58) maintains 'institutional regimes are not static but adapt to internal and external changes. Of particular interest . . . are the temporal variations on relationships between the institutional environment and the institutional arrangements and their effects on tourism'. Despite this argument, there has not been thus far a clear discussion within EEG linking the manner in which the overall dominant neoliberal paradigm that has been around since the early 1980s has served to condition the manner in which tourism has evolved in particular places. Specifically, even though there is strong evidence that the neoliberal project is not a 'one-size-fits-all global approach', but instead is mediated by local contingencies, there has not been a concerted effort to incorporate these discussions within an EEG lens of tourism's evolutionary trajectory. Thus, for instance, despite recognizing that one of the generic aspects of urban redevelopment efforts in the neoliberal era worldwide has tended to be the adoption of mega projects and events as well as signature cultural-tourism solutions (see Richards and Wilson 2007), the question remains: How do certain destinations manage to break the mould and create their own new paths? What role, if any, do certain non-traditional stakeholders such as members of the informal economy play in determining new directions in a destination's tourism product? Emerging evidence from South Africa shows that this is an important aspect of tourism-economy research, with further scope for empirical work globally (Rogerson and Letsie 2013).

Closer examinations of intersectoral knowledge transfer

Larsson and Lindström (2013: 1551) have provided a rare examination from an evolutionary perspective of how knowledge transfer between two unrelated economic sectors, namely boat building and tourism, can 'spur innovation in experience production'. They show that, despite the apparent disconnect between the two sectors (at first glance, what does building boats have to do with tourist visits after all?), there are, in fact, several interlinkages that are worth fleshing out. Though their study took place in a relatively small scale rural place, it provides food for thought in extending such an approach to far more complex settings (e.g. metropolitan regions), where tourism is often hard to disaggregate from a number of other sectors.

Closing thoughts: the future is looking bright for the economic geography of tourism

We began this book with the paraphrased quote 'why is tourism not an evolutionary science', originally derived from Veblen's (1898) famous question relating to economics. The contributions within this volume have, we hope, demonstrated that indeed one can view tourism in an evolutionary sense and the conceptual lens for doing this is through EEG. Ambitiously, we believe that such an approach goes a long way towards scholarship bridge construction, as it truly strengthens the ties between tourism and economic geography (Ioannides and Debbage 1998). It does so by offering researchers the ability to comprehend the evolution of tourism as part of a complex system of multiple co-evolving sectors as they are mediated by various forces. Having said that, we also realize we have only just now begun to scratch the surface of this intellectual approach and sincerely hope that more researchers immerse themselves in this line of inquiry.

References

Bianchi, R. (2009). 'The "critical turn" in tourism studies: A radical critique'. *Tourism Geographies* 11, 484–504.

Bianchi, R. (2012). 'A radical departure: A critique of the critical turn in tourism studies'. In J. Wilson (ed.) *The Routledge Handbook of Tourism Geographies*. London: Routledge (pp. 46–54).

Boschma, R. and Martin, R. (2010). *The Handbook of Evolutionary Economic Geography*. Cheltenham, UK: Edward Elgar.

Britton, S. (1991). 'Tourism, capital and place: Towards a critical geography of tourism'. *Environment and Planning D: Society and Space* 9, 451–78.

Brouder, P. and Eriksson, R. (2013). 'Tourism evolution: On the synergies of tourism studies and evolutionary economic geography'. *Annals of Tourism Research* 43, 370–89.

Brouder, P. (2014). 'Evolutionary economic geography and tourism studies: Extant studies and future research directions'. *Tourism Geographies* 16(4), 540–5.

Brouder, P. and Fullerton, C. (2015). 'Exploring heterogeneous tourism development paths: Cascade effect or co-evolution in Niagara?' *Scandinavian Journal of Hospitality and Tourism* 15(1–2), 152–66.

Brouder, P. and Ioannides, D. (2014). 'Urban tourism and evolutionary economic geography: Complexity and co-evolution in contested spaces'. *Urban Forum* 25(4), 419–30.

Butler, R. (1980). 'The concept of a tourist area cycle of evolution: Implications for management of resources'. *The Canadian Geographer* 24(1), 5–12.

Butler, R. (2006). *The Tourism Area Life Cycle, Vols. 1 & 2*. Clevedon, UK: Channel View Publications.

Christaller, W. (1964). 'Some considerations of tourism location in Europe: the peripheral regions–underdeveloped countries–recreation areas'. *Regional Science Association Papers* 12(1), 95–105.

d'Hauteserre, A.M. (2006). 'A response to "Tracing the commodity chain of global tourism" by Dennis Judd'. *Tourism Geographies* 8, 49–53.

Debbage, K.G. and Ioannides, D. (2012). 'The economy of tourism spaces: A multiplicity of "critical turns"'. In J. Wilson (ed.) *The Routledge Handbook of Tourism Geographies*. London: Routledge (pp. 149–56).

Essletzbichler, J. (2012). 'Generalized Darwinism, group selection and evolutionary economic geography'. *Zeitschrift für Wirtschaftsgeographie* 56(3), 129–46.

Gibson, S. (2008). 'Locating geographies of tourism'. *Progress in Human Geography* 32(3), 407–22.

Gibson, S. (2009). 'Geographies of tourism: Critical research on capitalism and local livelihoods'. *Progress in Human Geography* 33(4), 527–34.

Gormsen, E. (1981). 'The spatio-temporal development of international tourism: Attempt at a centre-periphery model'. In International Geographical Union (ed.) *La Consommation d'Espace par le Tourisme et sa Préservation: Actes*. Aix-en-Provence: Centre des Hautes Études Touristiques (CHET) (pp. 150–70).

Hall, C.M. (2011). 'Policy learning and policy failure in sustainable tourism governance: From first- and second-order to third-order change?' *Journal of Sustainable Tourism* 19(4–5), 649–71.

Hall, C.M. and Page, S. (2009). 'Progress in tourism management: From the geography of tourism to geographies of tourism: A review'. *Tourism Management* 30, 3–16.

Herod, A. (1997). 'From a geography of labor to a labor geography: Labor's spatial fix and the geography of capitalism'. *Antipode* 29(1), 1–31.

Hjalager, A.M. (2010). 'A review of innovation research in tourism'. *Tourism Management* 31, 1–12.

Ioannides, D. (1994). *The State, Transnationals, and the Dynamics of Tourism Evolution in Small Island Nations*. Unpublished PhD dissertation. New Brunswick, NJ: Rutgers University.

Ioannides, D. (2015). 'City planners as political entrepreneurs: Do they exist; can they exist?' In I. Narbutaite Aflaki, E. Petridou, and L. Miles (eds) *Entrepreneurship in the Polis: Understanding Political Entrepreneurship*. London: Ashgate (pp. 43–54).

Ioannides, D. and Debbage, K.G. (1998). *The Economic Geography of the Tourist Industry: A Supply-Side Analysis*. London: Routledge.

Ioannides, D. and Debbage, K.G. (2014). 'Economic geographies of tourism revisited: From theory to practice'. In A.A. Lew, C.M. Hall, and A.M. Williams (eds) *The Wiley Blackwell Companion to Tourism*. Chichester, UK: John Wiley and Sons (pp. 107–19).

Ioannides, D. and Holcomb, B. (2003). 'Misguided policy initiatives in small-island destinations: why do up-market policies fail?' *Tourism Geographies* 5(1), 39–48.

Larsson, A. and Lindström, K.N. (2013). 'Bridging the knowledge-gap between the old and the new: Regional marine experience production in Orust, Västra Götaland, Sweden'. *European Planning Studies* 22(8), 1551–68.

Lew, A.A., Hall, C.M., and Williams, A.M. (eds) (2014). *The Wiley Blackwell Companion to Tourism*. Chichester, UK: John Wiley and Sons.

MacKinnon, D., Cumbers, A., Pike, A., Birch, K., and McMaster, R. (2009). 'Evolution in economic geography: Institutions, political economy, and adaptation'. *Economic Geography* 85(2), 129–50.

Milne, S. and Ateljevic, I. (2001). 'Tourism, economic development, and the global–local nexus: Theory embracing complexity'. *Tourism Geographies* 3(4), 369–93.

Miossec, J.M. (1977). 'Un modele de l'espace touristique'. *L'Espace Geographique* 6(1), 41–8.

Mosedale, J. (2006). 'Tourism commodity chains: Market entry and its effects on St. Lucia. *Current Issues in Tourism* 9(4/5), 436–58.

Mosedale, J. (2014). 'Political economy of tourism: regulation theory, institutions, and governance networks'. In A.A. Lew, C.M. Hall, and A.M. Williams (eds) *The Wiley Blackwell Companion to Tourism*. Chichester, UK: John Wiley and Sons (pp. 55–65).

Narbutaite Aflaki, I., Petridou, E., and Miles, L. (eds) (2015). *Entrepreneurship in the Polis: Understanding Political Entrepreneurship*. London: Ashgate.

Nelson, R.R. and Winter, S.G. (1982). *An Evolutionary Theory of Economic Change*. Cambridge, MA: Harvard University Press.

Papatheodorou, A. (2004). 'Exploring the Evolution of Tourism Resorts'. *Annals of Tourism Research* 31(1), 219–37.

Pearce, D. (1989). *Tourist Development*. New York: Longman Scientific and Technical.

Plog, S.C. (1973). 'Why destination areas rise and fall in popularity'. *The Cornell Hotel and Restaurant Administration Quarterly*, November, 13–16.

Richards, G. and Wilson, J. (eds) (2007). *Tourism, Creativity and Development*. London: Routledge.

Rogerson, C.M. and Letsie, T. (2013). 'Informal sector business tourism in the global south: Evidence from Maseru, Lesotho'. *Urban Forum* 24(4), 485–502.

Rogerson, C.M. and Rogerson, J.M. (2014). Urban tourism destinations in South Africa: Divergent trajectories 2001–2012. *Urbani Izziv* 25(Supplement), 189–203.

Shaw, G. and Williams, A.M. (1994). *Critical Issues in Tourism: A Geographical Perspective*. Oxford: Blackwell.

Shaw, G. and Williams, A.M. (2004). *Tourism and Tourism Spaces*. London: Sage.

Smith, S.L.J. (1998). 'Tourism as an industry'. In D. Ioannides and K.G. Debbage (eds) *The Economic Geography of the Tourist Industry: A Supply-Side Analysis*. London: Routledge (pp. 31–52).

Stansfield, C.A. (1978). 'Atlantic City and the resort cycle: Background to the legalization of gambling'. *Annals of Tourism Research* 5(2), 238–51.

Tufts, S. (2004). 'Building a "competitive city": Labour and Toronto's bid to host the Olympic Games'. *Geoforum* 20, 47–58.

Veblen, T. (1898). 'Why is economics not an evolutionary science?' *Quarterly Journal of Economics* 12(4), 373–97.

Wilson, J. (ed.) (2012). *The Routledge Handbook of Tourism Geographies*. London: Routledge.

Wilson, J. and Anton Clavé, S. (2013). Geographies of tourism: European Research Perspectives. Bingley: Emerald.

Wolfe, R.I. (1952). 'Wasaga Beach – the divorce from the geographic environment'. *The Canadian Geographer* 2, 57–66.

Zampoukos, K. and Ioannides, D. (2011). 'The tourism labour conundrum: Agenda for new research in the geography of hospitality workers'. *Hospitality and Society* 1(1), 25–45.

Index

Note: Tables are indicated in bold; figures and illustrations in italics.

For Product Safety Concerns and Information please contact our EU
representative GPSR@taylorandfrancis.com Taylor & Francis Verlag GmbH,
Kaufingerstraße 24, 80331 München, Germany

Printed and bound by CPI Group (UK) Ltd, Croydon, CR0 4YY
08/05/2025
01864347-0001